Land Ownership Inequality and Rural Factor Markets in Turkey

THE ECONOMICS OF THE MIDDLE EAST

Series Editor: Dr. Nora Ann Colton

The Middle East has seen much more economic change than sociopolitical change over the past few decades in spite of the continuous political instability that is often highlighted by the press. Collectively the region is best known for producing and exporting oil. While the oil industry significantly impacts the region through generating wealth and movement of labor, it also has become the agent of change for endeavors such as development and diversification. With higher rates of growth occurring more in the East than in the West, the Middle East sits on the crossroads of this divide, acting as a bridge between these two market places.

This series is dedicated to highlighting the challenges and opportunities that lie within and around this central region of the global economy. It will be divided into four broad areas: resource management (covering topics such as oil prices and stock markets, history of oil in the region; water; labor migration; remittances in the region); international trade and finance (covering topics such as role of foreign direct investment in the region; Islamic banking; exchange rate and investments); growth and development (covering topics such as social inequities; knowledge creation; growth in emerging markets); and lastly, demographic change (covering topics such as population change, women in the labor market, poverty, and militancy).

Dr. Nora Ann Colton is principal lecturer in international business and management as well as a Middle East expert at the Royal Docks Business School, University of East London. Prior to joining the University of East London, Dr. Colton was a professor of Economics and Business at Drew University as well as the director of Middle East studies. Dr. Colton has conducted extensive fieldwork in the Middle East and was a Carnegie scholar in 2009 and visiting professor of Economics at the American University of Beirut.

Editorial Advisory Board

Sohrab Behdad—Professor and John E. Harris Chair of Economics, Denison University

Karen Pfeifer—Professor Emerita of Economics, Smith College

Ghassan Dibeh—Professor of Economics, Lebanese American University, Editor, *Review of Middle East Economics and Finance*

Roger Owen—A. J. Meyer Professor of Middle East History, Harvard University

Serdar Sayan—Professor of Economics, Director, Graduate School for Social Science, Tobb University of Economics and Technology, Turkey

Islamic Banking and Finance
By Omar Masood

Land Ownership Inequality and Rural Factor Markets in Turkey: A Study for Critically Evaluating Market Friendly Reforms
By Fatma Gül Ünal

LAND OWNERSHIP INEQUALITY AND RURAL FACTOR MARKETS IN TURKEY

A STUDY FOR CRITICALLY EVALUATING MARKET FRIENDLY REFORMS

Fatma Gül Ünal

First published in 2012 by
PALGRAVE MACMILLAN®
in the United States—a division of St. Martin's Press LLC,
175 Fifth Avenue, New York, NY 10010.

Where this book is distributed in the UK, Europe and the rest of the world,
this is by Palgrave Macmillan, a division of Macmillan Publishers Limited,
registered in England, company number 785998, of Houndmills,
Basingstoke, Hampshire RG21 6XS.

Palgrave Macmillan is the global academic imprint of the above companies
and has companies and representatives throughout the world.

Palgrave® and Macmillan® are registered trademarks in the United States,
the United Kingdom, Europe and other countries.

The views expressed herein are those of the author and do not necessarily
reflect the views of the United Nations.

ISBN: 978–0–230–12021–1

Library of Congress Cataloging-in-Publication Data

Ünal, Fatma Gül.
    Land ownership inequality and rural factor markets in Turkey : a study
for critically evaluating market friendly reforms / Fatma Gül Ünal.
        p. cm.—(The economics of the Middle East)
    ISBN 978–0–230–12021–1 (hardback)
        1. Land tenure—Turkey. 2. Land use, Rural—Turkey. 3. Rural poor—
Turkey. 4. Land reform—Turkey. I. Title.

HD846.5.Z7U53 2012
333.309561—dc23   2011044511

A catalogue record of the book is available from the British Library.

Design by Newgen Imaging Systems (P) Ltd., Chennai, India.

First edition: May 2012

10 9 8 7 6 5 4 3 2 1

Printed in the United States of America.

In loving memory of
My paternal grandmother, Fatma,
who was an agricultural laborer,
My first economics teacher at Bogazici University,
Demir Demirgil, who made me fall in love with
economics and taught me the importance of
asking good questions.
My maternal aunt, my half-mother, Hayriye Zeren,
who taught me the important thing in life is to fight with
all you have, even if you lose in the end.

And in honor of
my last economics teacher at University of Massachusetts,
Amherst, J. Mohan Rao, for teaching me to ask questions
with my heart and to answer them with my head,
finally, to my beloved family İsmail Hakkı,
Zehra, and Halil Ata Ünal.

Contents

TABLES

APPENDIX A

PREFACE

This book is about inequality in agriculture. It analyzes the interconnection between inequality and rural factor markets. Its scope is the intersection of agriculture and inequality. It investigates the effectiveness and efficiency of land and labor markets in spreading economic opportunities within agriculture and, thereby, in reducing rural poverty and inequality using Turkey as a case study. Therefore, the core theme in this book is the "connectedness"[1] between land ownership inequality and how markets mediate economic opportunities to people. The main issue we focus on is how existing inequalities perpetuate inequalities through markets, and limit markets' ability to function well, that is to distribute economic opportunities to those who are efficient producers. The main argument is that rural factor markets are prone to reproducing initial inequalities rather than redressing them because of existing inequalities in land—and thereby power as land begets political and economic power. In addition, economic and social determinants of participation in tenancy and labor markets are analyzed as they are affected by landownership inequality. This book distinguishes itself from the existing literature on rural markets inequality nexus by being one of the very few studies that provides empirical evidence using micro household data, and also by providing a unique index to measure the extent of how well markets distribute economic opportunities. Moreover, it is one of the few studies that look at the causes of rural inequality not only as an outcome of malfunctioning markets but as a reason of the process itself that creates inequality. Last but not least, another important contribution of the book is the fact that, one of the backbone chapters of the book, the section where we look at allocative efficiency in Turkish agriculture by testing for an inverse size-yield relationship across farms, is the first and only existing study on Turkey.

In the first chapter, we focus on why looking at agriculture and particularly land ownership inequality is important for Turkey and for the developing world overall, which Turkey is part of. First, we situate Turkey as a major international agricultural producer with a key regional role particularly for Middle East and North Africa (MENA) region as 27 percent of all arable land in MENA is within Turkish borders along with major water sources. Next, we emphasize the importance of looking at the agricultural sector by underlining the most recent developments in the poverty composition of Turkey, as poverty has been rising fastest in the agricultural sector in Turkey, particularly after the most recent agricultural reforms. We then elaborate on how land ownership inequality evolved with a historical analysis starting from Ottoman times with a focus on the changing role of agriculture and agrarian relations in Turkey. We conclude this chapter by looking at another factor that has been prominent in shaping the socioeconomic landscape in Turkey, and also MENA, the rise of political Islam.

The second chapter provides a portrait of the agricultural sector with a focus on income and asset inequalities in rural Turkey. It is a brief descriptive baseline of the existing situation of the inequality of endowments and income in rural Turkey with geographic and agroclimatic background for each seven rural regions (Marmara, Mediterranean, Central Anatolia, East Anatolia, Black Sea, Southeastern Anatolia, and the Aegean).

The third chapter develops a nonlinear probit model to examine the determinants of contract choice in Turkish agriculture. We first test the validity of the agricultural ladder hypothesis for contract choice (between fixed rent tenancy and sharecropping), and look at the impact of female workers in the household on the household's contract choice. We find a negative correlation between adult female workers in the household and the likelihood of engaging in both tenancy types. The study shows significant differences among households that engage in sharecropping and fixed rent tenancy. Those who have more access to credit, are relatively wealthy (whose food intake is higher), are more integrated into markets, and are more likely to engage in fixed rent tenancy as opposed to sharecropping. Those who are poorer, have less diversified incomes, have limited access to product and credit markets, own smaller land parcels, and live in villages where ownership of land is skewed, and have a higher probability of engaging in sharecropping tenancy. In general, land ownership inequality plays an important role in inducing households to participate in both types of tenancies. This impact is much stronger for fixed rent tenancy. We argue that this result may be associated with absentee landlordism, which has become more prevalent in Turkish agriculture in recent years as the adoption of neoliberal reforms has meant the withdrawal of government support for small landowners. Absentee landlords might favor fixed rent tenancy as a means of addressing supervision problems, thus producing the relationship we observe between land ownership inequality and fixed rent tenancy. In chapter 4, we evaluate performance of markets from a pure economic stand point, by testing for inverse size-yield relationship. Prevalence of inverse size-yield relationship is a manifestation of market malfunctioning in rural contexts, because it suggests decreasing yields per acre as the size of farm gets larger; markets malfunction in the sense that they fail to allocate resources (e.g., land) to those who are most efficient (e.g., small farmers). The empirical exercise is a simple econometric exercise within different demographic, technological, and regional contexts using the micro household data. This is a novel exercise that has not been done before for Turkey. Furthermore, this exercise yields a very robust and crucial finding of inverse size-yield relationship in Turkish context. In addition, our results suggest that one of the factors we consider, land fragmentation (number of parcels), has a positive impact on productivity in Turkish agriculture. This is a much debated issue on productivity and there are very few empirical studies on this particular issue. These findings are especially important because they signal the "poverty" of agricultural policy making in Turkey.

After establishing the inefficiency of rural factor markets in the previous chapters, the fifth chapter involves looking at the role of land ownership inequality in this efficiency. This is the core part of the book in which we address the overall hypothesis of *connectedness* between markets and inequality. The model we employ has been modified from Rao (2005),[2] and Benjamin and Brandt (1997). The basic idea of the methodology is to construct a mainstream account of the functioning of rural markets and of incomes derived from such markets, and then comparing the theoretically predicted outcomes with the actual outcomes. From this construction we estimate an inequality index for both incomes (predicted and actual), and then utilize the differences to construct a measure for evaluating market effectiveness, which we call MMM (Market Malfunctioning Measure) in rural Turkey. We then look at the relationship between MMM and land ownership inequality to see if land ownership inequality is instrumental in the failure of markets to distribute resources to the most efficient with a simple econometric exercise while controlling for heterogeneity of population density, infrastructure availability, and ease of access to urban centers. Our results suggest a very strong association of land ownership inequality and the failure of markets to distribute economic opportunities to those who can use them best according to economic valuation.

The sixth and the last chapter of the book consists of a summary of the findings and policy implications. In this chapter, we also include a brief analysis of what kind of economic opportunities may exist for agrarian-based economies in the face of agroclimatic and demographic challenges of the twenty-first century and with two fast growing giant economies, such as India and China. In this chapter, we argue that agriculture will have a much more important role to play in development than it used to, and also that, countries with significant agricultural production would benefit to use their strengths in agriculture to reap the benefits of a new world order in agriculture.

ACKNOWLEDGMENTS

This book has been five years in the writing. The core research in this book is from my doctoral studies at the University of Massachusetts, Amherst. Throughout this relatively long journey, there have been many people who supported me immensely. First and foremost, let me acknowledge J. Mohan Rao, my then PhD advisor, for his mindful guidance and enthusiastic support for my doctorate research. He has been an inspiration to me as an economist and a human being. Another very important person who made this particular research possible is Levent Yener, who was the director of Agriculture Reform Implementation Program in the Ministry of Agriculture, Turkey, in 2006, who provided me with the access to Quantitative Household Survey (QHS) dataset.

I am also indebted to my many colleagues and friends at several institutions that have become part of my life since 2006, at University of Massachusetts, Amherst, Levy Economics Institute, and United Nations Development Programme Regional Bureau for Asia and the Pacific in New York. I feel extremely fortunate to have been a part of institutions and environments in which I have been surrounded by colleagues who continue to contribute to my intellectual journey enormously. My fellow colleagues and friends, particularly Elizabeth Ramey, Sevinc Rende, Samuel Bowles, James Boyce, Michael Ash, Lynda Pickbourne, Alan Gainteby, John Strickland, Ebru Erberber, and my young friend Dilek Genç, deserve very special thanks for brainstorming with me and for helping me to improve my work.

I particularly want to extend my gratitude to Political Economy Research Institute at the University of Massachusetts, Amherst, and The Institute of Turkish Studies in Georgetown University for funding parts of this research. I also want to acknowledge the Levy Economics Institute of Bard College for providing me space to conduct my research and particularly extend my thanks to Rania

Antonopoulos and Dimitri Papadimitriou for their mentorship, support, and friendship at the institute.

Finally, I want to thank my family, my parents Zehra and İsmail Ünal, and my brother Ata for their support and for believing in me, and letting me be who I am.

1

INTRODUCTION: WHY AGRICULTURE?

My grandmother was a peasant woman, an agricultural worker, and a landlord's second wife. One day a government official came to our village—Harmandali, a tiny village in Central Anatolia—and on entering my grandfather's homestead, he saw my grandmother working barefoot, her feet covered in sheep manure. "Hanim, Hanim,"[1] he said, "what kind of a landlord's wife are you, your feet all covered in sheep dip?" Fatma, my grandmother, responded with great wit and without hesitation, "Mr. Officer, Mr. Officer," she said, "the one whose feet not covered in sheep dip cannot find anything to eat."

I grew up in an apartment where, frequently, some poor person would knock on the door, asking for money, food, or clothing. I do not remember a single time my mother turned any one of them down, nor do I remember asking her why people are so poor. But I don't think I will ever forget how my heart pounded in excitement when my economics professor wrote down an equation for poverty on the board in my third year of college in Turkey—an equation with amounts of milk, meat, and some unknown variable x. I was quite naïve. I thought as a social "scientist" is supposed to think: "Great, if I have the equation, I can solve for the unknown variable x." I had, after all, the required math skills to solve an equation with one unknown.

It turns out that solving the equation of poverty is much more complicated than solving a math equation. I am not sure if there is any magical route to solve poverty, but I am certain that many of those who work hard in agriculture are not guaranteed "something to eat," even when they are knee-deep in sheep manure, whether in Turkey or any other part of the world:

There are still about 1.4 billion people living on less than US$1.25 a day, and close to 1 billion people suffering from hunger. At least 70 percent of the world's very poor people are rural, and a large proportion of the poor and hungry are children and young people....Agriculture plays

a vital role in most countries—over 80 percent of rural households farm to some extent, and typically it is the poorest households that rely most on farming and agricultural labor. (IFAD 2011, 16)
Rural poverty rose to 39 percent in 2009 in Turkey, 4.2 percent higher than what it was in 2002. Poverty is highest in the agricultural sector with 33 percent of its population living under poverty in 2009. (TUIK 2011)

1. CENTRAL QUESTION

This book is not an attempt to find answers to the basic question of why some are poor and some are not. Its focus is on inequality of land ownership in agriculture. Land concentration on its own is enough to produce poverty, as land is crucial in employing labor and, therefore, in the income workers and tenants receive. Land concentration contributes to systematic differences in the institutions that allow access to investment in public goods, infrastructure, and economic opportunities (Deininger and Feder 2001; Engerman and Sokoloff 2002; Griffin et al. 2002; Baland and Robinson 2003).

This book is an exercise in linking inequality to the functioning of factor markets and to identify the ways in which rural markets in Turkey are failing not only the poorer classes but also the rural economy as a whole as a consequence of inequality in ownership of land. In an economy where agriculture is among the major sources of livelihood, it is clear that land ownership is important because of its productive capacities (Benjamin and Brandt 1997). Perhaps what is not so clear is how ownership of land plays a central role in the allocation of nonland factors of production, such as labor and capital, through rural factor markets, particularly in economies where land is the scarce factor compared to labor (Sen 1981; Griffin et al. 2002; Rao 2005).

The central question this study attempts to answer is this: Does land ownership inequality contribute to income inequality not only directly (via returns to land) but also indirectly via impacts on the functioning of rural land and labor markets?

2. AGRARIAN INEQUALITY AND RURAL FACTOR MARKETS: WHY IS IT RELEVANT TO ASK THIS QUESTION NOW?

Functioning of markets (i.e., the way markets distribute economic opportunities to people and, thereby, allocate productive resources and consumption goods and services) has been a fascinating topic for economists not only because the neoliberal agenda has (since the 1980s) offered "free markets" as a panacea to "free" the developing world from economic ills, such as inequality and poverty, but also because markets are a "many splendored thing."[2] Markets function in a way that captures all shades of socioeconomic life: policy, geography, culture, institutions, and even psychological problems.[3] In some contexts, markets function to increase inequality and poverty; in others markets help create a more equal and more affluent society. The market mechanism is an important determinant of the outcome but so are the starting positions of the participants: landlord or the landless men or women, Muslim or Christian, chieftain or shepherd, haves or have-nots. How markets mediate between the people and the economy depends not only on the structure and functioning of markets but also on the distribution and structure of the assets and income people have (Sarris 2001).

Studying the impact of land ownership inequality on the economic opportunities of people through rural factor markets in Turkey is interesting from three perspectives: international, regional, and national.

Internationally, many governments' and the international community's emphasis on Millennium Development Goal number one—to halve poverty by 2015—has led researchers and policy makers to focus on the agricultural sector more than any other. Furthermore, interest in agriculture has been rising in the face of food and energy crises. Food prices have risen to unprecedented levels during 2006–2008. Despite deflationary pressures caused by the most recent global recession in 2008, food prices have not come down to their precrisis levels in any country in the world. Compared to 2000, food prices are dramatically higher. From 2000 to 2009, despite no such rise in real incomes, food prices rose in Pakistan, India, China, Egypt, and Turkey by 130, 73, 53, and 68 percent, respectively (FAOSTAT 2010). As a result of the most recent food crisis between 2006 and 2008, another 100 million poor people were pushed into the ranks of the hungry in 2009 (IFAD 2011). Even though Asia and sub-Saharan Africa are home to the highest number of undernourished people, the Middle East and North Africa (MENA) registered the fastest increase (13 percent) (IFAD 2011). The factors behind such a significant rise in MENA were not solely due to the food crisis but were a combination of rising food demand, declining agricultural resources, declining farming population, and already-prevalent food security issues (IFAD 2011). According to International Fund for Agricultural Development (IFAD 2011), the world will have to produce 70 percent more food than it is producing today to feed its expected population of more than 9 billion by 2050. The environmental challenges of land degradation and climate change will further complicate the policy challenge of achieving food security for all.

Regionally, Turkey occupies a unique space as a major agricultural producer and an aspiring leader of the Muslim world, along with a possible membership in the European Union (EU). Despite its future inclusion being uncertain, if Turkey joins the EU, it means that not only Turkey, but also the EU are at the brink of a major socioeconomic change. There are other practical reasons for studying agriculture in Turkey. Turkey represents a good case study not only for Muslim countries but also for other developing countries. It is a typical developing country with a high proportion of its population still living in rural areas (30 percent) and one that is economically active (32 percent) in agriculture (FAOSTAT 2010). In addition, similar to many other developing countries in the world, the World Bank (WB) has strongly influenced development policies in Turkey since the late 1970s, and hence, Turkey offers good developmental policy lessons, particularly for those countries with large agrarian bases. Most recently, under the auspices of the WB, the reforms in agriculture, namely the Agricultural Reform Implementation Program (ARIP), which was implemented in 2001, represents a significant shift in agricultural policies in Turkey. As part of the neoliberal paradigm, the 2001 reforms made markets central to agrarian production, from resource allocation to output distribution (Aysu 2002; Cakmak 2004).

On the brink of accession to the EU, agriculture plays a significant role as home to the majority of the poor in Turkey. More than one-third of the rural population (39 percent) lives in poverty, and poverty has been most prevalent in the agricultural sector because of its low productivity, with only 9 percent contribution to the gross domestic product (GDP) in 2009 despite 26 percent[4] of the employment (World Bank 2011). Clearly, the prevalence of poverty in the agricultural sector could be a challenging issue not only for Turkey but also for Europe, given Turkey's possible accession, and for MENA. Hence, now is the perfect time to critically evaluate the effectiveness and efficiency of the markets, which were situated at the center of agricultural production by the latest reforms. Furthermore, now that the most recent global crisis has demonstrated the failure of the neoliberal paradigm, the time is perfect to discuss alternatives.

This book is structured as follows: the rest of the first chapter will situate Turkey within the MENA region as a major agricultural producer, and provide an overview of poverty in the region; section 3 in this chapter will provide a history of the land ownership structure in Turkey. Chapter 2 provides a portrait of the agricultural sector with a focus on income and asset inequalities in rural Turkey. Chapter 3 will underscore the economic and social determinants of participation in agricultural factor markets, focusing on land tenancy. Chapter 4 examines allocative efficiency in Turkish agriculture by testing for an inverse size-yield relationship across farms, and chapter 5 explores the interconnection between land ownership inequality and the functioning of rural factor markets in Turkey. Finally, in the last chapter, we take account of the analysis, point out the challenges and opportunities for Turkey within MENA and the EU, and, most importantly, evaluate the most recent agricultural policies in Turkey in light of the findings. Additionally, the last chapter suggests paths to structural transformation for developing countries by comparatively looking at Egypt, Tunisia, India, Pakistan, and China, and discusses possibilities for agriculture-based development under the shadow of the two giant economies of China and India.

2.1. Turkey as an Aspiring Regional Leader in MENA: Water and Agriculture

MENA[5] is a diverse region socially, culturally, and economically. It includes high-income countries, such as Qatar, Kuwait, and United Arab Emirates (UAE), with current per capita GDP exceeding $50,000, and also low-income countries, such as Yemen, Sudan, and Egypt, with current per capita GDP below $1,500 (World Bank 2011). The region consists of countries as populated as Tunisia, with over 100 million, and as small as Bahrain, with fewer than 1 million (FAOSTAT 2010). In total, MENA is home to 486 million people of diverse backgrounds—Jews, Muslims, and Christians; Armenians, Greeks, Turks, Persians, and Arabs; and Africans, Asians, and Europeans—and constitutes 7 percent of the world's population (AQUASTAT 2011). Political regimes in the region have been rapidly changing during the recent and ongoing Arab Spring, but there has long been political diversity: socialist regimes (Libya), monarchies (Morocco, Kuwait, Saudi Arabia, Jordan, Oman, and Bahrain), democracies (Israel, Algeria, Lebanon, and Turkey), Islamic Republics (Iran and Sudan), emirates (UAE, Kuwait, and Qatar), and republics (Sudan, South Sudan, Tunisia, and Egypt).

Despite its diversity on the socioeconomic, political, and cultural fronts, two common features significantly affect lives in MENA: water scarcity and lack of food self-sufficiency. It is the most water scarce and the least food self-sufficient region in the world (Allan 2002; World Bank 2007; Richards and Waterbury 2008; FAOSTAT 2010; Weinthal et al. 2010). Of the world's 20 most water-poor countries, 15 of them are in MENA (Moustakbal, 2009). Furthermore, 16 of the 21 MENA countries are under the water poverty threshold of 1,000 cubic meters per capita per year; the five exceptions are Turkey, Iran, Iraq, Sudan-South Sudan,[6] and Lebanon (AQUASTAT 2011). This already-scarce per capita water availability is expected to decrease by 30 to 70 percent (an average of 42 percent) by 2025 because of population growth (Sowers et al. 2010). Based on various studies on global warming, the region may experience a reduction of 10 to 40 percent in rainfall and an increase in temperatures, which would increase evaporation as a result of climate change (IPCC 2007; World Bank 2007; Weinthal et al. 2010). This is a significant problem for MENA because in much of the region, agricultural lands are considered semiarid, meaning they receive less than 400 millimeters of rain a year (Richards and Waterbury 2008). Additionally, rising populations with increased incomes (particularly after the first oil crisis of the 1970s), urbanization, climate change, and increased use of irrigation in agriculture have greatly increased the demand for water.

Agricultural production is the main consumer of water. Approximately 74 percent of all water resources are used for agricultural production in MENA as a whole. However, in 10 out of 21 countries in the region, agriculture accounts for 80 percent or more of the country's water consumption—in Sudan the figure is as high as 97 percent (AQUASTAT 2011). By world standards, devoting 74 percent of the region's water to agriculture is not exceptional: MENA comes after Central Asia (93 percent) and South Asia (78 percent) (AQUASTAT 2011).

However, what makes the water situation in MENA more bleak than in any other region is the water stress it is under. The region consumes more than its existing water resources. Food and Agriculture Organization (FAO) defines the pressure on water as "the percentage of total actual renewable freshwater resources withdrawn" (2011). MENA averages 395 percent, the highest in the world. It is the only region exceeding 100 percent. Despite similar proportions of water used by the agricultural sector, MENA's "pressure on water" ratio is six times more than Central Asia, which is the second highest in the world with 62 percent, 63 times more than sub-Saharan Africa, which consumes only 6 percent of its renewable water resources, and 294 times more than South America, which consumes only 1.4 percent (AQUASTAT 2011).

Naturally, water scarcity hampers the region's ability to achieve food self-sufficiency[7] and security.[8] Food self-sufficiency and food security are different: food self-sufficiency refers to the ability of a nation to meet its domestic food demand through domestic production. Food security refers to a country's ability to assure all its people access to safe and nutritious food that meets their food preferences and their dietary needs for an active and healthy life regardless of where that food is produced (FAO 2011). When water is scarce, it becomes more challenging to reach self-sufficiency in agriculture because of irrigation needs. However, there are different ways to achieve food security, which does not always require food self-sufficiency: nations could access food through international trade, and, in some not-so-desirable cases, food aid could help achieve food security as well. According to Richards and Waterbury (2008), despite being neither desirable nor possible, food self-sufficiency is politically irresistible in MENA and exacerbates water problems. For example, in the oil-rich countries of Saudi Arabia, Kuwait, and UAE, to achieve food self-sufficiency, the governments offered six times the international price of wheat in the early 1980s, about $1,000 per ton, at a time when it was selling in international markets for around $120 per ton. This produced spectacular results for this staple food crop to the extent that Saudi Arabia became the sixth largest exporter of wheat in the world by 1987 (Bonine 2001; Richards and Waterbury 2008). The vested interest of those who benefited from subsidies, mostly the landed elite, contributed to the pursuit of such policies despite the resulting increased pressure on water resources and the lack of any (broadly shared) economic justification (Richards and Waterbury 2008; Weinthal et al. 2010). After a decade, in the 1990s, when the reality of water scarcity sank in, policies shifted away from high subsidies to wheat production in the name of food self-sufficiency, which in turn helped reduce water usage by 50 percent from nonrenewable aquifers (Richards and Waterbury 2008). However, elimination of subsidies is replaced by liberal policies: now that world food prices are high and reflected in domestic markets, farming has become lucrative. Egyptian farmers, for example, have been increasingly cultivating rice, which creates more pressure on water.

MENA countries have been looking for solutions to ease their water-scarcity problem mostly through increasing supply as opposed to managing demand, through water desalination, importing "virtual water," and increasing and improving water storage facilities.

Virtual water is water embedded in other agricultural products. Through importing those products whose production requires higher water usage, MENA countries could ease some of their agricultural water demands. After its water crisis in 2000 following a major drought, Israel significantly changed its water management and reduced the share of water consumed by the agricultural sector from 68 percent in 2000 to 30 percent in 2009 (Weinthal et al. 2010).

Sea water desalination has become a more important source to satisfy the increasing water demand in the region, particularly in the Gulf and the Red Sea region, UAE, Bahrain, and Saudi Arabia, and more recently Israel (Fitchner 2011). MENA produces 60 percent of all the desalinated water in the world and has the most developed technology on desalination. According to the Fitchner (2011) report, 2,800 desalination plants have been producing 27 cubic meters of fresh water per day in MENA. This quantity is not adequate for the water demand in the region because desalination only satisfies 5 percent of the water demand, it is very expensive, and most of its financing depends on a nonrenewable resource—oil (Moustakbal 2009). However, existing desalination plants and projects that increase the use of renewable energy, such as solar thermal power, are available (Tolba and Saab 2009; Fitchner 2011).

Another strategy to ease water scarcity in the region is to increase recycling of domestic wastewater. Israel, Tunisia, and Jordan use 50, 30, and 12 percent, respectively, of recycled wastewater in the irrigation of their agriculture (Weinthal et al. 2010). Morocco, Egypt, and Saudi Arabia have been investing in dams, reservoirs, weirs, and other catchment technologies. These technologies are sometimes very large scale, such as the Aswan High Dam, or are very small-scale dams to catch runoff in specific wadis, such as in the Jordan Valley (Weinthal et al. 2010).

Water scarcity exacerbates conflict in the region over rivers between neighboring countries: the Jordan River system between Jordan, Israel, and Syria; the Euphrates and Tigris Rivers among Syria, Turkey, and Iran; and the Nile between Egypt, Sudan, and Ethiopia (Bonine 2001). Out of the 50 violent incidents in the last 50 years, 30 have been related to water between Israel and its neighbors (Moustakbal 2009). These conflicts within and among states have been devastating to local systems and communities.

Reform in water utilization is not an option for MENA—it is an exigency. As Richards and Waterbury (2008) have pointed out, low economic returns to water in agriculture when compared to industry indicate that the most effective way to adjust water usage is in the agricultural sector in the region. Agricultural trade will become more important—because it has to—given projected water scarcity. MENA already relies on food trade to meets its food demand; the region imports more than 50 percent of the food it consumes (FAOSTAT 2010). Turkey, with its relatively abundant water resources and large agricultural base, is definitely a good neighbor to have for countries in MENA. Although the regional solution has to go beyond Turkey, as we will discuss in the last chapter, the discussion can start with Turkey.

Turkey is a water-abundant country relative to others in MENA; it is home to 47 percent of all total renewable water resources[9] in MENA (AQUASTAT 2011). In contrast to the very high usage ratios elsewhere in the region, Turkey uses only 17 percent of its renewable water resources, which is the lowest in the region. The next highest share of MENA's water resources (27 percent) is within the borders of Iran, but Iran is under much higher water pressure than Turkey, as Iran uses 67 percent of all its renewable water. This puts Turkey at a unique advantage in the region.

As home to abundant water resources and more than one-fifth (22 percent) of all the arable land in the Middle East and North Africa, Turkey is a major agricultural producer by international standards (FAOSTAT 2010). Thirty percent of all lands are arable in Turkey, excluding pastures (FAOSTAT 2010). It ranks in the top five producers of 30 different products in the world. Turkey produces 2.2 percent of the world's agricultural GDP despite harvesting only 55 percent of its arable land, which is 25 percent less than China and 15 percent less than Pakistan and India[10] (FAOSTAT 2010).

2.2. Turkey and MENA: Rising Poverty and Agriculture's Changing Role

For most countries in the region, the agricultural sector still continues to provide employment for a significant share of the population. In some, such as Sudan, the proportion of people employed in agriculture is as high as 35 percent (IFAD 2011). On average for MENA, agriculture's share in employment is 22 percent, and its share in GDP is 7.4 percent (World Bank 2011; IFAD 2011). Unfortunately, the sector is also home to the 40 percent of those living in extreme poverty, a topic we take up in greater detail in the next section (IFAD 2011). Thus, economic policies affecting the role and perceived importance of agriculture in the economy are crucial for a large number of people who are often among the most vulnerable.

From a historical perspective, compared to earlier economic policies on agriculture, a clear shift has been made toward increased emphasis on the role of agriculture in development. The 1940s emphasized support of agriculture via prices set by states, mostly to protect the rural populations from the repercussions of the Great Depression, which caused a significant decline in world agricultural prices. The 1950s were marked by industrialization. The agricultural sector was assigned the passive role of providing industry with the surplus needed for investment (Lewis 1954; Ranis and Fei 1961). The 1960s witnessed a paradigm shift to agriculture as an active player in development rather than as merely a passive contributor to industry. Mechanized agriculture provided markets and other linkages to industrial growth (Johnston and Mellor 1961). The linkages agriculture provided fostered the view of balanced growth rather than acceptance of industry's exploitation of the agricultural sector. Concurrent with this development, evidence on the inverse-size-yield relationship in India (Mazumdar 1965; Sen 1966; Khusro 1973; Rudra and Bandapadhyaya 1973) also constituted the economic justification for small farms being considered as a path to growth out of poverty and provided the rationale for land reforms in traditional agrarian societies. The late 1960s and early 1970s ushered in modernization in agriculture, marked by machines replacing labor and, combined with the Green revolution, created mass unemployment in capital-poor, labor-rich countries such as Turkey (Koymen 1999).

The 1980s were the beginning of neoliberal policies; agriculture started to disappear from academic and political spaces. The Malthusian forecast was proven wrong: high-yield varieties, along with increased use of technology, produced enough food for everyone. Therefore, there was no need for policy makers and social scientists, or at least for those who were vocal and visible, to pay attention to the sector anymore. If anything, the sector was seen as a bucket with a hole, a waste of public funds. Hence, developing countries' economies needed to be "structurally adjusted" to spur development—when governments faced fiscal problems, agricultural subsidies were cut. In the 1990s, development policies were aimed at improving rural lives and correcting urban bias by "getting the prices right," or agriculture vis-à-vis exchange rate devaluation, abolishing export taxes, reducing trade barriers, and opening national borders to imports from heavily subsidized developed countries. Agriculture as a sector was on the periphery and secondary to the more important issues of fast industrialization and modernization.

The policies of the early 2000s focused on property rights (De Soto 2000) and on advocating for an increased role for nongovernmental organizations (NGOs) managed by some "white guy in shorts"[11] who was trained to accomplish what "corrupt" governments could not in the Third World: eliminate poverty and other developmental problems by empowering and emancipating peasants, with no accountability to any authority other than their donors. The state was seen as an inefficient and corrupt arm of aristocracy intertwined with the landed elite. In some countries it was, but not in all. Furthermore, the neoliberal model crucially depended on the unrealistic assumption that NGOs and the private sector were reliably honest in the same countries where corruption was widespread throughout the state machinery. Because of their rather fantastical beliefs and the resulting policy neglect, governments, the Bretton Woods Institutions, and the international development community were caught unprepared for the 2006 food crisis that devastated an already impoverished rural population. The situation worsened with the global financial crisis of 2008. The following section sheds light on those who got hardest hit in MENA by these two crises, with a particular focus on Turkey.

2.2.1. Poverty and Inequality in MENA and Turkey

To those without practice decoding poverty statistics, poverty may not seem prevalent in MENA. Poverty data is difficult to obtain for most of the countries in the region. Only 10 out of 21 countries have official data on poverty and inequality: Algeria, Egypt, Iran, Iraq, Jordan, Morocco, Syria, Tunisia, Turkey, and Yemen. According to Richards and Waterbury, the oil-rich countries of the Gulf are "black holes of ignorance" when it comes to poverty (2008, 274). So, unfortunately, when talking about MENA poverty, the discussion is limited to less than half of the countries and approximately 75 percent of the population.

Based on data available from these ten countries, extreme poverty (i.e., the $1.25 a day poverty rate) is highest in Yemen with 17.5 percent. In all other countries, extreme poverty rate is less than 7 percent, lowest in Jordan with only 0.4 percent (table 1.1). In MENA, overall 14 million people live in extreme poverty. Of those living in extreme poverty, 40 percent live in rural areas (IFAD 2011).[12]

However, when poverty is measured based on different benchmarks, such as $2.00 a day, or the national poverty line, the poverty picture significantly changes. When we apply a $2.00 a day poverty line, in Yemen, for example, the proportion of the poor jumps from 17.5 to 47 percent, and the total poor population in MENA jumps from 14 million to 60 million (World Bank 2011). When the national poverty line is the criterion, 18 percent of all Turks are considered poor; a significant jump from 2.7 percent based on the $1.25 a day

Table 1.1   Poverty in MENA

	Year	$1.25 A Day Poverty Rate	$2 A Day Poverty Rate	Rural Poverty*
Algeria	1995	6.79	23.61	22.6 (95)
Egypt, Arab Rep.	2005	1.99	18.46	22 (08)
Iran, Islamic Rep.	2005	1.45	8.03	n/a
Iraq	2007	4.02	25.31	22.9 (07)
Jordan	2006	0.38	3.46	13.3 (08)
Morocco	2007	2.5	13.97	9 (07)
Syrian Arab Republic	2004	1.71	16.85	n/a
Tunisia	2000	2.55	12.08	3.8 (05)
Turkey	2005	2.72	9.05	18.1 (09)
Yemen, Rep.	2005	17.53	46.6	34.8 (05)

Note: *Based on national poverty line.
Source: World Development Indicators (2011).

poverty measurement. Furthermore, based on national poverty lines, which are based on individual national calculations for each country, the total number of poor people rises to 64.5 million (World Bank 2011).

Poverty is mostly concentrated in pockets of particular constituencies in MENA. It is more common among the uneducated, the socially vulnerable such as female-headed households, widows, crowded families, the landless, agricultural laborers, and private sector workers, and more recently in urban areas (Richards and Waterbury 2008; IFAD 2011). According to the most recent global report on rural poverty, it is particularly common among the asset-less: those who do not have cattle, land, or chickens (IFAD 2011). Poverty is also concentrated spatially, such as the rural parts of Upper Egypt and the mountains and steppes of Morocco or northwest Tunisia (Richards and Waterbury 2008).

2.2.1.1. Poverty in Turkey

Poverty in Turkey is concentrated among the rural population. Based on the most recent poverty survey conducted by the State Statistics Institute of Turkey, the urban poverty rate, based on the national poverty line, is low and falling. It dropped from 11.3 percent in 2002 to 6.6 percent in 2009. Rural poverty, on the other hand, rose from 34.48 percent in 2002 to 38.7 percent in 2009. When poverty is measured in relative terms (i.e., those who are below the median income), the rise in poverty for rural Turkey is more striking, from 19.9 percent in 2002 to 34.2 percent in 2009. This suggests increased inequality along with poverty in rural areas. Particularly in recent years, poverty hit the rural unemployed hardest: the poverty rate among the rural unemployed rose from 35.4 percent in 2008 to 51.9 percent in 2009, which is five times more than the 12.4 percent poverty rate among the urban unemployed (TUIK 2011). Sectorally, poverty is also most common in agriculture. Thirty-three percent of those who work in agriculture are poor, as opposed to 9.6 percent in industry and 7.2 percent in the service sector nationally. In rural areas, only the service sector has seen a significant reduction in poverty, from 34.2 percent in 2002 to 20 percent in 2009. In agriculture there has been little change, from 36.8 to 35.4 percent, and in rural industry, poverty has risen from 25.6 to 27.3 percent from 2002 to 2009. The picture is strikingly different in urban areas; from 2002 to 2009 poverty in the urban agricultural sector declined from 33.7 to 13.3 percent; in industry, from 18.8 to 6.4 percent; and in services, from 21.9 to 4.7 percent (TUIK 2011).

Disaggregating the data on poverty in rural agriculture brings to light an interesting pattern, one that tells us something important about the political economy of recent agricultural reforms. The slight overall reduction is achieved because poverty among the employers in rural Turkey has declined significantly, from 15.3 percent in 2002 to 8.5 percent in 2009. On the selling side of the labor market, though, poverty increased among day laborers from 45.3 percent in 2002 to 46.12 percent in 2009. Among waged and salaried workers in rural areas, poverty rose from 18.3 to 21.3 percent, and declined very little among unpaid family workers and the self-employed (TUIK 2011).

This is contrary to the trend in urban Turkey, where poverty has declined in all categories of labor market; day laborers, waged and salaried workers, self-employed, employers, and unpaid family workers all experienced a reduction from 2002 to 2009 (TUIK 2011).

Additionally, in both rural and urban Turkey, poverty among women and female children is more prevalent than among men, but the disparity is more pronounced in rural Turkey. Forty percent of rural women are poor, as opposed to 19 percent of urban women. The poverty trend among rural women is not comforting either; poverty rose from 34 percent in 2002 to 40 percent in 2009. Poverty has risen the fastest for female children under six, from 37 to 51 percent, while male child poverty has increased from 36 to 47 percent in rural Turkey between 2002 and 2009. There is a clear neglect of the rural areas, and particularly the agricultural sector in Turkey.

One of the most recently added links on the chain that connects rural poverty to economic policies is the Agricultural Reform Implementation Program (ARIP), which started in 2001. The mechanism by which such a policy may have resulted in increasing poverty will be analyzed in detail in the following chapters. For now, suffice to say that ARIP is only the most recent policy adding to the immiserization of rural populations and those who work in agriculture, which started in the 1980s.

When the first oil crisis in the 1980s resulted in fiscal troubles for the state, agricultural policies took a turn for the worse. This was the beginning of the Bretton Woods–based stabilization and development programs, welcoming neoliberal economic policies to Turkey under the guidance of the WB and the International Monetary Fund (IMF).

Even though the WB's role in Turkish agriculture dates back to 1950, the nature of the bank's involvement changed in the 1980s. Overall, the WB offered five credits for dams, irrigation, and other agricultural infrastructure projects. Until 1985, all the WB's funding remained project based (Aysu 2002). The fifth of these credits, which came in 1985, was different from the previous ones because, for the first time, the credit was given for the whole sector and not just for a single project; it was titled "agriculture sector adjustment credit". The money was given on the condition that the state cut public spending on the sector.[13] The state changed its protective attitude and started to abolish price supports to agriculture. In 1970, 30 agricultural products were supported by the state, but this number was reduced to 22 in 1985, to 13 in 1988, to 10 in 1990, and to 3 in 1994 (Aysu 2002). By the end of the 1980s, trade liberalization and IMF policies were making Turkish agriculture dependent on imported fertilizers. At the same time, the Turkish lira (TL) was continuously depreciating against the dollar, causing a continuous rise in costs.

The 1990s and the beginning of the twenty-first century have not offered much to the agricultural sector, with one exception: the implementation of a huge irrigation project in the southeastern region of Turkey. The Southeast Anatolia Project (SAP, in Turkish Guneydogu Anadolu Projesi (GAP)) is a regional development project and includes 10 percent of all the cultivable land in Turkey. GAP was conceived in the 1980s with two ultimate goals: first, reducing poverty as a result of increased agricultural output due to increased irrigation, and second, integrating the ethnically diverse Kurds, Arabs, and Turkish people of the region.

During the 1990s, state support continued to decline. After the 1994 financial crisis and the following devaluation of the Turkish lira, the state limited its price support only to a few products, such as sugar beets, tobacco, and cereals. In 1996, the only products that received price support from the state were wheat, alfalfa, corn, tobacco, sugar beets, and poppy capsule. The total support to agriculture was on a declining trend: in 1995, $5 billion; 1996, $2.6 billion; 1997, $3.4 billion; 1998, $3.3 billion; 1999, 2.9 billion; and 2000, $1.4 billion (Aysu 2002). Agricultural policies became even more market friendly in the early 2000s (Cakmak 2004). Under the auspices of the WB in 2001, Turkish state began the implementation of ARIP, which replaced producer subsidies with direct income support, and this was phased out in 2008. ARIP resulted in the elimination of most government subsidies in agriculture and put emphasis on the role of markets as the sole decision-making mechanism in production and distribution in the agricultural sector. Rather than providing subsidies in the form of procurement prices and cheap credit for inputs such as fertilizers and oil, these direct transfers were given to every landowner possessing up to 500 *donums*, which is quite a large land plot.

Additionally, ARIP's implementation came along with the privatization of state economic enterprises in agriculture. The legislation on privatization of tobacco (TEKEL) and sugar (TurkSeker) has been completed and sales are partially realized.[14] The privatization of state economic enterprise for tea (CAYKUR) and milk (SEK) is also completed. Crop production declined sharply beginning in 2001. Turkey was now on its way to a free market system in agriculture.

Continuous neglect of the agrarian sector resulted in mass rural-urban migration, which was part of a state-led policy pioneered under the leadership of Turgut Ozal (1983–1993) to create a reserve army of labor for urban industrialization. Between 1995 and 2000, based on the 2000 population census, net migration velocity (i.e., the number of people who migrated to a region in every thousand persons) from northern regions of the Black Sea was 50, followed by 48 from northeastern Anatolia. Istanbul was highest among those that experienced immigration, with 46, followed by western Marmara, with 26. In the end, migration brought crime, poverty, and frustrated people as a result of the state's incapacity to create jobs and provide infrastructure for those who migrated. Consequently, national unemployment rates surged from 8.4 percent in 1988 to 14 percent in 2009, remaining over 10 percent for the entire period from 2002 to 2009, peaking after the global crisis at 14 percent and finally declining to 9.4 percent in 2011 (TUIK 2011; World Bank 2011). Another alarming development that has come with neoliberal policies is the declining labor force participation and employment to population rates, both of which have declined significantly, from 59 to 51 percent from 1980 to 2009, and from 53 to and 43 percent from 1991 to 2008,[15] respectively (TUIK 2011; World Bank 2011).

Market-centered organization of agriculture is doomed to fail in creating employment, output increase, and achieve overall resource allocation efficiency when structural inequalities, particularly inequalities in landownership are high in rural societies. Instead, such policies end up creating socioeconomic problems. This is exactly what has been happening in rural Turkey since ARIP. Economic policies and political power are very much imbedded, particularly in developing countries where institutions of democracy and participation in civic life through civil society organizations are not fully developed. Hence, looking at how landownership inequality has evolved and influenced the choice of agricultural policies in Turkey is necessary. The following section provides this historical perspective.

2.3. Turkey's Agrarian Relations through a Historical Lens (1500s to Present)

To understand the structure of landownership in modern Turkey, we need to understand two things. First, landownership cannot be understood without an understanding of the relations of production (i.e., the socioeconomic relationships among people and between people and land). Second, we need to understand the process of agrarian transformation and in particular the role of state policy. The landownership structure of the current Turkish Republic has its roots in the land structure of the Ottoman Empire, from which Turkey emerged after the declaration of the republic in 1923. Hence we will narrate the evolution of landownership inequality and agrarian transformation starting from Ottoman times.

Most entries in the literature on agrarian change in Turkey revolve around one of two views: that the agrarian transformation was the result of the class struggle between peasants and landlords and that change was brought about through state policies, along with the slower movements of technology, population, changing factor endowments, political dynamics, and market prices as reflected through state policies (Aricanli 1976; Inalcik 1978; Kongar 1992; Aksoy 1998; Koymen 1999; Karaomerlioglu 2000).

According to many in the literature, landholding in the Ottoman Empire can be characterized as a constant struggle between the state and the individual for control of agricultural lands (Inalcik 1978; Kongar 1992; Aksoy 1998; Karaomerlioglu 2000). The state had two main reasons to concern itself with the control of land: national security concerns and wealth generation for capital formation and state finances because the Empire was entirely dependent on agrarian production for its finances and for the maintenance of its military forces, called *sipahi* forces.

Private landownership didn't exist on the lands of the Empire until the decline of the Ottoman Empire in the late sixteenth century. Land was owned by the state and used by people in a tenure-like system. According to Inalcik (1978), Islamic Law (*Shari'a*), parallel with the state laws (*orfi kanun*) issued by the Sultan of the Empire, provided the legal framework for landholding of agricultural lands. On the one hand, Islamic Law protected the freehold rights of the individual, and on the other hand, state laws implemented state control on agricultural lands.

Agricultural production was organized in the *cift-hane* system. *Hanes* were peasant households, each of which was given a *cift*, or *ciftlik* (i.e., a plot of land sufficient to sustain one peasant family, including rent payments to the state). The sizes of *ciftliks* were dependent upon the fertility of the land and varied from 60 to 150 *donums*.[16] The usage rights of the land belonged to the household head, usually the eldest male. Upon the death of the household head, the land remained under the ownership of the state, and the usage rights were collectively held by the heirs of the deceased head of household.

The *cift-hane* system was an integral part of the *timar* system, the basic military institution in the classical period of the Empire. In the *timar* system, agricultural production and, hence, land were collectively controlled by the state and the mounted soldier of the imperial army, who was called *sipahi*. Every *sipahi* was assigned a *timar*, which was an area of land cultivated by peasants, from whom he was entitled to collect a fixed amount of rent. He would then transfer some of his tax revenues to the state and keep the rest for himself as his salary and also to cover the costs of his armed men (i.e., the part of the imperial army under his command). Similar to the *ciftlik*, the *timar* was fixed, nontransferable, and indivisible. A *sipahi* didn't have the ownership rights to the land, but he had some authority over the use of it and over the organization of rural life and agricultural production on his *timar*.

The *timar* system was common in Anatolia and the Balkans. It provided both military force and state revenue to the Empire, and was closely monitored by a traditional bureaucracy. This particular organization of agricultural production was well suited to the sociopolitical conditions of what could be called the Middle East Empire tradition. It achieved control by giving autonomy to local powers within a geographically spread empire while providing revenue to the state.

Up to this point, the Ottoman agrarian structure seems like a classical feudal mode of production. The peasants turned over a portion of their agricultural production to the *sipahi* in return for military protection. However, the Ottoman mode of agricultural production differed from a feudal structure in two distinct ways. First, the land and labor of the farmer (*reaya*) were protected by the state against third parties who might attempt to convert these lands into privately owned farms and reduce the peasants to laborers, sharecroppers, or serfs. Second, Ottoman law guaranteed a tenant, who is described as a married man and his male heirs, the right to enjoy, permanently and freely, the use of state-owned lands, called the *miri* lands, as long as these lands were used under specified conditions. The *miri* gave peasants a fallback option. The *miri* lands were different than *cift hane* and the *timar* because they were common lands and could be used by anyone for individual purposes.

The *miri* lands emerged for the purpose of maximizing the Ottoman state's revenue from agricultural production. First of all, those who could claim the *miri* lands needed to improve these lands substantially since these lands were lower in quality, for example, waste lands, swamps, stony fields, or arid lands. Hence, those who were to claim a piece of *miri* land were expected to invest via construction of canals or drying the swamps so that land would become cultivable. The second condition for claims on the *miri* land was the sultan's permission. The sultan granted his permission with a special document stating usufruct rights on the reclaimed land. The state encouraged such reclamations to extend arable land and eventually state revenue.

These *miri* reclamations were the first seeds of inequality in land access and eventually its ownership. Investment in the *miri* lands required capital, and those who had capital were mostly members of high rank in the military and/or the ruling elite. So, these lands were reclaimed not by the tillers but by absentee elite, who are close to the palace, and by those who already had wealth to fulfill the preconditions to claim land. Mostly, these absentee landowners lived in cities and monitored their reclaimed *miri* property by a hired farmer/manager, who lived on the land with his family and was considered to be the highest authority on the farm. As a result of this policy, the first seeds of unequal private access to land were sown into the structure of agrarian organization and the society, supported and institutionalized by the state.

The first signs of private property emerged in the weakening empire in the sixteenth century when *miri* land reclamations were extended from use rights to landownership rights. As the empire weakened, *miri* lands came partly under the control of private individuals. Sultans, who lacked the power to challenge local elites, ended up granting certain rights of control to the individuals on such lands. Alongside this *miri* land formation came the establishment of *waqf* lands. *Waqf* lands were originally state lands in the form of property grants, which were subsequently turned into trusts for religious endowments by influential figures in the palace or by those close to palace circles.

Even though the *cift hane* and *timar* systems still existed, land granting became more widespread through the sixteenth century. Surprisingly, these changes in the legal status of land didn't involve a change in agrarian organization (i.e., there was no change in the organization of labor). This was surprising because one would expect private ownership of land to lead to more capitalistic relations of production, such as use of wage labor in agriculture. Instead, the relationship between the farmer and private individuals or the farmer and the *waqfs* was the same as it had been under the *timar* system. The only thing that changed was the identity of the people who were collecting rent in the form of dues. Those who collected rent never attempted to change how production was organized; no other land tenure systems, such as sharecropping or land leasing, were allowed. According to Inalcik (1978), this change-resistant attitude of the Empire toward the organization of agriculture caused its stagnation for three hundred years.[17]

The imperial weakness that allowed the emergence of private property persisted and led to additional changes in the structure of landownership. At the end of the sixteenth century, social unrest rooted both in ethnic differences and in the economic interests of the leaders and erupted in a series of conflicts called the Celali uprisings. One result of the uprisings was the transfer of land ownership from absentee owners to local powers. The Celali uprisings emerged from the efforts of large Kurdish landlords to seek independence in the Eastern Anatolia region of the empire, and the weakened state of the empire made it easy for the uprisings to succeed. Once autonomy was achieved, landlords in the region increased taxes on agricultural production to such burdensome levels that it was difficult for the peasants to survive, which consequently resulted in the out-migration of peasants from their villages. This development left the lands under the absolute authority and domination of local Kurdish landlords. Corruption in local governments also contributed to this ownership shift. Many peasants who were in need of credit and indebted lost their rights to cultivate the land to local notables and to military chiefs through a simple decision of the local court, which again the local elite controlled. The people who were implementing the laws took the opportunity to enrich themselves by granting themselves the *miri* lands. Hence, usurers, mostly town-based military or religious leaders (*ulama*), took over peasants' use rights on agricultural lands, and over time, such lands turned into privately owned properties concentrated in the hands of the local elite.

The shift in landownership from the state to the local powers created the need for the first land reform in Ottoman history. Sultan Ahmet the First issued laws in 1609 known as "land reconstruction" (*arazi islahati*), which entitled tillers to the agricultural lands and encouraged the migrated peasants to go back to their villages and reclaim what they had lost. However, neither the sultan nor the state had enough authority to enforce these laws, and, thus, the redistribution attempts of the empire failed (Inalcik 1998).

After the Celali uprisings, the transformation of the landownership structure from state owned to privately owned continued at a relatively faster pace. The influential people among the military in their provinces appropriated the lands abandoned by the villagers as a result of the Celali disorders. Consequently, private landownership emerged incrementally in the Ottoman Empire. Earlier, use rights changed hands, while ultimate ownership of the land remained with the state. Now, landownership also changed hands from state to local powers.

Another major transformation in the structure of landownership came with a so-called lease-out system. Inalcik (1978) argued that this was the most important of all changes. Starting with the accelerating decline in the early seventeenth century, pressured by financial bottlenecks, the treasury of the empire leased out a growing number of *miri* lands to individuals for a life term, which later became virtually like property. This was the end of state control because a class of leasers intervened between the peasants and the state. Leasers became landlords, and peasants became tenants. By this transformation, the relationship between landholder and farmer underwent a profound change. Now, leasers had a motivation to maximize profits because, as owners of the means of production, they were entitled to keep the residual from agricultural production.

However, a lifetime lease was a short time in agriculture, so the ambition to get the maximum out of the lands caused exploitation of the peasants and the lands. The state was aware of this problem and proposed a remedy that changed the structure of landownership yet again. The state extended the term of leases, hoping that leasers would take better care of the lands, which ended up strengthening the asset position of landlords. The leasing-out system became more widespread than ever before and was popularly supported by the ruling elite. Most of the leaseholders emerged as a new class of provincial notables and new type of "entrepreneurs" in land reclamation and expansion of plantation-like farms.

The last attempt to redistribute land in the Ottoman Empire was connected to efforts to save the falling empire. In 1848, the state issued a law declaring that all land belonged to the state and was to be used by only the tillers. It was a fleeting and futile gesture. Not only was the state powerless to implement this law, but also, in 1858, only ten years later, the sultan acknowledged private ownership of land and recognized its exchange in the market as legal.[18]

Based on the landownership structure and the organization of agrarian production, it is argued in the literature that the Ottoman economy and social structure were transformed from an Asiatic mode of production to a European capitalistic one (Inalcik 1978; Koymen 1999). The emergence of the new ownership structure from the ruins of the old *timar* system was analogous to the passage from feudalism to capitalism in Europe. However, the shift in Europe was initiated bottom up (Inalcik 1978), while the transformation of the agrarian structure in the Ottoman Empire was from top to bottom. Aricanli (1976) argues that the state played a major role in the transformation with the purpose of expanding the base of the Ottoman state revenue. Policies about reclaiming the *miri* lands are a good example of this policy, as is the Land Code of 1858. As Aricanli (1976) points out, title deeds of 1858 did not imply unconditional and unbreakable private property rights. The condition to keep the title was to till the land, and there was no ceiling for the size of land that could be owned. This condition clearly serves the goal of increasing the revenue base for the Ottoman state without colliding with the local powers.

Another transformation in Ottoman agriculture came as a result of changes in global agricultural prices. The empire initiated a policy to follow an export-oriented strategy with the expectation of increasing its revenues further. Food prices were high between the years 1800 and 1840. During the Napoleonic wars and the Greek War of Independence, maritime trade along the shores of the Eastern Mediterranean was disrupted (Tabak and Keyder 1998). This disruption caused a shortage, exacerbated by the Egyptian invasion of Syrian provinces, and food prices remained high during this period. Commercialization increased the revenue of the producer, and therefore, the state did everything to enhance export-oriented agricultural production, such as allowing land concentration and producing beyond self-sufficiency.

Anatolian agriculture was rapidly commercialized in the nineteenth century, and migration policies were used to help this commercialization process (Onal 2010). The agricultural labor force was mobilized by forced migration from the Balkans and the Crimea Anatolia, a process that continued into the twentieth century.

As a result of these state policies, or in some instances as a result of the Ottoman state's weaknesses, large landed property eventually materialized in the twentieth century. Concentrated landownership was most common in the southeastern regions of Anatolia, mainly in Cukurova (i.e., the most fertile land in Anatolia). But other forms of large landed estates in Eastern Anatolia were a result of nonpenetration of the state.

When the Ottoman Empire conquered Eastern Anatolia from the Karakoyunlular tribe during the early years of the 1500s, the Ottomans allowed a form of governance called *derebeylik*. The institution of *derebeylik* allowed Kurdish landlords not only the ownership of land but also total autonomy over domestic governance. In return for their freedom, the landlords were to pay taxes on agricultural output. The purpose of this policy was to raise state revenue without causing further conflict between the Ottoman state and the Karakoyunlular state. The Ottoman Empire had little interest in investing in these provinces, and large landlords had local governing authority; thus, keeping the status quo was in the landlords' interest. Even today, these semifeudal relations exist in the Kurdish populated areas of Turkey as remnants of the political choices made in the Ottoman times. This ownership structure granted to Kurds is also the reason why the land concentration of these regions is among the highest in today's Turkey. The semifeudal structure within the Eastern Anatolia region, combined with high landownership inequality, also enhances "the Kurdish problem" since land concentration brings other socioeconomic problems, especially unemployment and/or underemployment in a by and large agrarian population. Later, during the republic years, the need for the Kurdish population to be integrated into the Turkish nation was used to emphasize the need for land reform.

Following the First World War, in 1923, the Turkish Republic emerged from the ashes of the Ottoman Empire after a four-year War of Independence. During the war, large landlords provided manpower and matériel to the independence army. The power of the landlords was not the only reason for the success of independence but neither was it negligible.

In the early years of the republic, the nationalist leaders tried to Westernize the country and create a national identity out of the remnants of the Ottoman Empire via top-to-bottom reforms. The formation of the republic, as well as implementation of the reforms, depended on the support of local powers. Thus, one of the first things the new state did was to abolish the agricultural tax to show its support for local powers and to ease the burdens on a population already traumatized by the war. When the war ended, those who were commanders during the war became local representatives in parliament, forming the ruling elite of the republic. As it happens, these were the same people who were the local elite during the Ottoman Empire.

Given the necessity of rebuilding the postwar economy on a largely agrarian economic base, Kemal Ataturk, the founder of the republic, framed the political agenda on agrarian issues with his famous words: "the peasant is the master of our nation." Hence, the 1920s and 1930s were times of populist reforms and pro-peasant policies. By 1930, 15 million out of a population of 18 million were still in the agricultural sector, and clearly, if the Turkish Republic was going to industrialize, the majority of the resources for industrialization would have to come from the agricultural sector in the form of labor, raw materials, or revenues. These were all the young republic had to rely on for resources. Hence, the path to modern economic development had to go through a transformation of the agricultural sector. This was a beaten development path that had been followed by the world's most industrialized nations, and the leadership of the young republic was aware of it.

By the 1930s, during the Great Depression, Turkey's agricultural production fell into a crisis as a result of a dramatic collapse in world agricultural prices. The 1930s witnessed an increasing concern by the Kemalist elite with the well-being of the peasantry and agricultural production. These concerns were reflected in state economic policies supporting peasants and the agricultural sector.

Two types of measures were taken to address these concerns: economic and sociocultural. On the economic side, the state fixed agricultural prices in an effort to stabilize them and protect the producers from global market fluctuations. The state also established a bank—*T. C. Ziraat Bankasi* (Agricultural Bank of the Turkish Republic)—that focused on agricultural loans to provide cheap credit and input subsidies. The Agricultural Bank was specifically designed to support the agricultural sector, but an important corollary was that peasants supported state spending because the bank also operated as a savings institution for the rural population and hence, mobilized funds from remote rural places.

On the sociocultural side, both rural and urban projects were undertaken to increase awareness of rural problems among the urban population, as well as to educate the rural population. The most prominent project in urban Turkey was the foundation of "The People's Houses" (Halkevleri), in 1932. Their members were encouraged to go to the countryside to educate and enlighten peasants. On the rural side, in the late 1930s, the most significant project was the establishment of "Village Institutes" public schools for peasant children from grades 6 through 12. They were instrumental in transforming the uneducated rural population to an educated, productive agricultural society. The aim was not only to enlighten peasants but also to create a rural population who would be productive without much state support. Courses ranged from science and mathematics to practical matters about rural life and production, such as veterinary skills, basic nursing, and other useful information that would increase agricultural productivity. What was also revolutionary about these institutes was that, for the first time in Ottoman and Turkish history, education included a coed boarding school system. The schools were residential because of limitations to the road and transportation infrastructure in the young republic. Commuting was difficult if not impossible for most peasant children, so for continuing education, the children had to board at the school.

Unfortunately, in the 1960s, the governing right-wing party (i.e., the Justice Party AKP) closed the Village Institutes on the grounds that they were the cradle of communists and out-of-wedlock relationships. Although the Village Institutes were open only for a short period, they had a profound impact on Turkish politics, culture, and village life because they mobilized an immense human potential that no government had considered before. During the Ottoman times, peasants were seen only as a source of labor and revenue, and educating them was of no concern. Closing these schools was a sign of the strength of landed classes in the senate, and the resulting power dynamic played a crucial role in the making of the Turkish path to (under)development for many years to come.

However, despite the strength of the landed elite in the senate, the newborn republic had to redistribute land to the landless for both political and economic reasons. The first land reform of the young republic, dated back to the early 1920s, came immediately after the founding of the republic in 1923. The government distributed negligible amounts of land to specific groups, notably Muslim immigrants from the former Ottoman territories.

Economic conditions during the late 1920s, combined with political worries about stability, brought the second land reform attempt. One of the main concerns and the underlying political worry that put land reform on the agenda of the state was the increasing number of landless poor. Since the 1930s, an increasing proportion of the population was landless and poor. In 1934, more than 30 percent of 15 million peasants were landless. A study by P. M. Zhukovsky[19] shows that 5 percent of families owned 65 percent of all land in 1933.

Given the situation and the fact that Turkey was an agrarian society with the goal of developing to the levels of Western civilization, the distribution of land had to be more equitable. As a result, politicians started to acknowledge the need to provide land to the poor, and in the fall of 1929, the government, headed by Prime Minister Ismet Inonu, announced plans to distribute land to landless peasants, while it emphasized that under no circumstances would it aim to hurt big landowners whose production was efficient. The reason for not touching the large landowners was because of the organic relation between the ruling elite and large landowners and economic considerations. The state was grateful to whoever was producing something, especially for a treasury that was bankrupt after the Balkan and independence wars. An additional nationalist concern was the so-called Kurdish problem. Redistributing land, particularly in the eastern regions of Turkey, where both land and the Kurdish population were concentrated, would break the feudal relations of production and would eradicate Kurdish nationalism.

The new emphasis on peasants and land reform bore its first fruits in 1934 in the senate. The leadership, led by Kemal Ataturk, proclaimed that every Turkish family should have the right to a piece of land large enough to provide subsistence. In 1934, a more comprehensive "Settlement Law" was passed that opened the way to redistribute land from large to small farmers. However, large landowners in parliament successfully blocked the attempted redistribution. The campaign to prevent land redistribution was impressive and wide-spread. One senator from the city of Eskisehir, Emin Sazak, made an offer to donate thirty thousand hectares to the state if the state would give up its plan to redistribute land from the rich to the poor.

After the first failed land reform attempt of 1934, in November 1936, Ataturk declared that it was absolutely necessary for every Turkish farmer family to possess enough land to cultivate and earn a living. However, the government still encouraged the surplus generated by the big farms. In the spring of 1937, land reform issues occupied a central place in parliamentary discussions of the changes to the constitution. To make peasants active elements of the society, they had to be given their own land and be freed from working on other people's lands. These attempts can be seen as determinants of the development plan the leaders, particularly Ataturk and Inonu, had in mind. However, the plan was never implemented because of the political balance leaning toward the landed elite.

As soon as the war ended in 1945, despite considerable opposition, the government passed a law titled Law for Providing Land to Farmers (LPLF). The law made clear that government land and other productive lands were to be distributed first. Although the law stated that private land could be distributed only if other lands were not available, private holdings larger than five thousand donums were subject to redistribution, and this ceiling could be decreased to two thousand donums in regions where land was scarce. However, the law was also open to interpretation in that efficiently and rationally cultivated large holdings could be exempt from the law.

The most controversial item of the law, Article 17, which was added at the last minute, gave right of ownership to the tiller. Agricultural workers and sharecroppers could claim the land they worked on. The maximum amount offered to the tiller–tenants had a floor for the existing landowners rather than a ceiling for the tenant. Tenants could not claim land if the claim resulted in fewer than 50 *donums* of land for the landlord from whom they would claim. If implemented, this article would have redistributed vast amounts of land because share-cropping was widespread in Turkey. Unfortunately, the law lacked the genuine political will of the majority in the parliament. Article 17 never saw daylight. On the contrary, President Inonu appointed Cavit Oral, a big landowner who was among the strongest opponents of the law, as head of the Ministry of Agriculture, the agency responsible for implementing the law. As a result, in 1945, of the 22 million donums (20.2 billion square meters) of land distributed to landless peasants, only 56 thousand were taken from large landowners; the rest came from state-owned lands.

Along with the land reform attempt, the government also implemented "Farmer's Homesteads," which purported to create and maintain independent farmer families and secure the indivisibility of agricultural land between three and five hundred donums for each family. In Farmer Homesteads, land could be owned and inherited by only one person provided other members in the family would be financially compensated. These lands could not be sold before 25 years, nor could they be mortgaged. Last, but not least, Farmer Homesteads could not be rented out, and sharecropping was strictly forbidden. The government's first motivation for the development of homesteads was to stabilize production by stabilizing and protecting the land size and ownership. The second reason was to politically stabilize society. By creating and sustaining "rooted" families who relied solely on their labor and property, the government hoped to avoid a peasant revolution, which happened not so long ago in neighboring Russia in 1917.

However, even in the mid-1950s, the planned modernization via industrialization was still not on the horizon. In 1955, 77.4 percent of the labor force was in agriculture, contributing 40 percent to the gross national product (GNP) (Kongar 1998). The land reforms, meanwhile, had not reached everyone in agriculture. The first land statistics of the republic era date to the 1950s. According to these statistics, approximately 13 percent of households (i.e., 2,760,304 families) were landless peasants.

The 1950s was a benchmark decade in the mode of production for agriculture. After the Second World War, under the Marshall Plan, the United States was trying to keep communism away from Europe. Turkey's geostrategic location forced the United States to include Turkey among the recipients of aid through the Marshall Plan even though Turkey had not been in the Second World War.

The Marshall aid came in the form of tractors. The number of tractors increased immensely. In Turkey, there were approximately 9,900 tractors in 1951, and this number increased to 118,800 in 1971 and to 702,000 by the year 1991 (Koymen 1999). These tractors were concentrated in the richer western parts of Turkey, namely, Midnorth, Aegean, Marmara, and Mediterranean. These regions held 85 percent of all the tractors in Turkey in 1951. The percentage shrank to 67 percent by 1991 (Koymen 1999), but this change was due more to tractor satiation in the west than to more egalitarian policies.

Premature mechanization brought problems to Turkey. Koymen (1999) argues that the mechanization of agriculture ended up being disastrous for Turkey because of high unemployment in the agricultural sector, combined with the state's incapacity to create jobs as fast as mechanization freed agricultural labor. Alongside high unemployment, another negative impact of mechanization was increased concentration of lands: those who could afford tractors grew faster and bought more lands. Sixty-nine percent of the tractors were owned by those who had more than 100 donums of land in 1963 (Koymen 1999).

With the increased mechanization, the 1960s could be considered the period of transition to modern agriculture. In those years, not only tractors but also pesticides, fertilizers, irrigation systems, and intensive cultivation were implemented into production. The transition was facilitated by state policies, such as commodity price supports, that protected the agricultural sector from global competition.

After the 1945 LPLF, the government made a few more failed attempts at land reform in the period up to 1973. Each time a land redistribution law was proposed, the strong opposition of the landed elite in the parliament blocked implementation.

Agricultural surveys conducted in 1952, 1963, and 1980 show that 62 to 72 percent of families owned less than 50 donums, and land concentration was on an upward trend: those who owned more than 200 donums rose from 28 to 35 percent (Kazgan 1999).

By the 1970s, private property and a concentrated landownership structure had been established. Changes in agriculture since then have resulted mostly from changes to state policy and the increasing intervention of international organizations, such as the IMF and the WB. Since the 1980s, as protection from global market competition has been withdrawn, changes in landownership have come mostly as an adjustment strategy by farmers responding to changing market dynamics.

2.4. Turkey, Islam, and the EU

During the 1980s, another prominent development in both the Turkish and MENA's sociopolitical and economic landscape was the rise of political Islam. The term "political Islam" may be a misnomer: if "political" means relating to the social organization and public affairs of a society through governance "then Islam is inherently political" (Richards and Waterbury 2008, 362). Different from other world religion systems in its core, Islam dictates laws to govern public affairs through *Shari'a* laws.

Islam has always played a prominent role in shaping the sociopolitical and economic life in MENA. When the last Islamic empire, the Ottoman Empire, fell at the end of the First World War, Islamic identity started to gain stronger ground as a form of resistance to the European invasion and colonization (Owen and Pamuk 1999; Richards and Waterbury 2008). With the defeat of the Ottoman Empire, the modern nations of MENA came into being in the twentieth century. In the formation of the MENA nations, Arabism and Islam formed the only common base of social and national identity. Later, particularly after the 1980s, the increasing marginalization of the developing countries by globalization and neoliberal economic policies has resulted in increased radicalization of Islam in many MENA countries (Hakimian and Moshaver 2001).

Turkey was never colonized, and the top-to-bottom reforms of nation building based on the Turkic identity after the birth of the new republic in 1923 prevented political Islam from becoming influential in socioeconomic and political life. Thus, for historical and cultural reasons, Turkey has been more resistant to radical and violent forms of Islam than have the other societies of MENA despite its 99 percent Muslim majority, most of whom are Sunnis (Rabasa and Larrabee 2008; Meral 2010). However, along with other developing countries, Turkey was not immune to the marginalization resulting from the new economic order brought by globalization and the neoliberal paradigm. It was exactly during the 1980s, when neoliberal economic policies started to play an important role in Turkish economic policies, that political Islam started its ascent. Ironically, radical Islam entered the Turkish political stream through Germany as a result of political asylum granted to the former mufti of Adana, Cemalettin Kaplan. In Germany, he founded the Union of Islamic Communities and Societies, whose mandate was establishing an Islamic state in Turkey (Rabasa and Larrabee 2008).

According to Rabasa and Larrabee (2008), the recent victory of the governing Justice and Democracy Party (AKP), led by Recep Tayyip Erdogan, has its roots in the changing socioeconomic dynamics of Turkey, changes that began under Turgut Ozal, who introduced neoliberal policies in the 1980s. As part of the neoliberal agenda of the state, Ozal inaugurated privatization of State Economic Enterprises (SEEs). Privatization of SEEs has led to the mushrooming of conservative Istanbul-based entrepreneurs whose roots were in rural Turkey (Rabasa and Larrabee 2008). The neoliberal paradigm and market-centered organization of the economy did not necessarily clash with the rise of political Islam in Turkey or in other Muslim countries. Islam is not against any particular type of economic regime, such as socialism versus capitalism, but against a non-*Shari'a* way of organizing society (Pfeifer 1997).

On the contrary, neoliberal policies helped the rise of political Islam in Turkey. In the face of fast rural-urban migration resulting from the neglect of the rural sector and agriculture and increasing unemployment due to the state's inability to generate sufficient employment, urban poverty and inequality have increased during the early years of neoliberal policies (Gurses 2007). Rising poverty aided the rise of AKP. The urban poverty problem was addressed through high provision of welfare subsidies (*sadaka*) by religious groups, which were funded by this newly emerging business class from rural Anatolia. These welfare subsidies have helped AKP to gain support, particularly among the urban poor who were originally rural migrants. These events also partially explain why urban poverty has been significantly declining in Turkey since the 2000s when compared to rural poverty. In our view, the urban poor have been in a Stockholm syndrome–like situation. Stockholm syndrome describes the phenomenon of captives falling in love with their captors. Just as in the syndrome, the feelings of sympathy by the urban poor toward AKP government are irrational but developed because of the risk to survival. The rural poor were impoverished because of AKP-backed neoliberal policies, and this impoverishment helped strengthen the urban political base of the AKP, who are hungry for welfare provisions. However, in very few cases do poor people's votes make a difference in governance. Turkey is not one of them. It was actually the support of the urban middle class that has been behind AKP's political success.

One factor in AKP's success to get the middle class votes was its moderate approach to Islam, combined with the party's so-called economic success. According to Meral (2010), even though AKP was an offshoot of a more radical movement of Islam, represented by *Milli Görüş* and the *Refah Partisi* in Turkish politics, AKP was different. It does not have the utopia to unite all Muslims under one flag like *Refah Partisi* had (Rabasa and Larrabee 2008; Meral 2010). The leadership of AKP knows that such a vision would not find political support at home. According to a 2006 study by Turkish Economic and Social Studies Institute (TESEV), even though the proportion of those who identify themselves as Muslim first is 44 percent, those who are in favor of *Shari'a* are only 9 percent. Furthermore, among

AKP voters, those who are opposed to *Shari'a* are 70 percent. These figures illustrate that AKP votes were not for Islamic ambitions.

Meral (2010) argues that in its attempt to develop relations with MENA and the Muslim Central Asian countries, such as Azerbaijan, the main motive behind AKP's foreign policy has been economics and not religion. The increasing wave of globalization and neoliberal economic policies help further this rediscovered alliance. Even though there are religious-based interpretations of AKP's increasing relations with its Muslim neighbors, it is true that as a result of open borders and increased trade, a new entrepreneurial business class has emerged in Turkey from the Anatolian plains.[20]

A couple of historical occurrences also helped strengthen Recep Tayyip Erdogan's image as the aspiring new leader of the Muslim world. During the 2009 Davos meetings, known for his volatile temperament, Recep Tayyip Erdogan abruptly left the stage during Israeli prime minister Shimon Peres's speech after rebuking Peres. Erdogan was criticized both at home and abroad for such politically incorrect behavior, but in reality, he found much sympathy, if not support, among Muslims (Meral 2010). However, the Davos incident did not hurt the existing trade relations between Israel and Turkey. Not until recently, after the flotilla crisis in 2010, did tourism and trade suffer between the two nations. Some see the Turkish leader as the new Ataturk of the Muslim world, backed by a strong economic and political clout, who arrived at last to change the Middle East dynamics in favor of Palestine either through soft power or hard power. Additionally, Turkey's strong relations with the West make Turkey the best suitor for mediation to further the increasingly polarizing Israeli-Arab dialogue.

A secular Muslim country since its inception in 1923, Turkey has always aspired to be part of Western civilization, both economically and culturally. Until now, it has aligned significantly more with the West and almost ignored the Muslim world. Turkey is an active member of many social, economic, and political supranational institutions: the United Nations (1945), the Council of Europe (1949), NATO (1952), the Organization for Economic Co-operation and Development (1961), the Organization for Security and Co-operation in Europe (1973), the Western European Union (1992), and the European Customs Union (1995). Turkey was officially recognized as a candidate for full membership to the EU in 1999. Based on the Copenhagen Criteria, negotiations between Turkey and the EU started in 2006; however, progress has been very slow due to political issues regarding Cyprus[21] and freedom of the press (Morelli 2011).

Even though the European Council has never officially acknowledged it, 70 million Muslims joining EU have been at the center of European anxiety. Such anxiety is evidenced by the 2005 referenda in France and Holland. When the outcome of the referenda turned out to be in favor of keeping Turkey out of Europe, the possibility of Turkish membership significantly declined (Rabasa and Larrabee 2008).

Having started on already sour grounds, since the negotiations started in 2006, out of the 35 chapters, only 14 have opened, 1 closed (on science and research), and 8 are frozen. AKP has been putting significant effort into complying with the Copenhagen Criteria, which supposedly helped democratize and increased civil society participation in the country (Morelli 2011). However, the EU claims that the progress has not been enough. In November 2010, when the European Council released its assessment of Turkey's progress toward fulfilling the Copenhagen Criteria, particularly pointing out the Cyprus issue, it has become clear to AKP that EU membership may never happen for Turkey or at least not anytime in the near future (Morelli 2011).

This political stalemate increased the momentum toward economic and political alliance between Turkey and its Muslim neighbors. Ironically, AKP's increased orientation toward the Muslim world has added to the existing discomfort within the EU and the United States, raising worries about Turkey's long-term global intentions and further stalling the accession progress (Morelli 2011).

Turkey's newfound active engagement with all its neighbors, and particularly with MENA, has been not mostly because of the EU stalemate or the increasing impact of political Islam. Turkey's new paradigm in foreign policy, namely the "strategic depth," has been more instrumental in this new direction. The intellectual architect behind this doctrine, previously an academic, Ahmet Davutoglu, almost single handedly transformed Turkish foreign affairs after becoming foreign affairs minister in 2009. Strategic depth simply meant to use Turkey's existing strategic strengths, such as its geopolitical location, its secular and Muslim population, and its legacy as the last Islamic Empire, to deepen Turkey's influence in a region that has been vastly changing since the end of the Cold War in 1989. Embarking upon the doctrine of strategic depth, Turkey started to strengthen its cultural, sociopolitical, economic, and historical relations not only with its Muslim neighbors in Central Asia, the Balkans, and the Middle East but also with Russia while keeping its ties with the EU and the United States (Rabasa and Larrabee 2008; Meral 2010).

This new role as an aspiring regional and global power is clearly illustrated by the Turkish leadership in their efforts to gain official recognition of Palestinian nationhood at the 66th General Assembly of the United Nations in New York during September 2011. Since the 2008 financial crisis, the European economy has been fragile due to Greece's debt problem, which further deepened from the financial troubles of Spain, Portugal, and Italy during 2011. The United States has been struggling to recover from the crisis, with little success in creating employment. The Middle East has been going through a major social change with the Arab Spring. The timing of Turkey's new aspirations as a regional leader and a global player could not have been better. Whether Turkey will rise to the challenge in such a diverse region is another matter that we will discuss later.

In the meantime, Turkey's high economic growth has been helping its aspirations, while countries around her have been going through socioeconomic problems. Turkey registered notably high annual growth rates in the earlier part of the last decade, averaging 5.4 percent starting from 2002 until the crisis hit in 2008, and it is rebounding much faster than its neighbors with 9 percent annual growth in 2010 and 11 percent year-on-year growth in the first quarter of 2011 (TUIK 2011; World Bank 2011). However, the GDP growth has been shadowed by high unemployment and unsustainable balance of payments problems, which increase its social and economic vulnerability.

3. Conclusion: Challenges and Opportunities

Can Turkey—an economically fast-growing country with a large but neglected agrarian base, high unemployment, a large deficit, and a crowded secular Muslim population, located strategically between the Christian and the Muslim world—lead MENA out of its problems achieving peace, water and food security, and economic development? Can political Islam and the Ottoman heritage be major strengths for Turkey to claim the regional and global role its current leader desires?

To answer the first question, we think not. Turkey has much economic and social vulnerability to claim the role of a leader. Turkey has domestic problems it needs to attend to, such as rural poverty, high unemployment, and an inefficient agricultural sector that has been deteriorating for some time. Muslim identity or affinity to MENA countries due to Ottoman legacy will not compensate for structural weaknesses in the economy. Without being a significant economic power, regional leadership is unlikely.

However, Turkey can play a prominent role in regional cooperation by using its cultural and historical alliance with MENA and its already existing strong ties with the West on a couple of issues. First, rural migration is a big problem for the MENA region, most of whom end up in Europe. Europe's increasing Muslim population creates the opportunity for Europe and Turkey to cooperate in addressing the social issues arising from migration. Second, given the extent of the problem of MENA's rising demand for agricultural products, rising food prices, and water scarcity, the solution does not lie within the hands of any single nation in the region. Agriculture as a development strategy confined within national borders is neither a viable nor a wanted strategy for MENA. Regional cooperation is a must, particularly to overcome challenges created by water scarcity. Despite its relatively abundant water resources, Turkey does not hold the key to water supply in MENA. If anything, Turkey may be categorized as a water-poor country by 2023 given its population increase to 100,000 million, reducing per capita water availability to around 1,125 millimeters per square meter (DSI 2009). However, opportunities are available if countries in the region cooperate. Turkey has vast experience in dam and reservoir technology because of its highly dammed rivers, and Gulf countries have the cutting-edge technology in water desalination. Turkey, surrounded by seas, would greatly benefit from cooperation with Gulf countries on know-how.

One of the most immediate requirements for food security and decreased poverty in the region is peace for cooperation (Bonine 2001). Peace can then unfold in the form of cooperation for water and can decrease each nation's need for self-sufficiency, leading to better lives for all. Turkey has been playing an increasingly significant role in mediations in the region. This will positively affect the region's and Turkey's socioeconomic stability.

As Bonine (2001) argues, the current discourse of food self-sufficiency and water sustainability has excluded the sustainability of communities from the discussion. The Arab Spring showed that healthy rural societies are crucial for stable regimes, which are crucial for economic development. Both in Turkey and in the rest of MENA, rural development must be prioritized for sustainable rural societies in the face of high unemployment in the nonfarm sector. Otherwise, the rise of political Islam, rather than build a platform for affinity, will only radicalize the region.

REFERENCES

Aksoy, S. 1998. *Osmanli ve Turkiye'de Toprak Reformu.* Tarim Hukuku, Ankara: Ziraat Fakultesi Yayini.

Allan, J. A. 2002. *The Middle East Water Question: Hydropolitics and the Global Economy.* New York: I. B. Tauris Publishers.

Aricanli, Tosun. 1976. "The Role of the State in the Social and Economic Transformation of the Ottoman Empire 1807–1918." PhD diss., Harvard University.

Aysu, Abdullah. 2002. *1980–2002 Turkiye Tarimind aYapilanma (ma) Tarladan Sofraya Tarim.* Istanbul: Su Yayinlari.

Baland, J. M. and J. A. Robinson. 2003. "Land and Power." In *BREAD Working Paper* No. 023. Durham: BREAD.

Benjamin, Dwayne and Loren Brandt. 1997. "Land, Factor Markets, and Inequality in Rural China: Historical Evidence." *Explorations in Economic History* 34(4): 460–94.

Binswanger, H. P., and K. Deininger. 1997. "Explaining Agricultural and Agrarian Policies in Developing Countries." *Journal of Economic Literature* 35(4): 1958–2005.

Bonine Michael, E. 2001. "Agricultural Development or Sustainable Agriculture: The Case of the Middle East." In *Rural Development in Eurasia and the Middle East: Land Reform, Demographic Change, and Environmental Constraint,* edited by Kurt E. Engelmann and Vjeran Pavlakovic, 210–38. Seattle: University of Washington Press.

Cakmak, Erol. 2004. "Structural Change and Market Opening in Agriculture: Turkey Towards EU Accession." *ERC Working Papers in Economics,* No. 04–10. Ankara: Middle East Technical University.

De Soto, Hernando. 2000. *The Mystery of Capital: Why Capitalism Triumphs in the West and Fails Everywhere Else.* New York: Basic Books.

Deininger, Klaus and Gershon Feder, 2001. "Land institutions and land markets." In *Handbook of Agricultural Economics,* edited by B. L. Gardner and G. C. Rausser, edition 1, volume 1, chapter 6, pages 288–331. Elsevier.

DSI. 2009. "Temel Politikalar ve Oncelikler, Toprakve Su Kaynaklari." Accessed on September 15, 2011, available at: http://www2.dsi.gov.tr/topraksu.htm

Engerman, Stanley L. and Kenneth L. Sokoloff. 2002. "Factor Endowments, Inequality, and Paths of Development Among New World Economies," *NBER Working Paper* No. W9259. Accessed on February 7, 2006, available at: <http://www.nber.org/papers/h0066.pdf>

Fichtner. 2011. "MENA Regional Water Outlook Part II: Desalination Using Renewable Energy." Accessed on May 20, 2011, available at: http://www.medrc.org/download/twb/FICHT-6911691-v3-Task_1-_Desalination_Potential.pdf

Food and Agriculture Organization of the UN. 2010. "FAOSTAT: The Global Information System on Water and Agriculture." Developed by the Land and Water Development Division of the Food and Agricultural Organization. Accessed on August 1, 2011, available at: http://faostat.fao.org/site/339/default.aspx

Food and Agriculture Organization of the UN. 2011. "AQUASTAT: The Global Information System on Water and Agriculture." Developed by the Land and Water Development Division of the Food and Agricultural Organization. Accessed on August 5 , 2011, available at: http://www.fao.org/AG/AGL/aglw/aquastat/main/index.stm

Griffin, Keith, Aziz Khan, and Amy Ickowitz. 2002. "Poverty and Distribution of Land." *Journal of Agrarian Change* 2(3): 279–330.

Gurses, Didem. 2007. "Türkiye'de Yoksulluk ve Yoksullukla Mücadele Politikaları" (Poverty in Turkey and the Social Policies to Combat Poverty), *Balıkesir Üniversitesi Sosyal Bilimler Dergisi* 17(1): 59–74.

Hakimian, Hasan and Ziba Moshaver, eds. 2001. *The State and Global change: The Political Economy of Transition in the Middle East and North Africa*. Richmond, Surrey: Curzon.

Inalcik, Halil. 1998. "Ciftliklerin Dogusu: Devlet, Toprak Sahipleri ve Kiracilar." In *Osmanli'da Toprak Mulkiyeti ve Tarim*, edited by Caglar Keyder and FarukTabak, 17–36. Istanbul: TarihVakfi Yurt Yayinlari.

Inalcik, Hanan G. 1978. *The Ottoman Empire: Conquest, Organization and Economy*. London: Variorum Reprints.

Intergovernmental Panel on Climate Change. 2007. "Climate change 2007: The Physical Science Basis." In Fourth Assessment Report of the Intergovernmental Panel on Climate Change, edited by Susan Solomon, D. Qin, M. Manning, Z. Chen, M. Marquis, K. B. Avery, M. Tignor, H. L. Miller. Cambridge: Cambridge University Press.

International Fund for Agricultural Development. 2011. "New Realities, New Challenges: New Opportunities for Tomorrow's Generation." Rural Poverty Report 2011, Rome, Italy. Accessed on September 10, 2011, at: http://www.ifad.org/rpr2011/

Johnston, B. and J. Mellor. 1961. "The Role of Agriculture in Economic Development." *American Economic Review* 51(4): 566–93.

Karaomerlioglu, Asim. 2000. "Elite Perceptions of Land Reform in Turkey." *The Journal of Peasant Studies* 27(3): 115–41.

Kazgan, Gulten. 1999. "2000 Yilinda Turk Tarimi: Biyoteknolojive GAP ne Getirebilecek?" In *Turkiye' de Tarimsal Yapilar 1923–2000*, edited by Sevket Pamuk and Zafer Toprak, 257–71. Ankara: Yurt Yayinlari.

Khusro, Ali M. 1973. *Economics of Land Reform and Farm Size in India*. India: McMillan Press.

Kongar, Emre. 1992. *Yirmibirinci Yüzyılda Dünya, Türkiye ve Kamuoyu*. Istanbul: SimaviYayınları.

———.1998. 21. *Yuzyilda Turkiye: 2000 li Yillarda Turkiye nin Toplumsal Yapisi*. Istanbul: Remzi Kitabevi

Koymen, Oya. 1999. "Cumhuriyet Doneminde Tarimsal Yapi ve Tarim Politikalari." In *75 Yilda Koylerden Sehirlere*, edited by Oya Baydar, 1–6. Istanbul: TC IS Bankasi Yayinlari, Tarih Vakfi Yayinlari.

Koymen, Oya and O. Meric. 1999. "Turkiye'deToprak Dagilimi Ustune Bazi Notlar." In *75 Yilda Koylerden Sehirlere*, edited by Oya Baydar, 75–80. Istanbul: TC IS Bankasi Yayinlari, Tarih Vakfi Yayinlari.

Lewis, Arthur. 1954. "Economic Development with Unlimited Supplies of Labor." *Manchester School of Economic and Social Studies* 22(2): 139–91.

Mazumdar, Dipak. 1965. "Size and Farm Productivity: A Problem of Indian Peasant Agriculture." *Economica* 32(126): 161–73.

Meral, Ziya. 2010. "Prospects for Turkey." Accessed September 15, 2011, available at: http://www.li.com/attachments/prospects%20for%20turkey.pdf

Morelli, Vincent. 2011. "European Union Enlargement: A Status Report on Turkey's Accession Negotiations." Congressional Research Service Report. Accessed on September 19, 2011, available at: http://opencrs.com/document/RS22517/.

Moshaver, Z, ed. 2001. *The State and Global Change: The Political Economy of Transition in the Middle East & North Africa*. London: Curzon Press.

Moustakbal, Jawad. 2009. *Water Resources and Climate Change in MENA Region*. Accessed on September 15, 2011, available at: http://www.cadtm.org/Water-resources-and-climate-change,5080.

Onal, Evrim, Nevzat. 2010. *Anadolu Tarımının 150 Yıllık Öyküsü*. YazılamaYayınevi / Türkiye Yazıları Dizisi: Istanbul.

Owen, Roger and Sevket Pamuk. 1999. *A History of Middle East Economies in the Twentieth Century*. Cambridge: Harvard University Press.

Pfeifer, Karen. 1997. "Is There an Islamic Economics?" In *Political Islam*, edited by Joel Beinin and Joe Stark, 154–66. Berkeley: University of California Press.

Rabasa, Angel and F. Stephen Larrabee. 2008. *The Rise of Political Islam in Turkey*. Santa Monica, CA: RAND Corporation.

Ranis, Gustav and John C. H. Fei. 1961. "A Theory of Economic Development." *The American Economic Review* 51(4): 533–65.

Rao, J. Mohan. 2005. "The Forms of Monopoly Land Rent and Agrarian Organization." *Journal of Agrarian Change* 4(2): 161–90.

Richards, Alan and John Waterbury. 2008. *A Political Economy of the Middle East*. Oxford: Westview Press.

Rudra, A. and B. Bandapadhyaya. 1973. "Marginalist Explanation for More Intense Labor Input in Smaller Firms." *Economic and Political Weekly* 8(2): 989–1004.

Sarris, Alexander. 2001. "The Role of Agriculture in Economic Development and Poverty Reduction: An Empirical and Conceptual Foundation." *The World Bank Rural Development Department*. Washington DC: World Bank.

Sen, Abhijit. 1981. "Market Failure and Control of Labor Power: Towards an Explanation of 'Structure' and Change in Indian Agriculture." *Cambridge Journal of Economics* 5(3–4): 201–28 and 327–50.

Sen, Amartya K. 1966. "Peasants Dualism with or without Surplus Labor." *Journal of Political Economy* 74(5): 425–50.

Sowers, Jeannie, Avner Vengosh, and Erika Weinthal. 2010. "Climate Change, Water Resources, and the Politics of Adaptation in the Middle East and North Africa." Accessed on September 15, 2011, available at: http://pubpages.unh.edu/~jlu36/ClimaticChangepiece.pdf

Tabak, Faruk and Caglar Keyder. 1998. *Osmanli Toprak Mulkiyeti ve Ticari Tarim.* Istanbul: Tarih Vakfi Yurt Yayinlari.

Tolba, Mostafa K. and Najib W. Saab. 2009. "Arab Environment Climate Change." Accessed on September 10, 2011, available at: http://www.afedonline.org/afedreport09/Full%20English%20Report.pdf

TUIK. 2011. Turkiye Istatistik Kurumu. "Yoksulluk Analizleri." Accessed on September 10, 2011, available at: http://www.tuik.gov.tr/PreTablo.do?tb_id=23&ust_id=7

Weinthal, Erika, J. Sowers, and A. Vengosh. 2010. "Climate Change, Water Resources, and the Politics of Human Security in the Middle East and North Africa." Accessed on September 5, 2011, available at: http://climsec.prio.no/papers/Weinthal%20et%20al.TrondheimpaperJune2010.pdf

World Bank. 2007. "Making the Most of Scarcity: Accountability for Better Water Management Results in the Middle East and North Africa."

World Bank. 2011. World Development Indicators Database. Accessed on September 1, 2011, available at: http://databank.worldbank.org/ddp/home.do?Step=12&id=4&CNO=2

2

A PORTRAIT OF TURKISH
AGRICULTURE: INEQUALITY AND
ITS DISCONTENTS

1. TURKEY'S AGROCLIMATIC FEATURES AND WATER RESOURCES: OPPORTUNITIES AND CHALLENGES FOR MENA

With its agroclimatic diversity and large amounts of arable land, Turkey has a great agricultural advantage to produce a rich variety of high-quality and high-quantity agricultural products.[1] Turkey ranks number one in the world for total quantity produced in poppy seeds, hazelnuts, apricots, and sour cherries; number two in cherries, quinces, vetches, cucumbers and gherkins, strawberries, watermelons (and other melons, including cantaloupes), leeks, other alliaceous vegetables, and figs; number three in pistachios, chickpeas, walnuts, chilies and peppers, green beans, chestnuts, spices, snails, lentils, apples, sheep milk, honey, tomatoes, beeswax, olives, spinach, dry onions, sugar beets, eggplants, stone fruits, berries, and tea (FAOSTAT 2010). In the MENA region, Turkey is the largest producer and exporter of agricultural products.

Its irregular topography is an important factor in the diverse climatic conditions that distinguish one region from another. Turkey's average altitude (1,132 meters) is higher than that of Asia (1,050 meters) and three and a half times higher than that of Europe (330 meters). The elevation differs from the west to the east, from 2,000 meters in the eastern plains to 875 meters in the capital city of Ankara in the central-west region. More than half of total land area is covered with mountains and the rest with plains, plateaus, steep and rugged lands, and flat hills. In terms of their tillage quality, lands in Turkey range from first-class tillage to class eight, no possible tillage. The topographic variation results in climate variation within short distances. Turkey has four distinctive seasons, four distinctive climate types, and three subclimate types in the Anatolian regions. The subtropical Mediterranean–type climate is characterized by hot, dry summers and rainy, mild winters, with little temperature difference between seasons. The Black Sea climate is humid and mild, characterized mainly by its year-round precipitation. Marmara's climate is dry with hot summers and with colder—compared to Mediterranean—and drier—compared to Black Sea—winters. The fourth type is a semiarid continental climate: most common in the Anatolia regions, in the East with very cold and snowy winters and relatively cooler summers due to high altitude, in the Southeast with very hot summers and relatively mild winters, and in central Anatolia with hot and dry summers, cold and dry winters, and wide daily and seasonal temperature differences.

Overall, because of the variation in climate, distribution of precipitation in Turkey is uneven across time and space. Most precipitation is concentrated during the months of December to April, but that changes from one year to another. Some areas, such as in the Central Anatolian inlands in Konya, get as little as fewer than 250 millimeters of precipitation per year, and the northeast Black Sea coast gets as much as 2,500 millimeters (DMO 2011).

1.1. Rivers and Lakes

Turkey has about 120 natural lakes. The largest and deepest one is Lake Van with a surface area of 3,712 square kilometers, followed by Lake Tuz in central Anatolia, which has a surface area of 1,500 square kilometers. Other large lakes in terms of surface area are Beysehir (656 square kilometers), Egirdir (482 square kilometers), Iznik (308 square kilometers), and Burdur (200 square kilometers). Additionally, the country is home to 673 dam reservoirs. The largest of these are Atatürk (817 square kilometers), Keban (675 square kilometers), Karakaya (268 square kilometers), Hirfanli (263 square kilometers), and Altinkaya (118 square kilometers). The first three reservoirs are on the Euphrates, and the last two are on the Kizilirmak River. Turkey is surrounded by three seas: the Mediterranean Sea in the south, the Black Sea in the north, and the Aegean Sea in the west. Turkey also has an inner sea in the northwest of the country called the Marmara Sea.

Many rivers rise and empty into seas within Turkey's borders. Rivers can be classified in relation to the sea basin they empty into. Some of the largest and longest rivers, such as the Euphrates and Tigris rivers, empty into the Gulf of Basra, while the Aras and Kura rivers empty into the Caspian Sea. Table 2.1 shows Turkey's major rivers but is not an exhaustive list of all rivers.

Based on geographic and climatic variation, Turkey is divided into seven regions: the Black Sea, Aegean, Mediterranean; East, Southeast and Central Anatolia; and the Marmara regions. With the exception of the Anatolian regions, all regions are named after the sea to which they are adjacent.

Home to approximately 8.5 million people out of the 73.2 million in Turkey, the *Black Sea* region is the third largest in terms of its surface area, with 146,000 square kilometers. Its mountainous geography has resulted in scattered dwellings in the mountains and inland plateaus. Cities are densely populated and concentrated on the coastline. The Black Sea region has the highest rate of rural population (70 percent) and lowest average population density, with 51 people per square kilometer, both of which are consequences of scattered population over a large area.

Climate is rather mild and humid. The Black Sea region gets the highest amount of precipitation in Turkey, with 2,500 millimeters; however, at times, precipitation may be as low as 1,260 millimeters in some years.

Agriculture is the major economic activity in the Black Sea region. The region produces 94 percent of the tea, 79 percent of the hazelnuts, 15 percent of the rice, 11 percent of the cabbage, and 10 percent of the tobacco produced in Turkey (TZOB 2011). In central sections of the region, the Carsamba delta provides a fertile ground for vegetables, grain, tobacco, and fruits.

Due to the limited availability of arable land and thus, inadequate nonfarm employment opportunities, the Black Sea region ranks number one in total number of people out-migrating to other regions. During 2009 to 2010, approximately 300 thousand people out-migrated from particularly the western parts of the region mostly to Istanbul, as well as other cities in Marmara and to the capital city of Ankara. The Black Sea region has the second lowest net migration rate with −11 per thousand people after Eastern Anatolia with −13 (TUIK 2011).

Located in the northwestern part of Turkey, *Marmara's* most unique feature is its location: bridging two continents, Asia and Europe, and connecting three seas, the Black Sea, the Marmara, and

Table 2.1 Major Rivers of Turkey

River	Origin	Mouth/Basin	Length	Tributaries
Kizilirmak	Eastern Anatolia	Black Sea	1,350 km	Delice, Devrez, Gok
Sakarya	Central Anatolia	Black Sea	824 km	Seydisu, Porsuk, Ankara
Yesil Irmak	Sivas	Black Sea	418 km	Cekerek, Kelkit
Coruh	North East Anatolia (MescitMontains)	Black Sea, and Georgia	438 km (417 km in Turkey)	
Simav	Aegean	Marmara	321 km	
Meric	Bulgaria	Aegean	480 km	Ergene
Gediz	Aegean	Aegean	401 km	SartCayi
Buyukmenderes	Aegean/Central Northwest Anatolia	Aegean	548 km	
Euphrates	Eastern Anatolia	Persian Gulf	2,800 km (1,263 km in Turkey)	Karasu, Murat
Tigris	East Anatolia	Persian Gulf	1,900 km (523 km in Turkey)	
Manavgat	Mediterranean	Mediterranean		
Seyhan	Mediterranean	Mediterranean	560 km	Zamanti, Goksu
Ceyhan	Mediterranean	Mediterranean	509 km	
Asi	Lebonon, Syria, Turkey	Mediterranean	240 km	Karasu
Batman	Turkey, Syria, Iraq, Iran	Persian Gulf	1,850 km	Batman, Cizre
Aras	Eastern Anatolia	Caspian Sea	1,072 km	
Kura	Eastern Anatolia	Caspian Sea	1,515 km	

Source: http://www2.dsi.gov.tr/topraksu.htm;
http://www.frmartuklu.net/ulkeler-cografyasi/180430-turkiyede-bulunan-nehirler-turkiyedeki-nehirler-ve-dokuldukleri-denizler.html;
http://www.geobilim.com/turkiyedeki-akarsular.html (accessed on August 22, 2011).

the Aegean, through the Bosphorus and the Canakkale Straits. Its surface area is the smallest in Turkey, 67,000 square kilometers, home to approximately 21 million people, of which 13.2 million live in Istanbul (TUIK 2011). Marmara has 25 percent of Turkey's population, the highest compared to other regions. As a result, Marmara has the highest population density, with 308 people per square kilometer, and Istanbul has eight times more than the regional average, with 2,551 (TUIK 2011). Due to its location, the region is the heart of the Turkish economy. Its well developed physical and social infrastructure with major airports and ports, railways, roads, hospitals, and schools, along with the largest nonfarm sector offers socioeconomic opportunities that are rarely matched in other parts of Turkey. Due to the economic and social opportunities available, Istanbul receives a significant amount of immigrants annually; during 2009 to 2010, close to half a million people (439,000) migrated to Istanbul, increasing by 100,000 people from the previous year (TUIK 2011). Even though the net migration (i.e., the difference between immigrants and out-migrants) was around 1,002,000 last year. The movement of approximately 800,000 people creates socioeconomic challenges, such as increased crime, lack of affordable housing, and difficulties in adaptation to urban life.

The Marmara region plays an important role in agricultural production as well. Sixty-four percent of all the sunflower seeds and half of all the rice are produced in Marmara around the Ergene and Meric Rivers (TZOB 2011). Other major agricultural products are corn, olives, wheat, peaches, tomatoes, tobacco, and dairy products.

The *Aegean* region is located in western Turkey and is the second most densely populated and the second most developed region after Marmara. Its surface area is 85,000 square miles, and it is home to more than ten million people (DSI 2009; TUIK 2011). The Aegean region is a prominent producer of agricultural goods. Major crops are seedless grapes, figs, cotton, tobacco, olives, sugar beets, grains, and poppy seeds. Eighty percent of figs, 60 percent of olives, 30 percent of apples, 24 percent of cotton, and 26 percent of watermelon that are produced in Turkey are from the Aegean (TZOB 2011). Other major economic activities in the region include tourism and mostly agriculture-based industries: food processing, textiles, oil industries, and small manufacturing.

In the *Mediterranean* region, similar to the Marmara region, agriculture-based industries are well developed. Textiles, paper, and food processing are the most prominent ones. The region is Turkey's largest citrus producer due to its suitable climate. Ninety percent of oranges and lemons and 75 percent of tangerines that are produced in Turkey are from the Mediterranean region. The region also supplies 43 percent of pistachios, 30 percent of tomatoes, 42 percent of cotton, and 26 percent of corn that is produced in Turkey (TZOB 2011). Other major agricultural products are cotton, chickpeas, tomatoes, and plums. Additionally, the Mediterranean region is a major attraction for domestic and foreign tourists due to its miles of sandy beaches and hot summers and the beautiful mountainous landscape.

Central Anatolia, which is like a bowl and located in the center of the country, is covered with plateaus and surrounded by mountains. The average altitude is around 1,000 meters. It is the second largest region in terms of surface area, with 151,000 square kilometers, and is home to more than 12 million people.

Central Anatolia receives 200 to 600 millimeters of precipitation and has very dry summers, cold and relatively dry winters, and significant temperature differences between seasons and within day and night.

Agriculture and industry constitute the major economic activities in Central Anatolia. The region is the main producer of cereals, particularly wheat. Large plateaus create an advantage for cereal production. Central Anatolia is considered the "wheat silo" of Turkey. Since wheat is the staple food crop for Turks, the region carries a strategic importance in food security and self-sufficiency for the country. Other agricultural products that are grown in the region are barley, green lentils, chickpeas, beans, potatoes, sugar beets, sheep milk, and angora wool.

The nonfarm sector is relatively developed when compared to the other Anatolian regions in Central Anatolia. Because of its central geographic place, both railways and highways are well developed. The presence of well-reputed higher education institutions and relatively developed industries, such as textiles, steel, sugar, and consumer durables, allows for an economically dynamic region. However, this dynamism is concentrated around the vicinities of a few large cities, such as Eskisehir and Ankara. Many villages inland and in rural parts are isolated from such socioeconomic opportunities.

Southeast Anatolia is located on large plains and lowlands. In terms of its surface area, it is the smallest region, holding 7.5 percent of land. Southeast Anatolia has the most arid soil despite getting more precipitation than, for example, Central Anatolia. The region receives on average 500 to 600 millimeters of rainfall. Rainfall increases above 1,000 millimeters in the northern areas adjacent to the Toros

Mountain range. However, due to very hot summers (averaging 30°C), evaporation is very high.[2]

Agriculture is important for Southeast Anatolia, as two-thirds of all economic activity in the region is from agriculture. Grains and legumes, which are suitable for arid conditions, are commonly grown, such as wheat, barley, and lentils. Southeast Anatolia produces 89 percent of lentils and almost half of cotton in Turkey (TZOB 2011). Olives, pistachios, cotton, sugar beets, and grapes are also cultivated in irrigated areas. Animal husbandry and livestock are also important to the economy.

Maybe more than in any other region, Southeast Anatolia has a large potential for increasing total output in agriculture. The region is home to the biggest investment project in the history of the republic and the largest irrigation project, the Southeast Anatolia Project (SAP), in Turkey. In fact, SAP is an "integrated development project which aims socio-economic development of the region through irrigation and energy weighted investments in the Tigris-Euphrates basin of Eastern Anatolia." (DSI 2009, 60). The SAP project aims for 22 dams and 19 hydroelectric power plants (HEPPs), which target the irrigation of 1.8 million decares[3] of arid land. Nicknamed the "locomotive of hydropower energy generation in Turkey" by Water State Works (DSI 2009), its current production through HEPPs under SAP supplies half of all the energy consumed in Turkey (DSI 2009).

However, the "integrated development" has an "urban bias." In 2009, only 26 percent of irrigation projects were complete despite 75 percent of completed power projects (DSI 2009). Of the total irrigation projects, 10 percent is under operation, and the rest, 62 percent, is still in the planning stage. Clearly, as seen from the completion rates, the nonfarm sector has the priority.

East Anatolia has the highest latitude among all the regions, with an average of 2,000 to 2,200 meters, surrounded by mountains. The highest mountain in Turkey, Mount Ararat (5,137 meters) is in East Anatolia. Because of its high altitude, winters are very long and cold, sometimes with 120 days of snow. The region gets 500 millimeters to 1,000 millimeters precipitation on average but, at the same time, is home to the driest plateau, Igdir, which receives less than 250 millimeters per year. East Anatolia has the largest surface area (171,000 square kilometers). Given that it is home to relatively few people at little more than 6 million, it has the lowest population density (36 persons per square kilometer) (TUIK 2011). East Anatolia has a very high ratio of rural population (70 percent), similar to the Black Sea region. Poor endowments in land and capital and inadequate physical and social infrastructure investment in the region result in significant out-migration to other regions and bigger cities rather than to urban areas within the region. East Anatolia, thus, has the lowest net migration ratio (−13).

Despite limited arable land due to the mountainous landscape and harsh climatic conditions, the major economic activity is still agriculture. The region's agricultural production does not constitute an important part in the economy of the country except for apricot production and some few other products. East Anatolia ranks number one in the world in terms of apricot production; it also produces sugar beets, walnuts, wheat, barley, cotton, and potatoes (2001). Similar to Southeast Anatolia, another major source of income is from cattle grazing and animal products. Red meat, milk, and wool production constitute 25 percent of all national production.

East Anatolia is the least developed region in Turkey. Its limited nonfarm employment opportunities are exacerbated by its climatic, geographic, and other sociopolitical challenges of being ignored for investment over many years. Long winters, difficult transportation, poor endowment, and distance to other major markets create a disadvantage for the region's integration into the national economy.

In 1998, a promising mobilization in pursuit of rural investment in East Anatolia started. Particularly after witnessing the economic development of the neighboring Southeast region as a result of SAP, East Anatolia has mobilized significant civil society organizations and academia. More than 300 academics from five universities, Ataturk, Firat, Inonu, Kafkas, and Yuzuncuyil, conducted a collaborative research project to determine the economic priorities of the region. This extensive study, which did an exhaustive survey of the existing physical infrastructure in comparison to the rest of Turkey, pointed out the urgent areas for development: increase domestic capital formation by way of industry and create employment for people. Besides low per capita income in the region, one of the most important economic problems underlined was out-migration. However, the study had a very limited focus on the issues of social infrastructure, such as the status of women, education, and health, and gave no attention to political issues, such as income and land distribution. Since its release in 2000, the report has generated discussion and made its way to the senate, however, with no significant recognition. To date, it has failed to be translated into implementation seemingly due to lack of political will.

To sum up, agriculture plays and will continue to play a significant but varying role for different regions of Turkey depending sometimes on natural obstacles, such as climate change, and sometimes on man-made vagaries, such as the political will (or lack thereof) to invest in certain regions, such as in Southeast Anatolia but not in East Anatolia.

2. ECONOMY AND SOCIETY IN RURAL TURKEY: A CLOSER LOOK

Rural Turkey, which constitutes approximately 25 to 30 percent of all the population, is home to crowded households.[4] For a closer look, we will utilize the most recent rural survey, namely, the Quantitative Household Survey (QHS), which was conducted by the World Bank in 2002, one year after ARIP was implemented. QHS is a very detailed dataset with 1,292 variables covering many aspects of rural life: production, consumption, earnings, savings, wealth, cultural life, and even perceptions of farmers' own welfare. The dataset includes five thousand rural households from 7 regions, 73 provinces, 389 towns, and 517 villages in rural Turkey.

As illustrated in table 2.2, the average size of a rural household is 5.7 members. Most crowded households are in Southeast Anatolia (8.1 members) and East Anatolia (7.8 members). The least crowded households are in Marmara, with 4.5 members. An average rural household is headed by a 50-year-old male. The dependency ratio, or mouths to hands ratio, is 1.45 mouths per pair of hands on average for Turkey. The dependency ratio is highest in Southeast Anatolia, with 1.80 mouths per pair of hands, and lowest in Marmara, with 1.31.

Turkish peasants work on a farm that is on average 92 decares. However, the three Anatolian regions, Central, East, and Southeast, have much larger farms, with 161, 132, and 122 decares per household, respectively. Nonetheless, per person land is not the highest in any of these regions. Marmara is the region with the least crowded households and has the largest farmland per person at 20 decares. However, peasants who end up with the least amount of land per person are from the Black Sea. Farms in the Black Sea region are almost half the size of the country's average, with 50 decares, and only 11 decares of operated land per person.

On average, 68 decares of out of every 92 decares of operated farmland are owned by the farmers. Fifty-seven percent of the owned land has titles. And interestingly, but not surprisingly, Southeast Anatolia, the poorest and one of the most unequal regions in terms of landownership distribution, has the highest ratio of titled land. In Southeast Anatolia, 77 percent of all owned land has a title, whereas

Table 2.2 Selected Variables for Rural Turkey

Region	Household (HH) Size	Household Head's (HHH) Age	Depend. Ratio	Ratio of Illiterate (%) HHH	Landless and Illiterate	Primary School (%) HHH
Mediterranean	5.6	50.4	1.41	9	8	67
Aegean	4.7	48.4	1.36	6	6	76
SE Anatolia	8.2	47.1	1.8	19	17	61
Marmara	4.5	52.2	1.31	5	2	73
Central An.	5.8	49.2	1.45	7	7	73
E. Anatolia	7.9	47.5	1.74	11	10	66
Black Sea	5.5	52.2	1.4	9	4	66
TURKEY	**5.7**	**50.1**	**1.45**	**9**	**7**	**70**

Region	Secondary School (%) HHH	College Degree Holders (%) HHH	Tractor Usage (%)	Per Capita Owned/Hold Land (in ha)	Per HH Owned Land (in ha)	Per HH Farmed Land (in ha)
Mediterranean	8	1	87	11/16	54.7	75.9
Aegean	5	0	81	14/18	50.5	63.7
SE Anatolia	9	0	88	13/16	94.5	122.3
Marmara	5	1	84	16/21	64.6	84.3
Central An.	6	1	90	23/34	105.4	160.8
E. Anatolia	5	1	92	16/19	113.5	132.4
Black Sea	6	2	47	9/11	41.2	50.2
TURKEY	**6**	**1**	**77**	**14/19**	**68.4**	**91.7**

Region	Percent of Landless Peasants (%)	Land Title Ratio (%)	Number of Plots	Indoor WC (%)	Indoor Plumbing (%)	Number of Households
Mediterranean	17	66	5.6	50	79	714
Aegean	16	66	6.8	42	81	887
SE Anatolia	18	77	4.0	30	50	490
Marmara	7	76	9.2	56	89	795
Central An.	19	74	11.5	33	72	901
E. Anatolia	10	53	6.3	31	44	331
Black Sea	11	56	7.6	88	81	1,179
TURKEY	**14**	**67**	**7.7**	**52**	**75**	**5,297**

Source: Quantitative Household Survey, 2002.

this ratio is 67 percent nationally (table 2.1). One reason for this could be the impact of SAP, which has been creating incentives for farmers to secure landownership, as irrigated lands yield higher returns and become more valuable. Farms are fragmented: 7.7 plots on average nationally. The highest fragmentation is in Central Anatolia, with 11 plots per farm, and the least fragmentation is in Southeast Anatolia, with 4 plots.

Housing is important for rural households; it provides shelter to the family and space for secondary production, such as processing grains for household consumption and dairy production. Certain amenities within the house, such as an indoor toilet or a plumbing system, indicate the welfare level of the household. Particularly for women, having a well-functioning plumbing system is important, as they are generally responsible for fetching water; in some cases, this may constitute the majority of women's work burden. Additionally, plumbing requires public investment, and hence, it may provide clues in most cases to the backwardness of the village.

In rural Turkey, 52 percent of all households on average have a toilet in the house, but the ratio varies significantly from region to region. In the Black Sea region, for example, 88 percent of houses have an indoor toilet, whereas this percentage in Central Anatolia drops to 33; in East Anatolia, to 31; and in Southeast Anatolia, to 30.

The picture for in-house plumbing is better than that for toilets (table 2.2). However, the same pattern exists for in-house plumbing: in the East, Southeast, and Central Anatolia regions, only 44, 50, and 72 percent, respectively, of all the houses are equipped with an in-house plumbing system. In the Marmara, Black Sea, and Mediterranean regions, this percentage is 89, 81, and 79, respectively. These three regions are also the poorest in terms of per capita income; hence it is not surprising to find lower ratios for the Anatolian regions.

3. REGIONAL AND NATIONAL ASSET AND INCOME DISTRIBUTION IN RURAL TURKEY

3.1. General Picture: Agrarian versus Nonagrarian Distribution of Incomes

A rural household in Turkey has an average per capita income of 1,840 YTL.[5] The three highest income per capita regions are the Marmara, Aegean, and Mediterranean, with 2,424 YTL, 2,281 YTL, and 2,057 YTL per capita income, respectively. The lowest income per capita regions are East Anatolia, Black Sea, and Southeast Anatolia, with 657 YTL, 1,388 YTL, and 1,471 YTL, respectively. A rural person who lives in the poorest region, East Anatolia, on average, earns two-sevenths as much as someone who lives in the richest region, Marmara. Seventy-five percent of the rural households in the dataset are agrarian households. A household who earns at least 50 percent of their total income from agricultural activities is considered an agrarian household. The highest percentage of agrarian households live in Southeast Anatolia, with 86 percent, and the lowest live in the Black Sea region, with 61 percent. Agrarian rural households average higher per capita income than nonagrarian rural households except in East Anatolia (table 2.3). Given limited farm and nonfarm opportunities in East Anatolia, this is normal.

Table 2.3 Descriptive Statistics, Per Capita Income, 2002 Rural Turkey (in YTL)

	Per Capita Income (A)	Per Capita Agricultural Income (B)	Per Capita Nonagricultural Income (C)	Ratio C/A (%)	Number of Households
Turkey	1,840	1,415	425	23	5,297
Mediterranean	2,057	1,703	744	36	714
Aegean	2,281	1,791	490	21	887
SE Anatolia	1,471	1,262	209	14	490
Marmara	2,424	1,942	482	20	795
Central An.	1,945	1,526	419	22	901
E. Anatolia	657	381	276	42	331
Black Sea	1,388	872	516	37	1,179
AGRICULTURAL HOUSEHOLDS					
Turkey	2,012	1,775	237	12	3,986
Mediterranean	2,271	2,071	201	9	569
Aegean	2,395	2,125	270	11	714
SE Anatolia	1,613	1,442	171	11	422
Marmara	2,578	2,278	299	12	650
Central An.	2,237	1,934	303	14	677
E. Anatolia	549	458	91	17	240
Black Sea	1,424	1,223	201	14	714
NONAGRICULTURAL HOUSEHOLDS					
Turkey	1,316	319.7	996	76	1,311
Mediterranean	1,216	260.1	956	79	145
Aegean	1,809	412.6	1,396	77	173
SE Anatolia	589	141.2	447	76	68
Marmara	1,737	435.6	1,301	75	145
Central An.	1,065	295.1	770	72	224
E. Anatolia	940	175.3	765	81	91
Black Sea	1,333	333.9	1,000	75	465

Source: Quantitative Household Survey, 2002.

Table 2.4 details the income distribution for rural households in Turkey. Rural Turkey's Gini coefficient for per capita income is 0.59. The most unequal region in terms of per capita income is Southeast Anatolia, with a 0.70 Gini coefficient, followed by the Mediterranean, with 0.68; Central East Anatolia, with 0.59; and the Aegean, with 0.57. Income is distributed most equally in the Black Sea region, with 0.51.

When we look at the components of household income for the whole sample, not surprising, we see that in most regions, the disequalizing component of personal income is nonagrarian income. Compared to urban settings, rural areas offer fewer opportunities

Table 2.4 Descriptive Statistics, 2002 Rural Turkey, Per Capita Income Inequality Indices

	Per Capita Income (A)	Per Capita Agricultural Income (B)	Per Capita Nonagricultural Income (C)	Number of Households
TURKEY	0.59	0.66	0.68	5,297
Mediterranean	0.68	0.74	0.76	714
Aegean	0.57	0.62	0.72	887
SE Anatolia	0.70	0.74	0.67	490
Marmara	0.54	0.60	0.66	795
Central An.	0.59	0.66	0.63	901
E. Anatolia	0.55	0.58	0.75	331
Black Sea	0.51	0.63	0.61	1,179
AGRICULTURAL HOUSEHOLDS				
TURKEY	0.61	0.62	0.70	3,986
Mediterranean	0.69	0.70	0.81	569
Aegean	0.56	0.57	0.70	714
SE Anatolia	0.71	0.73	0.69	422
Marmara	0.55	0.57	0.65	650
Central An.	0.59	0.61	0.66	677
E. Anatolia	0.56	0.56	0.77	240
Black Sea	0.58	0.60	0.69	714
NONAGRICULTURAL HOUSEHOLDS				
TURKEY	0.46	0.55	0.48	1,311
Mediterranean	0.51	0.65	0.51	145
Aegean	0.60	0.62	0.62	173
SE Anatolia	0.43	0.54	0.43	68
Marmara	0.42	0.49	0.45	145
Central An.	0.47	0.57	0.48	224
E. Anatolia	0.52	0.53	0.56	91
Black Sea	0.37	0.47	0.38	465

Source: Quantitative Household Survey, 2002.

for nonfarm employment, and hence, we see a more skewed distribution of per capita nonagrarian income. However, strikingly, in East Anatolia, the Aegean, and the Mediterranean, nonagrarian income distribution is significantly more unequal than in the agrarian sector. This shows that the ability to distribute economic opportunities in the nonfarm sector is very limited.

In East Anatolia, the distribution of nonagrarian income is 17 Gini points worse than that of the agrarian income; in the Aegean and the Mediterranean, distribution of nonagrarian income is 10 and 11 Gini points, respectively, worse. This is quite interesting because the Aegean and the Mediterranean regions provide significantly more nonfarm income opportunities than does East Anatolia. This may be explained by a common feature for the two more developed regions of the Mediterranean and the Aegean: both have the most unequal distribution of owned land, with Gini coefficients of 0.71 and 0.68, respectively (table 2.4).

Let us open Pandora's Box farther and see whether similar patterns are prevalent for agrarian households compared to the whole sample discussed earlier. Agrarian households have slightly more unequal income distribution on average when compared to the whole sample, with Gini coefficients of 0.61 versus 0.59, and much more unequal income distribution when compared to the nonagrarian sample (0.61 versus 0.46). This suggests that those whose incomes are mostly from nonfarm earnings in rural areas constitute a more homogeneous group in terms of income class. Given per capita incomes are much lower for the nonagrarian households, we can also claim that this homogeneous group is poorer (table 2.2). In other words, income opportunities to which poorer nonagrarian households have access are not very attractive in terms of monetary rewards.

As in the whole sample, among agrarian households, nonfarm income is distributed more unequally and hence has a disequalizing impact on overall per capita income. Furthermore, the same association between high landownership inequality and high nonfarm income is prevalent in the agrarian sample as well. The Mediterranean and the Aegean regions, the two most unequal regions for landownership inequality, and East Anatolia have the highest Gini coefficients, with 0.81, 0.70, and 0.77, respectively, for income (table 2.3).

A closer look at the agrarian sample makes the relationship between nonfarm income and its disequalizing impact more clear. Every single region, with the exception of Southeastern Anatolia, registers a high jump in inequality in nonfarm income when compared to agricultural income. Some of this increase is expected because not every household in the agrarian sample has nonfarm income as an additional source. However, in some regions, the increase in inequality is relatively higher in regions with high landownership inequality. The fact that Gini coefficients are lower without the nonagricultural income component suggests a very interesting dynamic for nonfarm income opportunities in rural Turkey. Among agrarian households, nonfarm earning opportunities are accessed by those whose agricultural earnings are higher. That is, the income gap is wider when we consider total income than when we consider only agricultural income. If those with lower agrarian incomes had higher nonagrarian incomes, the distribution would instead appear more equal when we consider total income. This suggests that most often, nonfarm income opportunities are asset based, not labor based. Another explanation could be that if these opportunities are for labor, they are for well-paid, high-skilled labor. In most cases, the poor rarely have access to decent jobs, which require education. Or the causal arrow could go the other way. People with nonfarm income might use that income to invest in their farms and make their farms more productive, thereby generating higher per capita agrarian income.

This disequalizing impact of nonagricultural income for agrarian households when compared to nonagrarian households tells us that markets that provide opportunities for nonfarm earnings are fragmented. Furthermore, the fragmentation is connected to the households' fallback position in agriculture. In other words, nonfarm income is making the rich richer among agrarian households but does not help the poor as much. Put differently, unequal distribution of assets can pose challenges to the poor as much as harsh agroclimatic and geographic realities can in accessing earning opportunities.

We can further our understanding of such patterns in income inequalities when we take a closer look at the distribution of factors of production (i.e., land, labor and capital, and income) from such assets for all three samples.

3.2. Sectoral Distribution of Assets and Income in Rural Turkey

3.2.1. Land

Land is more than just a productive asset. It is an asset of insurance, bondage, prestige, power, and wealth. Land is a portfolio asset, particularly in countries with undeveloped capital markets to hedge against inflation (Cornia 1985; Kaldjian 2001). It is a source of political power, which, in turn, produces economic benefits (Binswanger et al. 1995;

Karaomerlioglu 2000; Griffin et al. 2002). Last, but not least, it has nonmonetary value to people who live on or off of it because of ancestral ties. Hence, distribution of land is of the utmost importance for the economic, social, and political landscape of societies.

The largest average area of land owned per household is in East Anatolia, with 114 decares, followed by Central Anatolia, with 105 decares, and by Marmara, with 95 decares (table 2.5). This is significantly more than the countrywide average of 68 decares per household. The smallest amount of owned land per household is in the Black Sea region, with 41 decares. In the Mediterranean region, an average household owns 55 decares of land, which might seem significantly low compared to other Anatolian regions.

Central Anatolia has the highest per person land owned, with 23 decares of land. This is significantly higher than the national average of 14 decares. The land owned per person is also high in East Anatolia, with 16 decares (table 2.2). The least amount of land owned per person is again in the Black Sea region, with only 11 decares.

An apparent pattern appears that landownership per household is smaller in western parts of Turkey and larger in central, eastern, and southeastern parts. But regional variation is not as large as it first appears. The differences in land per household correspond to differences in household size so that, with the exception of Central Anatolia (23) and the Black Sea region (9), all other regions fall within a narrow range of 14 to 17 decares per person. Naturally, per capita land owned and land hold (i.e., farm size) is both higher for agrarian households than for nonagrarian ones: 15 versus 12 decares for owned land and 20 versus 13 decares for land hold.

Land is concentrated in rural Turkey (table 2.6). The Gini coefficient for landownership is 0.65 nationally.

The highest concentration is in the Aegean region, with 0.71, followed by the Mediterranean (0.68), Southeast Anatolia (0.64), and the Black Sea (0.64). The most equal land ownership distribution is in Marmara, with a Gini of 0.55, which is still quite high. Among the nonagrarian households, land is distributed less equally following a similar regional pattern.

If land markets were perfect and land were only a productive asset with zero noneconomic benefits, then asset inequality and income inequality would be identical. In perfect markets, the farmer should be indifferent to cultivating his own land or collecting the rent from leasing it out. There will be a more elaborate discussion on this in chapter 5, but right now, suffice to say that if returns to land came

Table 2.5 Descriptive Statistics, 2002 Rural Turkey, Assets

| | Land | Labor | Livestock | Capital | | Monetary Savings | Number of Households |
				Tractors	Harvesters		
TURKEY	68.4	3.2	2.4	0.44	0.03	15.8	5,297
Mediterranean	54.7	3.3	1.6	0.46	0.04	6.8	714
Aegean	50.5	2.7	1.9	0.47	0.01	26.3	887
SE Anatolia	94.5	3.9	1.1	0.3	0.04	0.9	490
Marmara	64.6	2.7	3.2	0.6	0.04	27.5	795
Central An.	105.4	3.2	2.6	0.63	0.05	8.7	901
E. Anatolia	113.5	3.8	4.1	0.24	0.01	0	331
Black Sea	41.2	3.2	2.5	0.24	0.01	21.3	1,179
AGRICULTURAL							
TURKEY	74	3.2	2.6	0.49	0.03	10.3	3,986
Mediterranean	54.8	3.3	1.8	0.52	0.05	8.8	569
Aegean	50.9	2.7	2.1	0.5	0.01	6.5	714
SE Anatolia	97	4	1.1	0.32	0.05	1	422
Marmara	69.8	2.8	3.7	0.65	0.04	33.5	650
Central An.	111.9	3.2	2.8	0.66	0.06	11.1	677
E. Anatolia	111.9	3.8	4.4	0.25	0.01	0	240
Black Sea	50.4	3.2	3.1	0.34	0.01	3.2	714
NONAGRICULTURAL							
TURKEY	51.6	3.1	1.6	0.26	0.01	32.3	1,311
Mediterranean	54.2	3.4	1.1	0.24	0.02	0	145
Aegean	48.7	2.8	1.3	0.32	0.01	115.8	173
SE Anatolia	78.2	3.4	0.8	0.12	0	0	68
Marmara	44.6	2.6	1.3	0.4	0.03	4.4	145
Central An.	82.9	3	1.8	0.54	0.02	0	224
E. Anatolia	119.5	3.6	2.8	0.22	0.01	0	91
Black Sea	28.3	3.1	1.7	0.11	0.01	46.7	465

Source: Quantitative Household Survey, 2002.

Table 2.6 Gini Coefficients, 2002 Rural Turkey, Assets

	Land	Labor	Capital				Number of Households
			Livestock	Tractors	Harvesters	Monetary Savings	
TURKEY	0.65	0.16	0.71	0.67	0.98	1.00	5,297
Mediterranean	0.68	0.16	0.78	0.66	0.96	1.00	714
Aegean	0.71	0.14	0.77	0.62	0.99	0.99	887
SE Anatolia	0.64	0.20	0.75	0.75	0.97	1.00	490
Marmara	0.55	0.12	0.66	0.51	0.97	0.99	795
Central An.	0.58	0.15	0.70	0.50	0.96	0.99	901
E. Anatolia	0.59	0.20	0.64	0.80	0.99	N/A	331
Black Sea	0.64	0.14	0.57	0.78	0.99	1.00	1,179
AGRICULTURAL HOUSEHOLDS							
TURKEY	0.63	0.16	0.71	0.63	0.97	1.00	3,986
Mediterranean	0.66	0.16	0.78	0.61	0.96	1.00	569
Aegean	0.71	0.14	0.77	0.58	0.99	1.00	714
SE Anatolia	0.64	0.20	0.75	0.73	0.97	1.00	422
Marmara	0.53	0.12	0.64	0.48	0.97	0.99	650
Central An.	0.57	0.14	0.7	0.48	0.95	0.99	677
E. Anatolia	0.57	0.20	0.62	0.79	0.99	N/A	240
Black Sea	0.60	0.15	0.58	0.73	0.99	1.00	714
NONAGRICULTURAL HOUSEHOLDS							
TURKEY	0.70	0.15	0.66	0.78	0.99	1.00	1,311
Mediterranean	0.75	0.14	0.74	0.83	0.99	N/A	145
Aegean	0.69	0.15	0.73	0.74	0.98	0.98	173
SE Anatolia	0.68	0.19	0.71	0.91	N/A	N/A	68
Marmara	0.64	0.13	0.72	0.65	0.98	0.99	145
Central An.	0.60	0.15	0.71	0.57	0.98	N/A	224
E. Anatolia	0.62	0.19	0.72	0.83	0.99	N/A	91
Black Sea	0.68	0.14	0.53	0.86	0.99	1.00	465

Source: Quantitative Household Survey, 2002.

only from its productive contribution, then distributions of income and assets should perfectly map. Clearly, this is not the case for rural Turkey. A comparison of tables 2.6 and 2.7 shows that, with the exception of the Aegean region, inequality in income derived from land is higher than its inequality in ownership.

Particularly in the Mediterranean region and Southeast Anatolia, income inequality from land is significantly higher than landownership inequality, with Gini coefficients of 0.81 and 0.75, respectively, in income distribution when compared to Gini coefficients of 0.64 and 0.68, respectively, in land assets. After the Aegean region, these two rank second and third most unequal regions in Turkey. Even though Southeast Anatolia shares the third rank with the Black Sea region, the former still has a dominant semifeudal structure, which

Table 2.7 Descriptive Statistics, 2002 Rural Turkey, Income Inequality Index

	Land	Labor	Capital	Number of Households
TURKEY	0.72	0.764	0.993	5,297
Mediterranean	0.75	0.805	0.995	714
Aegean	0.67	0.779	0.990	887
SE Anatolia	0.81	0.881	0.998	490
Marmara	0.66	0.747	0.989	795
Central An.	0.70	0.800	0.989	901
E. Anatolia	0.66	0.862	0.991	331
Black Sea	0.66	0.608	0.993	1,179
AGRICULTURAL HOUSEHOLDS				
TURKEY	0.69	0.829	0.991	3,987
Mediterranean	0.72	0.864	0.994	557
Aegean	0.64	0.807	0.990	726
SE Anatolia	0.80	0.897	0.997	424
Marmara	0.64	0.806	0.989	629
Central An.	0.66	0.839	0.987	701
E. Anatolia	0.66	0.899	0.990	262
Black Sea	0.64	0.734	0.990	688
NONAGRICULTURAL HOUSEHOLDS				
TURKEY	0.61	0.516	0.996	1,310
Mediterranean	0.72	0.563	0.994	157
Aegean	0.62	0.568	0.986	161
SE Anatolia	0.60	0.743	0.00	66
Marmara	0.57	0.475	0.991	166
Central An.	0.60	0.627	0.988	200
E. Anatolia	0.65	0.641	0.986	69
Black Sea	0.56	0.381	0.998	491

Source: Quantitative Household Survey, 2002.

clearly, the Southeast Anatolia Project (SAP) has not been very effective in breaking.

The fact that the Aegean region, the most unequal region, has a lower inequality in land income when compared to land inequality is intriguing. This may signal what Lipton and Newell (2004) call land underutilization in areas with high land concentration. Based on QHS (2002), in rural Turkey, on average, 15 percent of farmland is left fallow, and the amount of land left fallow increases with farm size. The ratio of fallow land for the Aegean farms that are larger than two hundred and smaller than five hundred decares is significantly higher than for similarly sized farms elsewhere (11 percent national average versus 20 percent for the Aegean). This explains relatively lower inequality when land incomes are compared to land assets despite a very skewed landownership in the region.

The agrarian sector is home to the most unequal distribution of land income when compared to the nonagrarian sector and to the whole country: 0.69, 0.61, and 0.65 Gini coefficients, respectively. For agrarian households, income inequality follows the same pattern as land asset inequality. For the nonagrarian sector, the relation between income inequality and asset inequality is reversed in Southeast Anatolia, Marmara, and the Black Sea; income inequalities from land are lower than asset inequalities.

3.2.2. Livestock

Livestock is another important asset in agriculture. It provides cash income but is also part of the consumption basket of rural households since it provides milk, meat, and manure, which can be used as fertilizer and/or fuel. In addition, in areas with little or no mechanization, cattle are used as draught animals to till the land.

On average, a rural household has 2.5 cattle. The highest number of cattle owned per household is in East Anatolia, with 4.1 (table 2.4). This is not surprising because the region's major agricultural activity is animal husbandry. The lowest number of cattle per household belongs to Southeast Anatolia, with only 1.1.

Livestock is distributed even more unequally than land (table 2.6). The Gini coefficient for livestock is highest in the Mediterranean region, with 0.78, followed by the Aegean region, with 0.77, and Southeast Anatolia, with 0.75 Gini. The lowest Gini is in the Black Sea region, with 0.57, and the rest of the regions have livestock Ginis ranging between 0.57 and 0.70. It is not surprising to observe that the top three ranking regions in cattle inequality are also the highest ranking regions in landownership inequality because land is essential for cattle grazing.

3.2.3. Machinery

The use of machinery has become very common in Turkish agriculture since it was introduced through the Marshall Plan in the late 1950s, as discussed in chapter 1.[6] On average, 77 percent of the farms use tractors (table 2.7). Seventy-seven percent of tractor use among all households is a very rough national average and not representative of regional differences. Tractor utilization in agriculture depends on geography, such as availability of flat surfaces, and also on the crop type. In the Black Sea region, only 47 percent of households use tractors because of the mountainous landscape. Hazelnuts, which are one of the main crops in the region, grow on trees in mountainous areas.

Tractor ownership is common among tractor users. On average, 66 percent of households own the tractors they use in Turkey. This ratio is lowest in Southeast and East Anatolia, with 34 percent and 42 percent, respectively, and highest in the Black Sea region, with 78 percent, followed by the Marmara region, with 74 percent, and Central Anatolia, with 73 percent (table 2.2).

Harvesters are not as commonly used and owned as tractors since they are more expensive machines and cannot be used as means of transportation as can tractors. Only 32 percent of households use harvesters. The highest usage ratio is in Southeast and Central Anatolia, with 61 percent and 58 percent, respectively. Central Anatolia grows mostly wheat, barley, and sugar beets, whereas Southeast Anatolia grows cotton, tobacco, alfalfa, and wheat. Both grain and cotton harvests are mechanized and make use of harvesters. The lowest harvester use is again in the Black Sea region due the region's hilly landscape, with only 11 percent. However, the highest ownership ratio of harvesters is in the Black Sea region, with 89 percent.

At a glance, there does not seem to be a significant pattern between the use of tractors and landownership or operational holding inequality. It is more likely that the use of tractors is determined by the crop type rather than by any other socioeconomic factor. Nevertheless, the ownership of tractors and harvesters does have a connection to land inequality. Out of the three highest ratios of nonownership among tractor and harvester users, Southeast Anatolia, East Anatolia and the Mediterranean region, two are also among the most unequal regions: Southeast Anatolia and the Mediterranean region.

3.2.4. Monetary Savings

Similar to the patterns in other assets, monetary savings, which include cash, savings accounts, stocks, and government bonds, are highest in the Marmara region, with 27.5 YTL per capita per year, and lowest in East Anatolia, with no savings (table 2.4). The second highest ranking region for per capita monetary savings is the Aegean, with 26.3 YTL, and the second lowest ranking is Southeast Anatolia, with 0.9 YTL. Both credit and monetary savings are extremely unequally distributed, with little variation: the Gini for credit per capita is 0.96 and the Gini for per capita monetary savings is nearly 1 for Turkey. None of the regions show a significant deviation from these numbers (tables 2.5 and 2.6).

Overall, distribution of capital is much skewed and shows a positive association with the inequality in landownership. Those who have land are more likely to have tractors, livestock, and monetary savings.

3.2.5. Labor

Labor is another important asset and most often, the only asset of the poor. Even though mostly lack of land results in poverty, the lack of labor within a household may also create problems, particularly for agriculture since agriculture in a developing country is very labor intensive. For each household in rural Turkey, on average, there are 3.2 working-age adults (i.e., the labor endowment per household); the highest number of working-age adults is in Southeast Anatolia, with 3.9, and the lowest number is in the Marmara and Aegean regions, with 2.7 (table 2.4).

For both the agrarian and nonagrarian sectors, neither the endowment nor the distribution has a wide variance. Labor is plentiful and is equally distributed. However, more important than the sheer quantity, quality is very important in evaluating the productive capacity of labor. Most people consider agriculture a low-skill profession, which is a mistake. Even cultivation of the crops that are simplest to grow requires proficiency to manage land, water, fertilizers, pesticides, and selection of most appropriate seeds to the agroclimatic conditions. Thus, the labor used in agriculture is rarely unskilled. Education has a positive impact on how productive a farmer can be, as he is able to read the directions on machine manuals or fertilizer packages. Further, a better educated person also has better chances of finding nonfarm employment, which adds to the value of labor as an asset since it increases its opportunity cost in agriculture.

Educational attainment is very low in rural Turkey. On average, 70 percent of household heads are primary school graduates, ranging from 76 percent (the Aegean) to 61 percent (Southeast Anatolia). Only 6 percent of household heads have a secondary school education, 5 percent have a high school education, and a mere 1 percent have a university degree. It is interesting to note that illiteracy is less common among landless household heads, with 8 percent of them illiterate as opposed to 9 percent nationally (table 2.1). This may be because of seeking upward class mobility by the landless through education since returns to education is quite significant for Turkey (Tansel 1999).

Distribution of labor income, or rather labor income from non-farm employment, is quite skewed. Labor income as it is embodied in agricultural production, such as the fruits of working on one's own farm, is not calculated here. Hence, high inequality in its distribution should not come as a surprise, particularly given that most of the households are agricultural and are relatively less likely to be engaged in off-farm employment.

Among the nonagrarian sector, naturally distribution of labor income is lower, and lowest is in the Black Sea region, followed by the Marmara region. Most unequal are the Anatolian regions, Southeast, East, and Central. The highest two are the most developmentally backward regions, Southeast and East Anatolia, with Gini coefficients of 0.74 and 0.64, respectively for labor income. This may signal a lack of off-farm employment opportunities for labor in these regions, particularly given the low per capita income level.

4. Conclusion

Existing inequalities in land and capital ownership, the resulting inequalities in the returns to these assets, and the regionally specific inequality patterns point out the challenges to and opportunities for the well-being of the rural masses. The analysis in this chapter leads to the conclusion that, particularly in the relatively backward Anatolian regions, the highest priority should be the provision of a more equitable asset structure. When the asset structure underlying the markets is unequal, such as in the case of Southeastern Turkey, even the most expensive and comprehensive infrastructure projects may not increase the well-being of the majority.

The demonstrated mismatching of inequalities between assets and income derived from those assets raises an important question about the potential outcomes of market-friendly reforms: If left to markets, when the starting position features tremendous inequality in the underlying asset structure and when the markets are underdeveloped, how efficient could agricultural production and resource allocation be in rural Turkey? The following chapter provides a closer look into land tenure markets given existing inequalities in land ownership in rural Turkey.

REFERENCES

Binswanger, H. P., K. Deininger, and G. Feder. 1995. "Power, Distortions, Revolt and Reform in Agricultural Land Relations." In *Handbook of Development Economics, Vol. III*, edited by J. Behrman and T. N. Srinavasan, 2661–763. Amsterdam: Elsevier Science.

Cornia, G. A. 1985. "Farm Size, Land Yields and the Agricultural Production Function: An Analysis for Fifteen Developing Countries." *World Development* 13(4): 513–34.

Devlet Meteoroloji Ofisi. 2011. "Climate of Turkey." Accessed on September 3, 2011, available at: http://www.dmi.gov.tr/files/en-US/climateofturkey.pdf

DSI. 2009. "Temel Politikalar ve Oncelikler, Toprakve Su Kaynaklari." Accessed on September 15, 2011, available at: http://www2.dsi.gov.tr/topraksu.htm

Eastwood, Robert, Michael Lipton, and Andrew Newell. 2004. Farm Size. Paper prepared for Volume III of the Handbook of Agricultural Economics. University of Sussex. Accessed on June 1, 2007, available at: http://www.sussex.ac.uk/Units/PRU/farm_size.pdf

Food and Agriculture Organization of the UN. 2010. "FAOSTAT: The Global Information System on Water and Agriculture." Developed by the Land and Water Development Division of the Food and Agricultural Organization. Accessed on August 1, 2011, available at: http://faostat.fao.org/site/339/default.aspx

Griffin, K., A. R. Khan, and A. Ickowitz. 2002. "Poverty and Distribution of Land." *Journal of Agrarian Change* 2(3): 279–330.

Kaldjian, P. 2001. "The Smallholder in Turkish Agriculture: Obstacle or Opportunity?" In *Rural Development in Eurasia and the Middle East: Land Reform, Demographic Change, and Environmental Constraints,* edited by K. Engelmann and V. Pavlakovic, 239–78. Seattle and Washington: University of Washington.

Karaomerlioglu, Asim. 2000. "Elite Perceptions of Land Reform in Turkey." *The Journal of Peasant Studies* 27(3): 115–41.

QHS. 2002. Quantitative Household Survey. Ministry of Agriculture, ARIP office, Ankara Turkey.

Tansel, A. 1999. "Türkiye ve Seçilmis Ülkelerde Egitimin Getirisi," (Returns to Education in Turkey and Selected Countries). *METU Studies in Development* 26 (3–4): 473–91.

Turkiye Istatistik Kurumu TUIK. 2011. "Nufus Istatistikleri." Accessed on September 10, 2011, available at: http://www.tuik.gov.tr/AltKategori.do?ust_id=11

Turkiye Ziraat Odalari Birligi. 2011. "Turkiye Tarim Profili." Accessed on July 15, 2011, available at: http://www.tzob.org.tr/tzob_web/turk_tarim.htm

3

SHARECROPPING OR
FIXED-RENT TENANCY?

1. INTRODUCTION

In a world with no uncertainty and perfect markets, where all inputs are divisible, there would be no room for tenancy in agriculture (Nabi 1985). In a perfect world, landless peasants could borrow money without collateral and purchase their own land, as opposed to being sharecroppers. In such a neoclassical world, the existence of tenancies could be explained only by the historical evolution of institutions. In the real world, however, markets are imperfect. Some factors of production are indivisible and/or not easy to market, such as cattle, machinery, and management skills. Furthermore, uncertainties exist due to weather and nature and those related to the labor market. As a result of market imperfections and the uncertainties of agricultural production, tenancy has become an important production arrangement in developing-country agriculture (Braverman and Stiglitz 1982; Byres 1983; Nabi 1985; Otsuka et al. 1993; Dasgupta et al. 1999).

Fixed rent and sharecropping are two forms of land tenancy. They differ in terms of who gets what portion of the output and who provides what proportion of the input. In fixed-rent tenancies, the tenant pays a fixed amount of cash as rent per unit of land and claims the entire crop. In sharecropping tenancy, the landlord provides land, and the tenant provides labor; they each claim a prearranged portion of the output. The ratio varies in different parts of the world, with the tenant's share typically ranging from 40 to 60 percent of the output; in Turkey the common practice is 50/50. The practice of sharing other inputs, such as fertilizers, seeds, machinery, and draft animals, also varies. In some cases, only one party (either the tenant or the landlord) supplies them; in other cases, these inputs could be equally supplied. Both types of contracts have advantages and disadvantages to the involved parties. An immense theoretical body of literature is available enumerating the reasons for and outcomes of different tenancies in terms of agrarian organization and production. But perhaps the most fascinating aspect of land tenancy for economists is its implications for resource allocation (Cheung 1969).

2. LITERATURE REVIEW

In studies of land tenancy, a great majority of the literature deals with sharecropping contracts in particular, as opposed to fixed-rent tenancy (Cheung 1969; Bardhan and Srinivasan 1971; Bhaduri 1973, 1983; Stiglitz 1974; Newbery 1977; Keyder 1983; J. Martinez-Alier 1983; Pearce 1983; Otsuka and Hayami 1988; Otsuka et al. 1992; Eswaran and Kotwal 1985; Smith 1994; Rao 2005). Maybe the reason for such immense interest in sharecropping is its existence dating back to long before Christ in many parts of the world, such as ancient India, China, and Greece. Or maybe such interest is due to its disappearance in some regions of the world, as in Europe and North America, and the fluctuation of its existence in some others, such as Turkey (Byres 1983).

Theorizing on sharecropping started with Adam Smith, who saw sharecropping as a transformed extension of the slave cultivation of ancient times, though quite different from slavery. Smith argues that sharecropping, or as it was then called in France, *metayers*, was different from slavery in a crucial way because tenants were capable of acquiring property (Smith 1994). However, according to Smith, the *metayer* system was still inefficient because the insecurity of tenure resulted in little incentive to invest.

The traditional view, which is known as the Marshallian inefficiency hypothesis, developed from the classical view. The traditional view considers sharecropping to be analogous to an ad valorem tax because the tenant has to give half of whatever is produced to the landlord. The Marshallian inefficiency argument posits that, because landlords and tenants share the output and because the tenant's marginal returns to effort and input are much less than the relevant marginal products, the tenant has less incentive to supply inputs than if he were the owner.[1] By the same token, landlords have less incentive to invest in land whenever the return to their investment is less than twice the marginal cost. Consequently, the equilibrium resource allocation resulting from share tenancy is less efficient than other forms of tenancy because resources are underutilized. As a result, fixed rent and owner cultivation, both of which supply the incentives to invest that sharecropping lacks, were seen as superior to sharecropping. However an interesting question many economists asked is this: If sharecropping were inefficient, then would it coexist with other tenancy forms?

One of the early responses to this question came from Johnson (1950), who argued that sharecropping was efficient. Under a sharecropping system with insecure tenure, tenants' incentive to invest comes from their desire to avoid costs related to moving, finding a new landlord, and possibly having to learn a new technique. In other words, Johnson (1950) believed sharecropping served a functional role, namely to discipline tenants.

However, as Johnson (1950) also acknowledged in his writings, his explanations have some limitations. First, the threat of eviction (i.e., insecure tenure) may not be a credible threat to discipline tenants if the inefficiencies resulting when a replacement tenant has to become familiar with the land and the crop are accounted for. When such inefficiencies are common, as they may be in agriculture, a landlord may not choose to change his tenants frequently, and hence, the functional explanation of sharecropping disappears.

Another efficiency-based explanation for why different tenancies exist came from Knight (1957), called the agricultural ladder hypothesis. According to the agricultural ladder hypothesis, inherent in the tenancy systems is the performance evaluation of the individual farmer, as different tenancies are seen as outcomes of different stages of experience and thus productivity. Very simply put, the agricultural ladder hypothesis posits that tenancies have a hierarchy based on productivity. In this hierarchy, landowners who own the land they cultivate occupy the highest rung, followed in order down the ladder by fixed-rent tenants, sharecroppers, and, finally, on the bottom rung, landless laborers who are employed in farming as day laborers.

The agricultural ladder hypothesis focuses particularly on the importance of management skills. According to the hypothesis, as the farmer becomes more experienced, he will be more productive and therefore more likely to have his own farm, thereby not engaging in tenancy for an additional source of income. Thus, the average age of the household head, which is used as a proxy for management skills, should be negatively related to the probability of sharecropping contracts (Knight 1957). The theory further claims that the management skills of the landlord are to be shared with the relatively younger sharecropping tenant, thus making the farm a place for vocational training.

The most comprehensive explanation, however, comes from the writings of Cheung (1969) on sharecropping being an efficient system to diversify risk. In his influential book, *The Theory of Share Tenancy*, Cheung (1969) argues that the mere existence of sharecropping, along with other forms of tenancy, proves that it is an efficient resource allocation mechanism in agriculture. Basing his arguments on Taiwan and China, Cheung (1969) argues that under the same property rights constraints, even though all tenancies yield the same efficiency of resource allocation, different tenancies coexist because of their different ways of handling risk. According to Cheung (1969), transaction costs differ among tenancies. Fixed-rent tenancy has bargaining costs; wage contracts have enforcement costs; and sharecropping has both bargaining and enforcement costs, which makes sharecropping a higher transaction-cost tenancy form. However, different levels of risk are associated with each tenancy type. In fixed-rent tenancies, the tenant bears all the risk, whereas in wage contracts, the landlord bears all the risk, and in share tenancy, risk is equally shared. Hence, despite differing transaction costs, because of the benefits in risk sharing, Cheung (1969) concludes that all types of tenure contracts are efficient.

As Pearce (1983) pointed out, Cheung's hypotheses have been subject to both criticism and extension and have generated considerable debate among economists.[2] Most of these critiques pointed out that transaction costs for sharecropping may not be higher than the other forms of tenancy, as the bargaining power of contracting parties in different tenancies may vary. First of all, returns to labor are not independent of labor effort in sharecropping, but they are in wage contracts; hence, it is unfounded to conclude that sharecropping has higher transaction costs than wage contracts. Furthermore, in developing countries with large labor surpluses, bargaining costs may not differ much among tenancy types. Alternatively, landlords may reduce the bargaining costs by choosing to have longer-term contracts, which would again reduce the transaction costs of sharecropping. In sum, if transaction costs are lower for sharecropping, then sharecropping contracts based on efficiency grounds should replace wage contracts. History proves the opposite. History also disproves Cheung's explanations centered around risk taking. As Otsuka et al. (1992) argued, if risk is so central to agricultural production and agrarian relations, then what explains the dominance of owner cultivation in developing-country agriculture?

Out of these debates and critiques emerged new explanations for both the prevalence and the disappearance of sharecropping tenancy, compared to fixed rent and owner cultivation. One explanation is the role of unmarketable inputs, such as management skills, female and child labor, and the ability to supervise labor (Bardhan 1980; Martinez-Alier 1983; Eswaran and Kotwal 1985; Morvadiri 1992). According to the authors cited, contracting parties are engaged in sharecropping tenancy to mitigate the effects of such inputs. Furthermore, by giving all participants a claim on the output, sharecropping contracts encourage the full use of resources. Landlords have an absolute advantage in management due to the experience of dealing with credit institutions and traders. While landlords are expected to use their management skills for the benefit of the contract outcome, similarly, tenants are expected to impose self-supervision because tenancy is a partnership. Everyone does what he is good at; hence, everyone wins. And therefore, sharecropping is sometimes more efficient than every other form of tenancy. In addition, from both the tenant's and the landlord's perspective, sharecropping further allows the utilization of otherwise unmarketable or not easily marketable and relatively immobile labor resources, such as female and child labor and cattle (Bardhan 1980; Martinez-Alier 1983; Morvadiri 1992).

Other explanations utilize both risk sharing and transaction costs to explain the persistence of sharecropping tenancy. Following from the work of Stiglitz (1974), Otsuka et al. (1992) supported the view that tenancy type is chosen based on two major factors: (1) where enforcement cost is high, fixed-rent tenancy is chosen and (2) when the tenant is risk averse, sharecropping is chosen. When capital markets improve, farmers can manage risk by diversifying their portfolios. Therefore, when credit or insurance markets develop, we can expect sharecropping to disappear (Stiglitz 1974).

Newbery (1977), who pioneered the "interlinking markets" hypotheses in contract choice theory, formulated a completely different explanation for the persistence of sharecropping, which Sen (1981) and Braverman and Stiglitz (1982) later developed. According to the interlinking market theory, sharecropping is not only a transaction in land but also in credit because rents and cost sharing are advanced in sharecropping tenancy. In areas where markets are not fully developed, such market linkages help reduce costs and risks related to agricultural production. First, such market linkages represent a partial solution to the need for intense labor use in agriculture; second, they are a partial solution to imperfections in credit markets, where the poor cannot borrow and lease-in through fixed-rent tenancy; and third, they ease output uncertainty. In addition, when credit markets are imperfect and the landlord is the supplier of credit, sharecropping tenancies could be more common because the landlord may prefer to employ a debtor tenant as a sharecropper to make sure he gets at least some of his loan back (Bardhan 1980). Hence, as Sen (1981) claims, sharecropping eases imperfections that factor markets cannot. Sen's (1981) and others' contributions to the literature are important because their studies provide the organic link to why sharecropping is prevalent in more backward areas.

On the other hand, Marxian theories of sharecropping provide the organic link to why backwardness is more prevalent in areas where sharecropping tenancy is common (Bhaduri 1973; Martinez-Alier 1983; Patnaik 1983; Pearce 1983; Rao 2005). The Marxian analysis of tenancy contract focuses on how the relations of production determine which contract type is preferable from the landlord's point of view (i.e., which tenancy type surplus labor can most easily be appropriated). The landlord owns the means of production, which grants him disproportionate bargaining power. He makes the choice of tenancy contract based on considerations of uncertainty, risk, bargaining power, and supervision costs and the way these elements affect the labor process and therefore his ability to appropriate surplus. Hence, inequality in the ownership or control of the means of production takes a central role in the determination of the contract choice (Rao 2005). In a theoretical study, Rao (2005) shows that when there is higher land inequality, the optimal choice of tenancy for a surplus-maximizing landlord would be sharecropping, as opposed to fixed rent for any given level of labor productivity.

A village is the most immediate socioeconomic environment a household interacts with, hence, inequality of land in a village affects social relations of production (Rao 2005) and economic opportunities (Mduma and Wobst 2005). Higher landownership inequality in the village may render the need to lease in more land not only because by definition of inequality, many have little and few have a lot, but also because inequality affects how local markets function. One of the ways landownership inequality affects markets is that it gives disproportionate power in relations of production in agriculture to a few (Griffin et al. 2002), and as Rao (2005), Braverman and Stiglitz (1982), and Bhaduri (1973) argue, landlords may use this power to extract surplus labor from tenants.

To maximize surplus labor, landlords control the labor process through various mechanisms. One of these mechanisms is to use tenants' disadvantage in accessing other markets as a threat to their survival. By either allocating smaller plots of land (Bhaduri 1973) or providing consumption loans to peasants, landlords strengthen the dependence of tenants to landlords for livelihood. Tenants have very few, if any, options for accessing other markets. Rural markets are isolated and hence, costly to access for employment opportunities. Similarly, tenants have limited access to formal credit markets because they lack collateral. When tenants need credit, they often borrow from the landlord at much higher interest rates than the formal market rate, which increases their dependency on the landlord for survival. Thus, landlords may even choose to prevent technical change so they can continue to benefit from usury in the role of creditor.

According to Bhaduri (1973), a landlord may resist technical change because additional returns to new investment may lower his returns on usury, as the tenant may not borrow as much due to an increase in productivity. Since the lender-landlord shares this productivity increase but not his usury income, lender-landlords rarely introduce new technology. Additionally, a tenant's increased bargaining power due to lower indebtedness and higher income may lower the rate of surplus extraction or even allow the tenant to entirely cut his ties to the landlord.

In the Marxian literature, sharecropping is seen as the product of socioeconomic contingencies and hence part of the historical fabric; as these contingencies disappear, so shall sharecropping (Pearce 1983). Such contingencies are seen particularly as a common phenomenon in precapitalist agrarian societies. Furthermore, Marxian analysis of tenancy contracts is different from the neoclassical analysis in the sense that Marxist work is not ahistorical and does not have an efficiency fetish, though efficiency is not disregarded (Rao 2005).

To sum up, the literature on sharecropping and land tenancy in general focuses on a handful of points: output risk, employment risk, indebtedness, and the power of landlords over tenants in extracting surplus labor and organizing agricultural production.

The model we have used based on this theoretical discussion is inclusive of macro determinants, such as landownership inequality, risk, and credit access and of micro determinants, such as the demographic structure of the household. Inquiry about the economic and demographic characteristics of tenants is where we turn next.

3. SHARECROPPERS VERSUS FIXED-RENT TENANTS: AN ECONOMIC AND DEMOGRAPHIC INQUIRY

In Turkey, 30 percent of agricultural land is cultivated by tenants through sharecropping or fixed-rent tenancy (QHS 2002). Most of the farmers in rural Turkey rent land on a fixed-rent contract rather than sharecropping. In a national sample of 5,297 households, 23 percent of farmers lease in land in fixed-rent tenancy while only 10 percent sharecrop. However, significant regional variation exists in this distribution. Fixed-rent tenancy is highest in Aegean, with 33 percent; followed by Marmara, with 30 percent; Central Anatolia, with 26 percent; and Mediterranean, with 25 percent. The Black Sea region has the lowest ratio of fixed-rent tenants, with 9 percent. Central Anatolia has the highest ratio of sharecroppers, with 16 percent, followed by Southeast Anatolia, with 14 percent. For the rest of the country, fixed-rent tenancy ranges between 6 and 9 percent (table 3.1).

3.1. Demographics

An initial inquiry into the ages of farmers who are engaged in different forms of tenancies does not provide a convincing picture in support of the agricultural ladder hypothesis in rural Turkey. On average, a sharecropper is 48, one year older than a fixed-rent tenant, a few months younger than an agricultural laborer, and only two years younger than an owner–cultivator. These age differences are not big enough to make a prominent difference in productivity-enhancing farm management, and in any case, the order does not confirm the ladder hypothesis.

A typical sharecropper household has an average of 5.8 members, similar to a fixed-rent tenant household (table 3.1). However, upon closer scrutiny, in all the regions except Central Anatolia, sharecropper households are less crowded than fixed-rent tenants. The difference is more pronounced in Southeastern and Eastern regions, where sharecroppers have 7.9 and 6.7 members versus fixed-rent tenants, with 9.4 and 6.8 members, respectively. Both sharecropper household heads and fixed-rent household heads are younger than the country average, 48 and 47 years versus 50 years for an average household in rural Turkey (table 3.1).

No significant difference is found between sharecropper households and fixed-rent tenant households in the number of workers; the number of workers in both households is close to the national average of 4.09 workers per household (table 3.1). In Southeast Anatolia, the number of female workers is higher than elsewhere, with 2.5 female workers, compared to the national average of 2. Only in East Anatolia ratio of female workers is higher, with 55 percent for sharecroppers (table 3.1).

Table 3.1 Selected Variables for Land Tenants

Region	SC (% in Total HH)	FT (% in Total HH)	Landless (% in Total HH)	SC Members	FT Members	SC HHH Age
Mediterranean	9	25	17	5.1	5.7	46.0
Aegean	9	33	16	4.8	4.7	46.6
SE Anatolia	14	18	18	7.9	9.4	45.7
Marmara	7	30	7	4.1	4.6	51.2
Central An.	16	26	19	6.1	6.1	49.1
E. Anatolia	9	19	10	6.7	8.6	44.1
Black Sea	6	9	11	5.9	6.3	49.0
TURKEY	10	23	14	5.8	5.8	47.8

Region	FT HHH Age	SC No of Workers	FT No of Workers	SC No of Female Workers	FT No of Female Workers	SC Dep. Ratio
Mediterranean	46.7	3.95	4.26	1.91	2.06	1.38
Aegean	45.6	3.74	3.5	1.89	1.75	1.33
SE Anatolia	43.5	4.93	4.93	2.49	2.74	1.81
Marmara	49.4	3.09	3.52	1.53	1.84	1.36
Central An.	47.7	4.46	4.01	2.3	2.17	1.39
E. Anatolia	43	4.32	4.83	2.34	2.69	1.66
Black Sea	48.5	4.08	4.07	1.98	2.27	1.54
TURKEY	46.9	4.14	4.07	2.09	2.06	1.47

Region	FT Dep. Ratio	SC Land Owned	FT Land Owned	SC Credit Per Decare	FT Credit Per Decare
Mediterranean	1.4	26.3	46.3	1.05	17.56
Aegean	1.36	28.2	60.2	8.16	7.57
SE Anatolia	1.77	40.6	66.8	0.21	0.19
Marmara	1.31	46.2	64	2.15	3.01
Central An.	1.46	107.2	105.8	2.15	1.25
E. Anatolia	1.77	85.8	67.4	0.25	0.45
Black Sea	1.39	21.8	36.7	3.74	6.69
TURKEY	1.45	57.1	66.6	2.87	5.93

Note: FT: Fixed Rent Tenancy; HH: Household; HHH: Household Head; SC: Share Cropping.
Source: Quantitative Household Survey, 2002.

The dependency ratio seems to be higher for sharecroppers, with 1.47 mouths per pair of hands; this ratio is lower than the 1.50 mouths-to-pair-of-hands ratio among the landless but higher than the ratio for any other group (table 3.1). From the initial investigation of household demographics, Turkish data seem to support Morvadiri's (1992) nonmarketable inputs explanation for the persistence of sharecropping. As his model would predict, sharecropping households more fully utilize female labor.

3.2. Assets, Credit and Income, and Landownership Inequality

3.2.1. Land

Sharecroppers own less land: 7 percent less land than fixed-rent tenants and 17 percent less land than an average farmer in Turkey (table 3.1). Some regional variation exists, such as in Central and East Anatolia, where the amount of land owned by sharecroppers is slightly higher than the amount of land owned by fixed-rent tenants. Elsewhere in the country, sharecroppers own small parcels of land.

3.2.2. Credit

A strong link seems to exist between the availability of credit and tenancy choice (table 3.1). Nationally, sharecroppers have less credit per decare, with 2.87 YTL, less than half of what fixed renters have, with 5.93 YTL, and less than half of the national average of 6 YTL per decare. The largest gap in terms of credit per decare is in the Mediterranean region: sharecroppers have only 1.05 YTL per decare credit, whereas fixed-rent tenants have 17.56 YTL, and the average across all rural households in the region is 12.9 YTL per decare. Curiously, there are a few regions in which sharecroppers have slightly higher credit per decare than do fixed-rent tenants: Central Anatolia, Southeast Anatolia, and Aegean.

3.2.3. Income

Income per capita for sharecroppers is one of the lowest in Turkey, ranking behind landless laborers. Sharecroppers' average income is 1,665 YTL per person, 45 percent less than fixed-rent tenants', and 11 percent less than the country's average of 1,840 YTL (table 3.2). The largest difference is observed in Mediterranean, where sharecroppers' income is 88 percent less than fixed-rent tenants', and 28 percent less than the regional average income among rural households. Looking at income per person can make sense of why Southeast Anatolian

Table 3.2 Selected Variables for Land Tenants

Region	SC Income Per Cap	FT Income Per Capita	SC Agr. Income Per Cap	FT Agr. Income Per Capita	SC Agr. Income Per Cap	FT NonAgr. Income Per Capita
Mediterranean	1,603	3,013	1,126	2,697	477	316
Aegean	2,545	2,462	1,958	2,062	587	401
SE Anatolia	592	1,301	493	1,137	99	164
Marmara	2,069	2,965	1,483	2,549	586	416
Central An.	2,014	2,465	1,618	2,062	397	403
E. Anatolia	617	995	402	818	216	177
Black Sea	1,161	1,571	849	1,312	313	260
TURKEY	**1,665**	**2,404**	**1,270**	**2,054**	**396**	**350**

Region	Land Ownership Gini	Land Holding Gini	Participation to Factor Markets (%) (All)
Mediterranean	0.68	0.64	41
Aegean	0.71	0.61	49
SE Anatolia	0.64	0.58	41
Marmara	0.55	0.54	39
Central An.	0.58	0.51	42
E. Anatolia	0.59	0.55	28
Black Sea	0.64	0.59	22
TURKEY	**0.65**	**0.6**	**37**

Note: SC: Share Cropping; FT: Fixed Rent Tenancy.
Source: Quantitative Household Survey, 2002.

households who are engaged in sharecropping have higher credit per decare. They make so little money compared to other groups that they might be in desperation-driven debt. A Southeastern sharecropper household is making 592 YTL, opposed to the regional average of 1,471 YTL per person per year. Only in the Aegean region, do sharecropper households make 3 percent more than the fixed-rent tenants, who earn 2,545 YTL, and 10 percent more than the region's average, with 2,281 YTL. Everywhere else they are making something in the range of 23 to 49 percent less than the fixed-rent tenant households make.

The difference in income per person between sharecroppers and fixed-rent tenants is more pronounced if we restrict our analysis to agricultural income (table 3.2). On average, a sharecropper household is earning 62 percent less agricultural income than a fixed-rent tenant earns. But the same pattern is not valid for nonagricultural income.

On average, a sharecropper household is making 11 percent more nonagricultural income per person than a fixed-rent tenant makes. Especially in Mediterranean, a sharecropper household is earning 34 percent more nonagricultural income than a household who is engaged in a fixed-rent tenancy contract is earning. Marmara and Aegean are regions that also have a significant difference of nonagricultural income per person for sharecroppers when compared to fixed renters or an average peasant. They make more money than the fixed renters make, 29 and 32 percent respectively (table 3.2). The fact that peasants from these regions make more money could point to the more prevalent off-farm employment opportunities.

3.2.4. Landownership Inequality

To start with, in most regions, a very clear pattern exists in per capita landownership distribution and agricultural market participation: market participation is higher in the regions with high landownership inequality, namely Aegean, Mediterranean, Southeastern Anatolia, and Central Anatolia. Particularly in the Aegean, where the landownership Gini coefficient is highest at 0.71, participation in factor markets through land tenancy and wage labor is also significantly higher than in the other regions, with 49 percent (3.2).

However, there are three exceptions to this pattern: Black Sea, East Anatolia, and the Marmara regions. In the Black Sea region and East Anatolia, the market participation rates are surprisingly low given the high degree of land inequality. In Marmara, on the other hand, market participation is surprisingly high given the relatively equal land distribution. There are two main reasons for the low market participation rate in the Black Sea region. First, farms in the Black Sea region are already small because of the mountainous landscape;, on average, 50 percent smaller than farms in Turkey. Second, because agricultural land is very limited, most laborers seek nonfarm employment, contributing to a significant amount of out-migration from the region. This is also supported by the high average combined—agricultural and nonagricultural—labor-market participation, with 40 percent. East Anatolia has a significantly lower market participation rate than does Central Anatolia (28 percent versus 42 percent) despite being almost equally unequal in landownership distribution, as measured with a Gini coefficient. Also, East Anatolia has a much lower proportion of landless residents than does Central Anatolia: 9 percent versus 19 percent, respectively. Marmara is the exception that swings the other way. It is relatively equal and has the lowest landlessness ratio but has high agricultural market participation. The reason why there is not a linear relationship between land owner-ship inequality and market participation may be due to differences in accessing credit markets.

A similarly clear pattern exists in per capita credit and rural factor market participation in Turkey: where credit per capita is higher, there is less participation in the labor and sharecropping tenancy markets and more participation in the fixed-rent tenancy markets. Since fixed-rent payments require cash—as opposed to sharecropping, in which output is shared in physical terms—such a pattern is unsurprising. It certainly makes more sense than the agricultural ladder model does and is better supported by the evidence in Turkey.

From this brief overview of the summary of statistics, we get a strong hint that the important factors influencing tenancy choice include landownership inequality, credit access, and initial land base (i.e., total amount of land a household owns).

4. THE MODEL: DETERMINANTS OF TENANCY IN AGRARIAN MARKETS

Based on the theoretical discussions, descriptive statistics, and the literature review, we have conducted probit regression analysis to look at the determinants of contract choice in Turkish agriculture using QHS 2002. The econometric specification that we test follows:

$$\text{Share cropping tenancy dummy} = c + \beta_i \sum X + \alpha_i \sum W + \Delta_i \sum Y + \pounds_i \sum Z + \mu_i \sum V + \varepsilon, \qquad (1)$$

where X is the vector of demographic variables, W is the vector of household wealth variables, Y is the vector of macro variables, V is the vector of regional dummies, ε is the error term, and c is the intercept.

In this nonlinear probit model, the dependent variable is binary, taking the value of "1" if the household sharecrops and "0" otherwise. The probit model estimates a probability distribution function that allows us to assess to what extent each independent variable affects the probability of a household participating in sharecropping.

For the regression analysis, we estimated four different models to control for demographics, wealth, market and macroeconomic context, and geographic variation. Each additional model adds on to the explanatory variables of the previous one, and all models are signifi-cant at the 1 percent level. We tested whether income risk matters in contract choice using a reduced sample of agrarian households selected to illuminate this point. These models are tested first for sharecropping and then for fixed-rent tenancy. The first model includes the household's demographic characteristics as explanatory variables. These characteristics include age of the household head, his education, and the average age of adult males and females in the household, as well as the dependency ratio, the proportion of female workers in the household, and the household's food self-sufficiency ratio (which will be elaborated in the following section).

The second model adds the household's wealth variables to the first model. We introduce total land owned, per capita protein and carbohydrate consumption, total number of cattle owned by the household, and total number of tractors owned by the household to proxy for wealth.

The third model adds macro variables as explanatory variables to the second model. Specifically, these macro variables are the land-ownership distribution in the village the household is operating in, credit per capita, an infrastructure index for the village, the ratio of the value of marketed crops in total crop production, and a risk variable. The risk variable is defined by adopting the technique used in an earlier study by Douglas and Lueck (1992): risk is measured by the ratio of agricultural income to total income. They argue that when a household is more diversified, they will be less averse to agricultural risk and hence more likely to engage in fixed-rent tenancy. Less diversified households will be less able to absorb agricultural losses and so will be more likely to limit their exposure to risk by engaging in sharecropping.

Finally, in addition to the variables discussed above, the fourth model includes regional dummy variables to account for variation based on regional features that may be due to agroclimatic characteristics of the region and/or sociocultural variables that cannot be captured by demographic or economic indicators.

We have used identical econometric specifications in looking at both tenancy types. The following discussion on the variables relates to both tenancy types.

4.1. Variables Used in Regressions

Age and education variables are introduced to control for the demographic characteristics of the household and to test for the agricultural ladder hypothesis. If the hypothesis holds, the average age of the household head should be negatively related to the probability of sharecropping contracts (Knight 1957). In addition, we introduce the average age of the adult males and females in the household to get a better grasp of the life cycle of the household. In rural Turkey, a much older male may be heading a crowded household with much younger adults because of cohabitation among kin.

Two more variables, share of self-sufficiency of total food consumption and dependency ratio, are introduced to control for women's housework burden. Share of self-sufficiency of total food consumption refers to the ratio of the monetary value of the food produced by the household to the monetary value of the food consumed by the household. A ratio of one or higher does not necessarily mean the household produces everything they consume, but it does mean that, by engaging in exchange, they can meet their food needs with their agricultural production. A higher ratio of self-sufficiency may negatively affect the agricultural labor supply of the household, particularly of women workers, since they would be engaged in household production. It is well observed that women make up the majority (80 percent) of unpaid family workers in Turkish agriculture (TUIK 2011). In an average household in Turkey, the care of dependents is overwhelmingly women's work. Given that female workers are constrained by hours in a day, a negative correlation exists between the amount of housework and fieldwork: doing more of one means doing less of the other. Hence, we might expect a higher dependency ratio to be associated with women doing less agricultural labor. Conversely, a higher dependency ratio may increase the financial distress of the household thereby compelling the household to direct as much labor as possible to earning more income. If this second possibility dominates the relation, then the relation between dependency ratio and land tenancy may be positive. Thus, we expect to find a negative coefficient for the self-sufficiency ratio, and we have no clear prediction for the sign of the coefficient for the dependency ratio.

The ratio of female workers to total workers is included to test for Bardhan's and Mordaviri's hypotheses regarding market imperfections. Bardhan (1980) argues that when credit and land markets are connected, landlords who are also money lenders would prefer to lease out their land in sharecropping contracts to a family they have lent money to since a rational landlord would try to guarantee at least some portion of the debt be paid back by providing employment and income to the borrower. Morvadiri (1992) argues that women's labor is less easily marketable than men's, so sharecropping may give landlords a way to benefit from female labor that they cannot otherwise access. Given Morvadiri's (1992) and Bardhan's (1980) claims, it is plausible to expect that landlords may not only choose tenants to whom they have lent money but also to households who have more adult females; female labor guarantees a stable labor supply and thereby stable production, and hence increased possibility of debt payment. As discussed in the literature, stable labor supply is particularly crucial during peak times, such as harvest. Female labor is less mobile due to customs, and females also have fewer, if any, opportunities to be employed in other rural markets. To test whether such a phenomenon exists in rural Turkey, whether indebtedness and having more female laborers increase the likelihood of engaging in sharecropping contracts, we introduced an interaction variable: the product of credit per capita and ratio of female workers. We expect to see a positive correlation between sharecropping probability and the interaction variable.

All else equal, we expect that households with smaller landownership would be more likely to lease-in land. As land owned gets smaller, so does the likelihood of earning a living from the owned land alone and hence the increased probability to engage in tenancy. As discussed in the literature, land tenancy is also a way to utilize indivisible inputs, such as farm machinery and cattle. This is particularly applicable to Turkish agriculture given that it is flooded with underutilized tractors thanks to cheap credit provided by the Marshall Plan (Keyder 1983; Koymen 1999). Therefore, a small farmer who cannot fully utilize his tractor on the land he owns is more likely to lease-in land. Hence, we expect a negative relationship between total land owned and land tenancy and a positive relationship between the number of tractors and cattle a household has and land tenancy.

Following the Marxist tradition, we further inquire if sharecropping is a feature of backward areas, where we proxy backwardness with poverty. More often than not, backwardness in rural areas manifests itself as poverty. All else constant, those who are poorer are more likely to sharecrop than lease-in land through fixed-rent tenancy not only because they have little access to the cash that is needed to pay the rent but also because poverty and backward agriculture go together with a higher incidence of sharecropping as argued by Mazumdar (1975) and Rao (2005).

We introduce a per capita food consumption variable to determine whether a farmer is poor or not. Using consumption levels to proxy for either income or wealth is common (Filmer and Pritchett 2001). We further the measurement of poverty by focusing on the protein and carbohydrate consumption levels since having a nutritious meal is different from having just a meal and is reflective of wealth. In particular, meat consumption is a very significant indicator of household wealth in Turkey. We expect a negative relationship between consumption levels and the probability of sharecropping since poorer farmers with limited options elsewhere are more likely to sharecrop.

The distribution of landownership is an important determinant of land tenancy contracts for reasons we have discussed earlier, and greater inequality in landownership is expected to have a positive relationship with the likelihood of engaging in land tenancy, particularly of sharecropping. Higher inequality may mean more control of the labor process by landlords, and landlords may expect higher profits from and hence prefer sharecropping over fixed-rent tenancy. However, in Turkey, the relationship between form of tenancy and landownership inequality may go the other way because of the following reason: the shrinking land base, along with unfavorable conditions for agricultural production as detailed in earlier chapters, and increased rural-urban migration, which has resulted in a mushrooming rate of absentee landlords in rural areas. Since labor supervision cost is not as big a problem in fixed-rent tenancy when compared to sharecropping, fixed-rent tenancy may be more prevalent with high landownership inequality.

On the other hand, following from Griffin et al. (2002), in extreme cases of inequality, land inequality translates into limited alternative sources of employment and income through monopsony in labor markets and monopoly in land markets. When this is the case, landlords may prefer to limit land access to keep the status quo in the village, as additional income to peasants may threaten landlords' position, and hence, less likelihood for any kind of tenancy.

The ratio of the monetary value of marketed crops to total crops (i.e., the crop marketization rate) is introduced to determine a household's ease of access to cash instead of credit. We expect sharecropping to be less likely when the household is more integrated into the market and has more cash. This variable will also help us see if sharecropping tenancy is more frequent in areas with less developed and connected markets.

The infrastructure variable is an index taking values up to 100. This index is calculated based on the part of the survey (QHS 2002) where households were asked to evaluate public services, such as irrigation canals, roads, veterinary support, and other services that are instrumental in agricultural production in the village, compared to what was available five years ago.[3] Availability of good quality infrastructure also helps a household to better integrate into markets; hence we expect a negative relationship between this variable and the probability of sharecropping but not fixed-rent tenancy, as better access to markets also eases access to alternative sources for credit.

Population density is a province-level variable and measures people per square kilometer for all towns and villages under the jurisdiction of the province. We expect this variable to be negatively related to sharecropping tenancy since in areas of higher population density, there is a greater tendency to develop techniques for intensive agriculture, which produces higher yields and incomes as discussed by Boserup (1965). Hence higher population density may reduce the likelihood of land tenancy (Boserup 1965).

Regional dummies are introduced to control for regional variations that may be due to agroclimatic and sociocultural heterogeneity. All else equal, it is expected that being a farmer in Southeast, East, and Central Anatolia increases the likelihood to sharecrop since sharecropping is a more common tenancy in backward agricultural regions. Those regions are backward compared to the Aegean and Marmara regions not only because of the way agriculture is organized but because Marmara and Aegean offer more off-farm opportunities to their populations, which increases options for farmers with less land who need additional earnings to survive. These differences cannot be captured by a poverty variable as a proxy.

4.2. Hypotheses

We would like to test several hypotheses by using the QHS 2002. The first hypothesis is that sharecropping is more common among those who are poor. Second, credit and cash access is negatively related to sharecropping but positively related to fixed-rent tenancy. Third, ownership of land is negatively related to the probability of land tenancy. Fourth, all else constant, ownership of means of production other than land (such as tractors and draft animals) is positively related to both tenancies. Fifth, agricultural ladder theories do not hold true for Turkey. Sixth, having access to female labor increases the probability of engaging in sharecropping contracts. Last, but not least, landownership inequality matters (i.e., it has a positive relationship with both tenancy types).

4.3. Regression Results and Discussion

4.3.1. Sharecropping

The regression results are based on a slightly smaller sample than was the original one (4,995 versus 5,297) due to missing observations in some of the explanatory variables. The descriptive statistics of the variables used are illustrated in table 3.3 and table 3.4 for the two samples (agrarian and combined) used in the regressions in Appendix A. Before we start to discuss the results, addressing a few methodological and statistical issues would be useful. First of all, the number of sharecroppers in Turkish agriculture is small. Only 332 sharecroppers are in the sample, of which 56 are also engaged in fixed-rent tenancy, as opposed to 4,663 nonsharecropper households. Hence the magnitude effects of our findings may be small. However, statistical significance as it is represented by correlations in patterns of variations may indicate important features of land tenancy and provide useful insights for policy.

The maximum likelihood estimates of the probit regression model for the sharecroppers are presented in table 3.5. Interpreting the coefficients of probit regressions is more complicated than regular Ordinary Least Squares (OLS) regressions. We will therefore discuss the changes in the probability of sharecropping based on level changes in the variables that turned out to be significant when all other variables are constant at their sample mean. Since all models are significant and the statistical significance of the variables does not change much across specifications, we confine the discussion to the last model, which is inclusive of regional variation, and the regression run using the full sample. We will report if and when there are considerable differences in our findings from model to model. Unless noted, all discussions are about the findings of the full model.

Age of household head indicates a significant positive nonlinear relationship to the probability of sharecropping. All other variables constant at their mean, increasing the household's age from the sample mean of 50 to 60 years of age increases the probability of sharecropping from 5 to 9 percent. The average ages of both female adults and male adults are negatively related to the probability of sharecropping; however, neither is statistically significant. The positive relationship between household head's age and the probability of sharecropping seems to point to the fact that the agricultural ladder hypothesis does not hold true for Turkey, or if there is an agricultural ladder, it is reversed as a result of some other socioeconomic factors. One such factor could be that older people have limited access to other off-farm earning opportunities, so they prefer more traditional arrangements to what is available within their immediate surroundings.

When estimation is restricted to the agrarian sample, the age of the household head remains significant, as in the full sample. Increasing the age from the sample mean of 49 to 59 increases the probability

Table 3.5 Regression Results for Sharecropping Tenancy

	Dependent Variable: Sharecropping Dummy (1)				
	I	II	III	IV	V
Household Size	-0.001	-0.013	-0.008	-0.008	-0.014
	-0.011	-0.012	-0.013	-0.013	-0.013
Head's Education	-0.162	-0.188	0.165	-0.165	-0.166
	-0.115	-0.116	-0.12	-0.12	-0.12
Head's Education Square	0.027	0.032	0.034	0.034	0.034
	-0.017	(0.017)*	(0.017)**	(0.017)**	(0.017)*
Head's Age	0.03	0.027	0.029	0.029	0.029
	(0.016)*	(0.016)*	(0.016)*	(0.016)*	(0.016)*
Head's Age Square	-0.0004	-0.0004	-0.0004	-0.0004	-0.0004
	(0.0002)**	(0.0002)**	(0.0002)**	(0.0002)**	(0.0002)**
Average Age Female[a]	-0.005	-0.005	-0.004	-0.004	-0.004
	-0.003	-0.003	-0.003	-0.003	-0.003
Average Age Male[a]	-0.003	-0.004	-0.003	-0.003	-0.003
	-0.004	-0.004	-0.004	-0.004	-0.004
Female Ratio[b]	-0.05	-0.067	-0.087	-0.087	-0.086
	-0.253	-0.252	-0.283	-0.283	-0.282
Dependency Ratio	0.296	0.228	0.271	0.271	0.267
	-0.268	-0.264	-0.272	-0.272	-0.271
Dependency Ratio Square	-0.086	-0.067	-0.078	0.078	-0.076
	-0.069	-0.067	-0.069	-0.069	-0.068
Self Sufficiency Rate	0.091	0.028	0.0091	0.009	0.008
	-0.093	-0.093	-0.1001	-0.1	-0.1
Total Land Owned		-0.001	-0.001	-0.001	N/A
		0	(0.000)*	(0.000)*	N/A
Per Capita Land Owned		N/A	N/A	-0.002	N/A
		N/A	N/A	-0.002	N/A
Log (Per Capita Consumption)[d]		-0.154	-0.119	-0.119	-0.119
		(0.061)**	(0.069)*	(0.069)*	(0.069)*
Total Cattle (HH)		0.014	0.012	0.012	0.011
		(0.006)**	(0.006)*	(0.006)*	(0.006)*

	(1)	(2)	(3)	(4)	(5)
Total # of Tractors	0.1673 (0.056)***		0.12194 (0.061)**	0.1219 (0.061)**	0.1176 (0.062)*
Population Density			0.00003 (0.0001)	0 (0.0001)	0.00003 (0.0001)
Village Land Distribution (Gini)			0.462 (0.167)***	0.462 (0.167)***	0.475 (0.168)***
Log (Per Capita Credit)			-0.147 (0.254)	-0.147 (0.254)	-0.146 (0.254)
Per Capita Credit * Female Ratio			0.16 (0.265)	0.16 (0.265)	0.159 (0.264)
Infrastructure Index [c]			-0.003 (0.006)	-0.003 (0.006)	-0.003 (0.006)
Agr. Income / Total Income			-0.583 (0.114)***	-0.583 (0.114)***	-0.584 (0.114)***
Share of Marketed Crops			-0.54 (0.077)***	-0.54 (0.077)***	-0.545 (0.077)***
Regdum_Medit				-0.208 (0.134)	-0.208 (0.134)
Regdum_Eagen				0.159 (0.11)	0.161 (0.11)
Regdum_BlackSea				0.104 (0.112)	0.111 (0.112)
Regdum_SE_Anatolia				0.219 (0.135)	0.217 (0.135)
Regdum_C_Anatolia				0.386 (0.105)***	0.381 (0.104)***
Regdum_E_Anatolia				-0.651 (0.213)***	-0.66 (0.213)***
Constant	-1.65 (0.544)***	1.74 (1.4)	1.11 (1.62)	1.11 (1.62)	0.68 (1.76)
Observations	4,995	4,995	4,995	4,995	3,801

Notes: *significant at 10%; **significant at 5%; ***significant at 1%. [a]Calculated for Adults Older Than 15. [b]Ratio of Females in Total Earners. [c]Protein and Carbohydrates Only. [d]In Annual Million TLs. [c]Max 100. Robust standard errors in parentheses.

Source: Quantitative Household Survey, 2002.

of sharecropping from 6 to 11.5 percent. In the agrarian sample, the education level of the household's head is also significant at the 10 percent level and is negatively correlated with the probability of sharecropping as expected. An illiterate farmer in the agrarian sample is much more likely to sharecrop than one with a primary school degree (13 versus 6 percent).

In the full sample, the ratio of female workers in the household is negatively correlated with sharecropping tenancy, but insignificantly. On the other hand, women's burden variables (i.e., the dependency ratio and self-sufficiency ratio) are positively correlated. In the agrarian sample, the share of female workers affects sharecropping tenancy positively but with no statistical significance. Even though we also observed for the agrarian sample what Morvadiri observed for a Central Anatolian village, we cannot provide robust statistical evidence to support our hypothesis that households with more adult females are engaged more in sharecropping.[4]

When we introduce the second set of explanatory variables, regression results are in support of the hypothesis on landownership and wealth as indicated by consumption. They are both negatively related to the probability of sharecropping tenancy. Ownership of farm capital, such as tractors and cattle, is positively related to the probability of being engaged in sharecropping, at the 1 percent significance level. Having one tractor, as opposed to having none, increases the probability of sharecropping by 1.5 percent; however, this variable completely loses its significance when we run the regressions for the agrarian sample only. Total land owned by the household is significant at the 10 percent level (i.e., the more land households own, the less likely they will sharecrop). However, the magnitude effect of total land owned is small. Increasing the amount of land from the sample mean of 70 donums to 280 donums decreases the probability of sharecropping by 1.3 percent, from approximately 5.1 to 3.9 percent. Interestingly, except for total number of tractors, none of the variables are significant in the agrarian sample among macro variables.

One interesting finding in the first three models, without controlling for regional heterogeneity, is about the impact of per capita food consumption. The more a household eats, the less likely they are to sharecrop. The relationship is significant at the 1 percent level for the three models using the full sample. For the agrarian sample, doubling per capita consumption from 100 YTL to 200 YTL reduces the probability of sharecropping from 5.2 to 4.4 percent. When we control for regional heterogeneity, the statistical significance of food consumption declines to the 10 percent level. For the agrarian sample, the same pattern is observed but only if we keep the observations regarding missing crop marketization rates.[5] Landownership distribution has a positive and significant relationship at the 1 percent level. A landless household who live in a village where all the land is owned by one landlord (i.e., Gini equals to 1) are twice as likely to engage in sharecropping tenancy when compared to a household who live in a village where everyone has equal amounts of owned land (i.e., Gini equals to 0). The probability increases from 3 to 6 percent. For the agrarian sample, the magnitude effect is higher as the probability of sharecropping increases, from 5 to 10 percent when Gini is 0 compared to when it is 1.

Being more integrated to markets reduces tenancy probability at the 1 percent level: marketing 85 percent of one's output versus marketing 45 percent reduces sharecropping probability to 4 from 6.4 percent.

Income risk mitigation, as measured by the proportion of total income derived from nonagricultural sources, is negatively associated with sharecropping tenancy at the 5 percent significance level, both for the full sample and for the agrarian. In the agrarian sample, increasing the ratio of nonagricultural income's share from the sample mean of 13 to 50 percent reduces sharecropping by 1.5 to 5 percent.

Living in Central and East Anatolian regions makes a farmer household more prone to engage in sharecropping tenancy as opposed to living in Marmara, where landownership inequality is lower and off-farm employment opportunities are greater. If we imagine a Central Anatolian farmer and a Marmaran farmer as demographically identical households, living in villages that appear statistically identical according to the variables included here, the Central Anatolian farmer has a 9.5 percent probability of sharecropping, making him twice as likely to sharecrop as his counterpart who lives in Marmara.

4.3.2. Fixed-Rent Tenancy

The results of the probit regression for fixed-rent tenancy are illustrated in table 3.6. There are 1,165 households who are engaged in fixed-rent tenancy, of which 56 of them also sharecrop. As in the previous section, unless specified, results for fixed-rent tenancy regression are discussed for only the full sample.

Having an educated household head positively affects the probability of engaging in fixed-rent tenancy. If the household head has finished primary school with a diploma (i.e., is officially recognized as a primary school graduate), as opposed to just having finished secondary school, the probability of fixed-rent tenancy drops to 19 from

Table 3.6 Regression Results for Fixed-Rent Tenancy

	Dependent Variable: Rent Dummy (1)					
	I	II	III	IV	V	VI
Household Size	-0.007	-0.022	-0.01	0.007	0.004	0.006
	-0.008	(0.009)**	-0.009	-0.009	-0.009	-0.01
Head's Education	0.373	0.332	0.282	0.236	0.234	0.258
	(0.091)***	(0.091)***	(0.094)***	(0.096)**	(0.096)**	(0.108)**
Head's Edc. Square	-0.048	-0.044	-0.039	-0.029	-0.029	-0.029
	(0.013)***	(0.013)***	(0.014)***	(0.014)**	(0.014)**	(0.016)*
Head's Age	0.002	-0.002	-0.003	0	0	-0.003
	-0.012	-0.013	-0.012	-0.012	-0.012	-0.013
Head's Age Square	-0.0001	-0.00004	-0.00003	-0.00004	-0.00004	0
	-0.0001	-0.0001	-0.0001	-0.0001	-0.0001	-0.0001
Average Age Female[a]	-0.009	-0.011	-0.01	-0.009	-0.009	-0.009
	(0.002)***	(0.002)***	(0.002)***	(0.002)***	(0.002)***	(0.003)***
Average Age Male[a]	-0.002	-0.004	-0.002	-0.004	-0.004	-0.005
	-0.003	-0.003	-0.003	-0.003	-0.003	(0.003)*
Fem. Ratio[b]	-0.229	-0.2	-0.198	-0.193	-0.195	-0.094
	-0.181	-0.185	-0.189	-0.193	-0.193	-0.213
Dep. Ratio	0.032	0.085	0.116	0.13	0.131	0.136
	-0.221	-0.217	-0.2	-0.196	-0.196	-0.209
Dep. Ratio Square	-0.005	0	-0.015	-0.01	-0.009	-0.011
	-0.055	-0.054	-0.049	-0.048	-0.048	-0.051
Self Suff. Rate	0.25	0.14	0.185	0.179	0.1835	0.1919
	(0.0674)***	(0.0691)**	(0.0708)***	(0.0737)**	(0.0736)**	(0.0811)**
Total Land Owned		-0.0003	-0.0003	-0.0004	N/A	-0.0003
		-0.0002	-0.0002	(0.0002)*	N/A	-0.0002
Per Capita Land Owned			N/A	N/A	-0.00026	N/A
			N/A	N/A	-0.00051	N/A
Log (Per Capita Cons.)[d]		0.075	0.029	0.092	0.088	0.119
		(0.045)*	-0.046	(0.049)*	(0.049)*	(0.053)**
Total Cattle (hh)		0.013	0.017	0.016	0.016	0.016
		(0.005)***	(0.005)***	(0.005)***	(0.005)***	(0.006)***

	(1)	(2)	(3)	(4)	(5)	(6)
Total # of Tractors	0.526 (0.042)***		0.431 (0.044)***	0.357 (0.045)***	0.346 (0.045)***	0.307 (0.050)***
Population Density			0 (0.0001)	−0.0001 (0.0001)*	−0.00013 (0.0001)*	−0.0001 (0.0001)
Village Land Distribution (Gini)			1.069 (0.123)***	1.145 (0.129)***	1.144 (0.129)***	1.226 (0.147)***
Share of Marketed Crops			0.011 (0.003)***	0.009 (0.004)**	0.009 (0.004)**	0.008 (0.004)**
Log (Per Capita Credit)			0.021 (0.004)***	0.006 (0.005)	0.007 (0.005)	0.008 (0.005)*
Infrastructure Index [c]			−0.664 (0.083)***	−0.635 (0.086)***	−0.637 (0.086)***	−0.739 (0.165)***
Nonagr. Income / Total Income			0.201 (0.063)***	0.258 (0.066)***	0.251 (0.066)***	0.335 (0.077)***
Regdum_Medit				−0.25 (0.081)***	−0.246 (0.081)***	−0.281 (0.088)***
Regdum_Eagen				0.049 (0.072)	0.053 (0.072)	0.002 (0.078)
Regdum_Black Sea				−0.686 (0.084)***	−0.675 (0.084)***	−0.699 (0.094)***
Regdum_SE_Anatolia				−0.474 (0.099)***	−0.483 (0.099)***	−0.564 (0.106)***
Regdum_C_Anatolia				−0.1 (0.075)	−0.112 (0.075)	−0.101 (0.082)
Regdum_E_Anatolia				−0.231 (0.108)**	−0.245 (0.108)**	−0.203 (0.120)*
Constant	−0.75 (0.436)*	−2.27 (1.066)**	−3.35 (1.099)***	−3.54 (1.167)***	−3.47 (1.165)***	−4.33 (1.278)***
Pseudo R square						
Observations	4,995	4,995	4,995	4,995	4,995	3,801

Note: *significant at 10%; **significant at 5%; ***significant at 1%. [a]Calculated for adults older than 15. [b]Ratio of females in total earners. Robust standard errors in parentheses.

Source: Quantitative Household Survey, 2002.

26 percent. If the household head is illiterate, the probability drops to 9 percent. Unlike sharecropping, having a younger household head increases the likelihood of engaging in fixed-rent tenancy, though this association is not statistically significant. Having younger female workers in the household however has a positive relationship with the dependent variable and is significant at the 1 percent level. For agrarian households, having younger male workers is significantly and positively associated with the likelihood of fixed-rent tenancy at the 10 percent level. The probability of engaging in fixed-rent tenancy for an agrarian household whose female members are on the average 10 years younger than the sample mean of 39 years old is 28 percent, 4 percent greater than for an average agrarian household.

Households with a higher burden of household production and those with more mouths to feed for a pair of working hands are more likely to engage in fixed-rent tenancy according to the signs of their coefficient estimates. However, only the self-sufficiency ratio is significant at the 5 percent level, and the magnitude of the effect is small. Nearly doubling the food self-sufficiency ratio from the sample mean of 0.26 to 0.50 increases the probability of fixed-rent tenancy only by 1.7 percent.

Some of the wealth variables similarly affect fixed-rent tenancy and sharecropping, while others differently affect the two forms of tenancy. The coefficient of the total amount of owned land is negative for fixed-rent tenancy, as it is for sharecropping, but only in the full model; and it is only significant at the 10 percent level. Quadrupling the total amount of land owned decreases the likelihood of fixed-rent tenancy by only 2 percent.

Unlike sharecropping, consumption of food (carbohydrate and protein per capita) has a positive correlation to the probability of fixed-rent tenancy at the 5 percent level of significance. For the normal sample, doubling per capita protein carbohydrate consumption from 100 YTL to 200 YTL increases the probability of fixed-rent tenancy from 19.5 to 21.2 percent.

Confirming our expectations, the number of tractors is positively and significantly associated with fixed-rent tenancy throughout all the models; all else constant at the sample means, having no tractor as opposed to having one decreases the probability of fixed-rent tenancy by 10 percent from 25 to 15 percent for the full sample and from 30 to 20 percent for the agrarian sample. Cattle ownership is also positively related. Having no cattle as opposed to having 2.4 (the sample mean) reduces the probability by 1 percent, and having 10 cattle increases it by 3 percent. Clearly and reasonably, having a tractor is more instrumental in engaging in fixed-rent tenancy, as cultivation and harvesting are relatively mechanized in Turkey.

Among the macro variables, population density, infrastructure, and risk variables are negatively related, while per capita credit and village land Gini are positively related to the probability of fixed-rent tenancy. With the exception of infrastructure, all are significant. Landownership inequality is significant at the 1 percent level, as it was for sharecropping, except the relationship is much stronger. A household who lives in a village of perfect equality has an 8 percent probability of fixed-rent tenancy, whereas a household who lives where there is perfect inequality has a 40 percent probability. For the agrarian sample, the probability rises even higher; an agrarian household who lives in a village of perfect equality has 10 percent probability of fixed-rent tenancy, whereas a household who lives where there is perfect inequality has a 50 percent probability.

Being well integrated into the markets increases the likelihood of fixed-rent tenancy at the 5 percent level, but the magnitude effects are small even for the agrarian sample. For an agrarian household, the likelihood of fixed-rent tenancy rises to 28 percent from 18 when all crops are marketed in return for cash as opposed to when no crops are sold.

Having access to credit increases the probability of fixed-rent tenancy because credit access helps ease the household's cash constraint, as most rent payments are in advance of harvest season. Having some credit at the sample mean of 64.6 YTL as opposed to none increases the probability of fixed-rent tenancy by 3.3 percent, from 19.6 to 23.9 percent. The infrastructure index is positively correlated with the probability of fixed-rent tenancy. Although it is not significant for the full sample, it is significant for the agrarian sample at the 10 percent level. A village with good infrastructure (index = 100) increases the probability of fixed-rent tenancy to 34 percent from the 24 percent probability associated with infrastructure at the sample mean of 68.

Risk, or income diversification, has a positive and significant impact on fixed-rent tenancy at the 1 percent level for both samples. A household who earns 28 percent of their income from nonagrarian activities has a 20 percent probability of fixed-rent tenancy, whereas one with 0 percent share of nonagricultural income naturally has more at 25 percent.

For fixed-rent tenancy, as in sharecropping, it matters where someone lives. Marmara is the comparison region. In the full sample, all regions other than Aegean are less likely than Marmara to be home to fixed-rent tenants. In the agrarian sample, the results are mixed. Black Sea, Southeast Anatolia, and Mediterranean have negative coefficients significant at the 1 percent level; East Anatolia is significant at the 5 percent level; and Central Anatolia not significant with a negative coefficient. Aegean has the only positive coefficient but not significant. If a farmer is from Southeast Anatolia compared to being from Marmara, all else constant, his chances to be engaged in a fixed-rent tenancy drops to 10 percent as opposed to 21 percent if he were from Marmara.

5. CONCLUSION AND POLICY IMPLICATIONS

Some patterns are common to participants in both forms of land tenancy. First of all, the agricultural ladder hypothesis does not hold for Turkish agriculture because age of the household head positively affects the probability of sharecropping but negatively affects fixed-rent tenancy. All three age variables are positively related to the probability of fixed-rent tenancy. By contrast, the age of the household head is positively related to the probability of sharecropping, but the ages of other household members are negatively related. This suggests that sharecropping households follow an older traditional pattern, with extended families cohabiting under a much older head of household.

Gender plays a limited role in land tenancy. Households with higher ratios of female members are at a disadvantage because the ratio of female workers negatively affects both tenancy types.

Education, not age, seems to help agricultural workers climb the ladder of agrarian hierarchy because household heads' education levels negatively affect sharecropping probability but positively affect the probability of engaging in fixed-rent tenancy.

As expected, even though magnitude effects are small, a significant pattern exists in Turkish agriculture: the smaller the land owned, the higher the probability a household will engage in land tenancy. Landownership inequality has a much larger impact than the absolute amount of land owned on the probability of both type of tenancies. This effect is more prominent for fixed-rent tenancy than for sharecropping. It is natural to see a much higher impact on fixed-rent tenancy as a result of the neoliberal policies "reforming" Turkish agriculture by withdrawing government support and leaving the small landowner to his own fate somewhere in between urban slums and rural poverty. With the increasing prevalence of absentee landlords who prefer to lease out their land in fixed-rent tenancy where supervision costs are relatively small, fixed-rent tenancy has become the more prevalent form of land tenancy.

Those who eat less are more likely to sharecrop than those who do not, as food intake is negatively related to sharecropping. For fixed-rent tenancy, this relationship is reversed. However, the poorest of the poor may still not get as much land access through tenancy since having tools such as a tractor or cattle positively affects the probability of sharecropping. In short, given food intake, those who have cattle and tractors are more likely to sharecrop than those who do not have such tools for agrarian production.

The findings in this chapter also suggest that, particularly for fixed renters, having access to credit matters. We confirm Mduma and Wobst's (2005) argument that having access to cash plays a role in a household's ability to pay the rent, and thus their probability to lease-in land through fixed-rent tenancy increases.

Diversification of income matters for both tenancies but in opposite directions. Increasing the share of nonagricultural income in total income (i.e., decreasing the vulnerability of the household to vagaries of agricultural production) reduces the likelihood of sharecropping but not the likelihood of fixed-rent tenancy. These findings are in line with the literature that sees sharecropping as a mechanism to share output risk.

Integration into markets also plays a role in choosing tenancy type. A higher ratio of marketed crops to total crop production results in a lower probability of sharecropping but a higher probability of fixed-rent tenancy. Therefore, we support the hypothesis that sharecropping is more prevalent when markets are not developed.

One of the most important contributions of this chapter to the literature is to look at the impact of village landownership inequality by using a national survey. Village land inequality affects both tenancies in the same direction: positively and significantly. Living in a more unequal village increases the probability of engaging in land tenancy for Turkish farmers. This relationship is particularly strong for agrarian households who are engaged in fixed-rent tenancy.

Based on the findings of this chapter, what seems to be instrumental in tenancy choice are structural macro variables. Those who are poorer have less diversified incomes, have limited access to product and credit markets, and have smaller lands; those who live in villages where ownership of land is skewed have a higher probability of engaging in land tenancy, particularly in sharecropping.

Given sharecroppers are poorer, the findings of this chapter suggest that policies that promote rural infrastructure, to facilitate better and easier access to credit, land, and goods markets, as well as non-farm employment, may improve the macroeconomic framework in which poor farmers operate.

REFERENCES

Bardhan, Pranab. K. 1980. "Interlocking Factor Markets and Agrarian Development: A Review of Issues." *Oxford Economic Papers New Series* 32(1): 82–98.

Bardhan, Pranab. K. and T. N. Srinivasan. 1971. "Cropsharing Tenancy in Agriculture: A Theoretical and Empirical Analysis." *The American Economic Review* 61(1): 48–64.

Bell, Clive and Pinhas Zusman. 1976. "A Bargaining Theoretic Approach to Cropsharing Contracts." *The American Economic Review* 66(4): 578–88.

Bhaduri, Amit. 1973. "A Study in Agricultural Backwardness Under Semi-Feudalism." *Economic Journal* 83(329): 120–37.

———. 1983. "Sharecropping as a Labor Process, Size of Farm and Supervision Cost." In *Sharecropping and Sharecroppers,* edited by T. J. Byres, 88–93. London: Frank Cass and Company

Boserup, Esther. 1965. *The Conditions of Agricultural Growth: The Economics of Agrarian Change under Population Pressure.* London: George Allen & Unwin Ltd.

Braverman, Avishay and Joseph Stiglitz. 1982. "Sharecropping and the Interlinking of Agrarian Markets." *The American Economic Review* 72(4): 695–715.

Byres, Terence J. 1983. "Historical Perspectives on Sharecropping." In *Sharecropping and Sharecroppers,* edited by Terence J. Byres, 7–42. London: Frank Cass and Company.

Cheung, Steven N. S. 1969. *Theory of Share Tenancy.* London W.C. I.: University of Chicago.

Dasgupta, Siddharta, Thomas O. Knight, and Alan H. Love. 1999. "Evolution of Agricultural Land Leasing Models: A Survey of the Literature." *Review of the Agricultural Economics* 21(1): 148–76.

Douglas, Allen and Dean Lueck. 1992. "Contract Choice in Modern Agriculture: Cash Rent Versus Crop Share." *Journal of Law and Economics* 35(2): 397–426.

Eswaran, Mukesh and Ashok Kotwal. 1985. "A Theory of Two Tier Labor Markets in Agrarian Economics." *The American Economic Review* 75(1): 162–77.

Filmer, Deon and Lant Pritchett. 2001. "Estimating Wealth Effects without Expenditure Data—Or Tears: An Application to Educational Enrollments in States of India." *Demography* 38(1): 115–32.

Griffin, Keith, Aziz Khan, and Amy Ickowitz. 2002. "Poverty and Distribution of Land." *Journal of Agrarian Change* 2(3): 279–330.

Johnson, D. Gale. 1950. "Resource Allocation Under Share Contracts." *The Journal of Political Economy* 58(2): 111–23.

Keyder, Caglar. 1983. "The Cycle of Sharecropping and the Consolidation of Small Peasant Ownership in Turkey." In *Sharecropping and Sharecroppers,* edited by Terence J. Byres, 133–45. London: Frank Cass and Company.

Knight, F. 1957. *Risk, Uncertainty and Profit.* New York: Kelley and Millan Inc.

Koymen, Oya. 1999. "Cumhuriyet Doneminde Tarimsal Yapi ve Tarim Politikalari." In *75 Yilda Koylerden Sehirlere,* edited by Oya Baydar, 1–6. Istanbul: TC Is BankasiYayinlari, Tarih Vakfi Yayinlari.

Koymen, Oya. and O. Meric. 1999. "Turkiye'de Toprak Dagilimi Ustune Bazi Notlar." In *75 Yilda Koylerden Sehirlere,* edited by Oya Baydar, 75–80. Istanbul: TC Is Bankasi Yayinlari, Tarih Vakfi Yayinlari.

Martinez-Alier, J. 1983. "Sharecropping Some Illustrations" In *Sharecropping and Sharecroppers,* edited by Terence. J. Byres, 95–105. London: Frank Cass and Company.

Mazumdar, Dipak. 1975. "Theory of Sharecropping with Labor Market Dualism." *Economica* 42(167): 261–73.

Mduma, John K. and Peter Wobst. 2005. "Determinants of Rural Labor Market Participation in Tanzania." *African Studies Quarterly* 8(1): 32–47. Accessed on July 1, 2006, available at: http://www.africa.ufl. edu/asq/v8/v8i2a2.htm

Morvadiri, Behrooz. 1992. "Gender Relations in Agriculture: Women in Turkey." *Economic Development and Cultural Change* 40(3): 567–86.

Nabi, Ijaz. 1985. "Rural Factor Market Imperfections and the Incidence of Tenancy in Agriculture." *Oxford Economic Papers, New Series* 37(2): 319–29.

Newbery, David M. G. 1977. "Risk Sharing, Sharecropping and Uncertain Labor Markets." *The Review of Economic Studies* 44(3): 585–94.

Otsuka, Keijiro and Yujiro Hayami. 1988. "Theories of Share Tenancy: A Critical Survey." *Economic Development and Cultural Change* 37(1): 31–68.

Otsuka, Keijiro, Hiroyuki Chuma, and Yujiro Hayami. 1992. "Land and Labor Contracts in Agrarian Economics: Theories and Facts." *Journal of Economic Literature* 30(4): 1965–2018.

———. 1993. "Permanent Labor and Land Tenancy Contracts in Agrarian Economies: An Integrated Analysis." *Economica, New Series* 60(237): 57–77.

Patnaik, Utsa. 1983. "Classical Theory of Rent and Its Application to India: Some Preliminary Propositions with Some Thoughts on Sharecropping." In *Sharecropping and Sharecroppers,* edited by Terence. J. Byres, 71–87. London: Frank Cass and Company.

Pearce, R. 1983. "Sharecropping Towards a Marxist View." In *Sharecropping and Sharecroppers,* edited by Terence. J. Byres, 42–70. London: Frank Cass and Company.

QHS. 2002. Quantitative Household Survey. Ministry of Agriculture, ARIP office, Ankara Turkey.

Rao, J. Mohan. 2005. "The Forms of Monopoly Land Rent and Agrarian Organization." *Journal of Agrarian Change* 4(2): 161–90.

Sen, Abhijit. 1981. "Market Failure and Control of Labor Power: Towards an Explanation of 'Structure' and Change in Indian Agriculture." *Cambridge Journal of Economics* 5(3–4): 201–28 and 327–50.

Smith, Adam. 1994. *An Inquiry into the Nature and Causes of the Wealth of Nations.* Toronto: Random House.

Stiglitz, Joseph. 1974. "Incentives and Risk Sharing in Sharecropping." *Review of Economic Studies* 41(2): 219–55.

TUIK. 2011. Turkiye Istatistik Kurumu. "Is Istatistikleri." Accessed on September 10, 2011, available at: http://www.tuik.gov.tr/VeriBilgi. do?tb_id=25&ust_id=8

4

TESTING FOR INVERSE
SIZE-YIELD RELATIONSHIP IN
TURKISH AGRICULTURE

1. INTRODUCTION: DOES SIZE
MATTER AND FOR WHAT?

Two of the most common characteristics of developing countries are
the large share of agriculture in their economies and poorly functioning and/or nonexistent factor markets. The intersection of these
two features produces the widely observed inverse size-yield relationship (IR) (Sen 1962, 1966; Mazumdar 1965; Berry and Cline 1979;
Sen 1981; Cornia 1985; Eswaran and Kotwal 1986; Benjamin 1995;
Helbertg 1998).

The *inverse relationship between farm size and yield per acre* (IR)
indicates that as farm size gets larger, yield per acre gets smaller.
When studying the link between farm size and yield, one needs to
be careful "to distinguish between the technical input-output efficiency from the broader question of resource utilization" (Berry and
Cline 1979, 5). As Berry and Cline point out, the former refers to the
technical relationship between inputs and outputs in the production
process. The latter is about the overall utilization of available land
resources and the related use of labor. In this inquiry, we choose to
focus on the allocative efficiency when testing for the inverse size-
yield relationship in Turkey.

The relationship between size and yield became a focal point of
agrarian debates after the 1960s when Farm Management Surveys in
India first established the empirical basis. Since then, the evidence has
been so widely observed by many others in different countries that
IR is considered a "stylized fact" of agriculture in developing countries such as Pakistan (Berry and Cline 1979; Heltberg 1998), Brazil,

Colombia, Philippines, India and Malaysia (Berry and Cline 1979), India (Rudra et al., 1973; Bharadwaj 1974; Khusro 1974; Bhalla 1979; Sen 1981), Haryana in North India (Carter 1984), North East Brazil (Kutcher and Scandizzo 1981), Java (Benjamin 1995), Paraguay (Masterson 2005), and 15 other countries (Cornia 1985).

Inverse size-yield has many crucial and far-reaching implications for rural development policy, which is in part why it has received considerable attention from development researchers. The most prominent implication is that prevalence of inverse size-yield may provide economic justification for redistributive land reforms, as policies to correct for IR imply both allocative efficiency and equity at the same time. If land productivity is higher in small farms and rural factor markets are not correcting for IR, then policies to eliminate it and promote economic growth call for redistributive land reforms. Land reforms have played a very important role in economic transformation, creating agricultural surplus, growing consumer demand, and creating political stability to maintain rapid industrialization for countries like Japan, South Korea, and Taiwan (Heltberg 1998).

Another important implication of IR in rural development policy is its outcome for employment. Sen (1999) argues that the choice of technology in agriculture is crucial for resource allocation and employment since, in most developing countries, the majority of the population is employed in agriculture. According to Sen (1999), certain types of technologies are more appropriate for countries in which labor is abundant, relative to other factors of production. Since small-scale farming is more labor intensive than large-scale farming, it leads to more employment.

In addition to the economic implications, another important implication of IR is deteriorating environmental conditions and disintegrating communities. Land concentration combined with mechanization in agriculture create a class of landless laborers who, lacking alternative means of procuring a livelihood, find the solution either in cultivating ill-suited and environmentally sensitive tracts of land in forests, uplands, and arid areas, or in migrating to other places in search of employment (Heltberg 1998; Kaldjian 2001).

Due to its policy implications for employment, efficiency, equity, and sustainability, IR has been one of the most important and hotly debated topics in agricultural economics for more than 40 years. Despite the abundance of research and discussion on the topic, as of yet, there exists no consensus on what causes the inverse-size relationship (Heltberg 1998; Sen 1999).

2. INTRODUCTION AND THE CLASSIC EQUATION OF THE IR RELATIONSHIP IN AGRICULTURE

In the IR literature, the most common equation that tests the inverse relationship between farm size and yield per acre is based on an ordinary least squares (OLS) regression of a simple model, such as the following:

$$Log(Q) = \alpha + \beta log(H) + u, \tag{1}$$

where Q is either the monetary value of total output or output per acre. H is net-operated farm size, which includes owned and leased land for each household. An inverse relationship exists when β is less than unity if Q is total output, and when β is negative if Q is output per acre.

Bardhan (2003) argues that one of the problems with such studies is the assumption of the homogeneity of farm output when, in fact, *output* is measured by the total value of a range of specific products produced. Such aggregation in monetary terms can create biased results, particularly when crop prices vary significantly across types of crops or across regions for the same crop. Market values for cash crops, for example, are typically higher than those for subsistence crops.

Segregating the data based on regions and geographical features might address both of these problems due to the nature of agricultural production. Certain soil types and climates are more suitable to grow certain types of crops, thus homogeneity of farm products is highly likely within regions where land heterogeneity is not enormous. Turkey makes a particularly good case for very distinct regional homogeneity in agriculture as a result of its agroclimate structure, as we have discussed in chapter 2.

By using either the exact, or some modified version, of the classical equation (1), many studies have found a significant negative relationship between per acre productivity and farm size for different developing countries. A natural question to ask then would be, why is IR so common in developing countries, and what accounts for such a relationship?[1]

In the IR literature, there are two main explanations for it: the misidentification hypothesis (Chayanov 1966; Srinivasan 1972; Bhalla and Roy 1988; Benjamin 1995; Lamb 2003; Assuncao and Braido 2004) and the factor market imperfection hypothesis (Sen 1962, 1966; Mazumdar 1965; Sen 1981; Cornia 1985; Eswaran and Kotwal 1986; Heltberg 1998; Benjamin and Brandt 2002).

2.1. The Misidentification Hypothesis

It is often argued that the IR is a statistical artifact due to omitted variables (Bhalla and Roy 1988; Benjamin 1995; Assuncao and Braido 2004). In the IR literature, debates center around two main reasons that are claimed to constitute the misspecification: (1) omitted land quality and (2) omitted farmer heterogeneity and mode of production.

2.1.1. Omitted Land Quality Hypothesis

Land quality arose as an issue for land productivity differences, because the IR has been observed as being more robust among villages than within villages (Cornia 1985; Benjamin 1995; Sen 1999). The heart of the omitted land quality argument is the observation that fertile lands can support higher population densities, which result in higher land fragmentation; hence, smaller farms are more productive due to the inherent fertility of land. In addition, smaller farms are more likely to have higher quality lands since the ones that are sold first during a financial bottleneck are lower quality, resulting in higher overall land quality for the remaining plots on the farm.[2] Given fragmented plots in land and higher population densities in a developing country's agriculture, it is crucial to account for land quality to eliminate the possibility of systematic correlation between land quality and farm size for a robust analysis of IR.

Unfortunately many datasets, particularly those for developing countries, lack information on land quality. Hence, indirect methods of accounting for land quality must be applied. These methods include relying on geographical disaggregation (Sen 1981; Carter 1984; Bhalla and Roy 1988), using price of land or share of irrigation as a proxy for land quality (Khusro 1974; Berry and Cline 1979), using village or plot fixed effects (Carter 1984; Heltberg 1998; Assuncao and Braido 2004), and employing instrumental variables to proxy for land quality (Benjamin 1995).

Studies including land quality in IR estimations divide land quality indicators into two categories: *exogenous*, or nature-made, such as soil type, existence of irrigation canals;[3] and *endogenous*, or man-made, such as introduction of tube-well irrigation and fertilizer use. Some argue that a clear distinction between exogenous and endogenous land quality is important, because man-made land quality incorporates labor input and has to be separated from nature-made land quality (Bhalla and Roy 1988). Consequently, when the distinction is not clear, what is observed as land quality might be the result of a blend of labor effort and land quality.

Another reason why smaller farms may have higher yield per acre may be due to crop intensity: a cropping pattern which favors crops with high value-added (Bardhan 1973; Griffin et al. 2002). Bhalla (1979) argues that since different crops require different labor and nonlabor input requirements, cropping pattern and farm size may dictate a nonrandom relationship. However, one problem in such studies is that cropping pattern is a choice variable and is part of the dependent variable.

One such study that looks at IR as an outcome of farmer choice is by Assuncao and Braido (2004). In their study, based on plot level panel data on India, they claim that the inverse relationship between productivity per acre and farm size diminishes when controlled for inputs, and that the "IR puzzle is solved."

From our point of view, despite the prevalence of literature, looking at technical efficiency rather than resource utilization is not very meaningful for developing countries. One reason small farms produce more value per acre is because land utilization is much higher on smaller farms since large farms cultivate less land in proportion to their size (i.e., larger farms have more idle land). Thus, even if small and large farms produce an equal value of output per acre cultivated when controlled for other inputs, this does not disprove the IR puzzle. We think that to look at technical efficiency by way of taking size of utilized land as the denominator of IR studies is not only far from solving the IR puzzle, but also not relevant in a developing-country context where overall land utilization is an important factor in economic development, since land is generally the scarce factor, as opposed to labor.

2.2.2. The Farmer Heterogeneity and Mode of Production Hypothesis

The farmer heterogeneity hypothesis explains IR by farmer characteristics. According to the literature, farmer heterogeneity could be due to the agrarian structure in which farm size is a proxy for mode of production (Chayanov 1966; Sen 1966), or due to farmers' preferences as determined by education, attitudes toward risk, and other socioeconomic factors (Srinivasan 1972; Banerjee 1999).

According to Chayanov (1966), a peasant family worker maximizes a different objective than any other worker; he/she operates under a peasant mode of production. A peasant's objective is subsistence, thus his/her objective function is to minimize the effort given to the subsistence needs as determined by the dependency ratio within the household (i.e., the ratio of mouths to working hands). Given farm size, a crowded family with a higher dependency ratio generates higher yields per acre, and as the dependency ratio changes based on the life cycle of the household, so does the effort and yield per acre. The peasant mode of production is particularly relevant where rural factor markets are not developed and/or are totally missing. In the absence of markets, peasants cannot optimize resources or accumulate wealth by way of market exchange. Thus, there is no monetary incentive to produce more than what is required for subsistence. Hence, given the objective of subsistence combined with missing rural markets, neoclassical tools for maximizing profit would be meaningless in analyzing peasant behavior.

Despite its strength in delineating a separate mode of production for peasants based on strong empirical evidence and paving the road for labor-based theories of IR, Chayanov's (1966) pioneering work in explaining productivity per acre, founded on household demographics and life cycle, is inadequate. It does not provide much insight into why, given size and dependency ratios, some farms stay large beyond subsistence needs of the household. In addition, it is not completely true that there are no labor markets in traditional agriculture; even among the very small farms, hiring labor during peak times is a common practice to avoid crop losses. A Chayanovian explanation for IR also ignores macroeconomic, social, and cultural determinants of labor supply, such as unemployment, social norms against female laborers, and/or sociopolitical structure of the province within which the household operates (Mazumdar 1965; Sen 1981; Cornia 1985; Agarwal 1994).

The second strand of literature on farmer heterogeneity focuses more on educational differences among farmers and farmers' behavioral differences toward risk taking. Schultz (1964) claims that the productivity of farmers could be increased by educating them. Education increases productivity because farmers can read the instructions on machines, and thus are more able to apply productivity-enhancing techniques (Sen, 1999). Furthermore, having the know-how regarding fertilizer and pesticide use could make a positive impact on productivity. However, the IR puzzle still remains as small farms are likely to lack access to such machines and/or modern inputs, such as fertilizers and pesticides, and small farmers are more likely to be less educated.

Differences in productivity could also be due to differences in risk aversion. Given risk aversion decreases in wealth, small farmers are more likely to be risk averse in the face of agricultural uncertainty. According to Srinivasan (1972), this uncertainty combined with risk aversion leads to IR as small farmers. Given two choices of income source, self-cultivation (which is more uncertain) versus wage labor (which is certain), Srinivasan (1972) claims that since smaller farms are self-cultivated, they are more productive because smaller farmers are more risk averse.[4] Bardhan (1973) offers a good critique, arguing that output uncertainty in agriculture, which is due to weather or natural disasters, affects large farms that use wage laborers as well. Hence, differentials in risk, which are contingent upon size, is not a convincing explanation for IR.

Banerjee (1999) indicates that farmer characteristics matter in the sense that they are related to farm size; tenants with larger land plots are more efficient because they are more likely to own and use tools that help raise productivity.

Others such as Agarwal (1994), Alderman et al. (1995), Deere and Magdalena (2001), and Masterson (2005) introduce gender differences in farm productivity. Female farmers may experience different access to economic opportunities which, in turn, results in different crop choices, and yields per acre.

2.2.3. The Factor Market Imperfections Hypothesis

The most common explanation in the IR literature is the hypothesis of imperfect factor markets. Mainstream theory suggests that through perfectly competitive markets, all factors of production are fully utilized and receive their marginal contribution, and resources are allocated efficiently across alternative uses (Schultz 1964; Conning 2000). At this point, assuming all farms operate under the same production function with constant returns to scale, a really interesting question is then, why do markets not *distribute land* toward small farms where *land is relatively more productive than labor* and distribute labor toward large farms *where labor is relatively more productive than land*? A Pareto improvement, and also an increase in technical efficiency of the system as a whole, could occur when small farmers trade in labor for land with large farms up to a point where *marginal rates of technical substitution are equal* in each and every farm; this will eliminate IR. The obvious answer is because markets are imperfect and do not allocate resources efficiently, hence IR prevails. What is less obvious is which factor market is the culprit and which factor causes IR.

The main theme in the imperfect markets-inverse-size-yield literature is that small and large farms use different proportions of inputs due to different factor prices—resulting from imperfections of markets—which then give different incentives to farmers operating on different scales (Mazumdar 1965; Sen 1966; Berry and Cline 1979; Sen 1981; Cornia 1985; Eswaran and Kotwal 1986; Griffin et al. 2002; Benjamin and Brandt 2002). As argued by Cornia (1985), the prices of land and capital are generally higher for small farmers whereas the price of labor is higher for large farmers, resulting in usage of different proportions of inputs by farms according to their resource position (access to and the cost of production factors).[5]

According to Cornia (1985), small farmers apply more labor per unit of land than large ones in several ways. First, small farmers engage in more intensive use of labor in each crop activity. Second, they cultivate a larger portion of their land. Third, they use land more intensively by employing such techniques as multicropping. Last but not least, small farmers are more apt to undertake productivity-enhancing practices, such as land terracing, canalization, and other land infrastructure projects, which require more input of labor per acre to get maximum possible returns from their lands. Hence, IR is due to better utilization of both primary and intermediate inputs, and Cornia (1985) shows that IR relationship is particularly pronounced when farm size changes from medium to large.

As pointed out by Bardhan (1973), what may be the more interesting question about IR is why smaller farms use more input per acre, hence produce higher yields per acre. Addressing this question entails assessing the institutional framework of traditional agriculture in developing countries and examining market imperfections more closely.

A detailed analysis of the reasons for factor market imperfections in developing countries is beyond the scope of this chapter, however it is useful to mention a few. To start with, no market is scale neutral. Input and output prices differ based on scale. In addition, land markets may exhibit imperfections because land is more than just a productive factor, as we have explained earlier in chapter 2. Land is an asset of insurance, bondage, prestige, power, and wealth. In short, the price of land is almost always above its expected economic returns.

Capital markets may be imperfect since formal credit requires collateral. Thus, capital markets favor haves over have-nots. In addition, large farmers have greater access to machinery due to scale effects and/or government contacts, which may provide more favorable access to capital (Cornia 1985).

Labor markets may exhibit imperfections because of transactions and segregated markets due to gender or cast norms. Despite willingness to hire in or out labor, farmers may not partake in the labor market simply because they cannot afford job or worker search costs. Second, large farmers incur higher costs than the market wage rate because of the supervision required in agriculture, thus they do not hire labor as much even in the absence of search costs.

To sum up, labor is cheaper for small farmers, and land and capital are cheaper for large farmers. Factor market imperfections that produce different prices for large and small producers may reinforce and be reinforced by the exercise of market power. Both land and capital tend to be priced higher for smaller producers in developing countries, because it is much easier to form a monopoly in land and capital markets than it is in labor markets. This is not only because labor is the relatively abundant factor but also because unemployed land and capital can survive if left idle, but unemployed labor cannot survive without food. This leaves laborers with a weaker bargaining position vis-à-vis capital, thus favoring large farmers.

Most researchers who identify rural market imperfections as the culprit for the IR recognize that it is the combination of imperfections in all markets that results in IR. However, Sen (1981) claims that only one factor— labor—takes the brunt of the burden of all factor market imperfections. Peasants compensate for the lack of land and credit markets by putting more labor into production, thereby resulting in higher yields per acre (i.e., IR).

2.2.3.1. Labor-based hypothesis

The first labor-based explanation in the IR debate emerges from Arthur Lewis' (1954) seminal article, "Economic Development with Unlimited Supplies of Labor," in which he assumes zero marginal productivity or, in other words, zero marginal cost of labor in agriculture, and introduces disguised unemployment in agriculture.[6] Picking up the concept of zero marginal productivity from Lewis (1954) and applying the intersectoral duality between industry and agriculture to intrasectoral duality between large and small farms, many agricultural economists have tried to explain the existence of IR as a result of the intense use of labor in agriculture: that is, the lower cost of labor in smaller farms leads to its intense use, thereby resulting in higher yields per acre (Sen 1966; Bardhan 1973; Bhalla 1979; Sen 1981; Carter 1984; Cornia 1985; Heltberg 1998; Benjamin and Brandt 2002).

Understanding the reasons behind the intrasectoral duality of wages provides hints regarding the labor dynamics in a country. Sen (1966) explains this duality in terms of subjective, *real costs of labor.*

Marginal disutility of labor for peasants on small farms is smaller than the marginal disutility of workers on commercialized, larger farms because of labor surplus. Labor surplus results in fewer hours or less effort for the family worker, hence a lower real cost of labor. Mazumdar (1965), on the other hand, explains the duality by lower opportunity cost of labor on small farms due to unemployment. Maybe the most common explanation for intrasectoral wage duality is about labor supervision (Rudra et al. 1973; Sen 1981; Feder 1985; Eswaran and Kotwal 1986; Banerjee 1999). Labor supervision in agriculture is costly since workers keep moving in a large open field unlike in industry where both the worker and the machine are confined in a relatively small area. It is because of labor supervision costs that large farms do not use more labor input per acre. Labor is hired in large farms to the extent that it can be supervised by family members. This puts family labor at the center of labor-based hypotheses.

As argued by Sen (1981), two issues require special attention in labor-based explanations of IR; first, different tenure types and second, technology. Different tenure types have different labor dynamics. For example, in the tenancy literature, it is argued that sharecropper tenants provide less effort since they do not have full claim to the output. The reasons for the inefficiency in sharecropping range from Marshallian disincentive to lower crop intensity per acre. Thus, treating farms as if they have identical modes of production might result in biased results.

Second, technology is important, as given family worker per acre, land-augmenting technology (such as irrigation and use of fertilizer) increases labor input per acre, resulting in a lower ratio of family labor to total labor (assuming labor is hired to compensate for the need to increase labor input). Labor-augmenting technology, such as mechanization, would reduce labor input per acre and increase the ratio of family to total labor. Hence, if one does not control for technology, even though the family labor input is the major factor behind IR, the relationship cannot be captured statistically.

Once IR is established by equation (1)-type regressions, another way to test the validity of labor-based explanations is to analyze whether labor input has an inverse relationship with farm size using the following equation (Berry and Cline 1979; Benjamin 1995; Barret 1996; Lamb 2003):

$$Log \ (labor \ per \ acre) = \alpha + \beta \ Log \ (size) + u, \tag{2}$$

Equation (2) can also be used to test the relation between other intermediary inputs, such as fertilizers and capital, as dependent variables
to test for systematic variation with farm size.

Based on the rich and extensive literature on IR, our conclusion
is that in the context of developing-country agriculture, labor-based
theories are better able to explain IR. The crux of the debate on IR,
as well as the possible solution, is not about scale advantages or unemployment (Sen 1981). IR reflects inability of land and credit markets
to solve the labor surplus on small farms. Hence, evidence of IR is
an indicator of two things: allocative inefficiency and connectedness
between the ownership of assets and the distribution of resources
through markets. It is because of this connectedness that those who
are poor in land but rich in labor (and thus can reap higher yields from
their land) fail to lease-in more land to utilize their labor. The reason
for market imperfection—the failure of markets to allocate resources
efficiently—cannot be corrected through rural markets, because markets function connected to existing inequalities. In other words, it
is due to connectedness that markets fail allocative efficiency, which
demonstrates itself by the existence of IR. Labor-based theories point
to this failure more than any other existing explanation for IR.

There are no empirical IR studies on Turkey, only beliefs about
large farms being more productive than small ones. Productivity problems in Turkish agriculture are ascribed to a number of intertwined
causes, ranging from "an ill-defined 'backwardness' among farmers
and peasants, the variability and vagaries of nature, declining soil fertility, and the legacy of Ottoman-era practices to a variety of much
more contemporary administrative, technical, social, and operational
inadequacies" (Keyder 1984; Aydin 1987). Notably, the Food and
Agriculture Organization (FAO) (1999) and Cakmak (2004) claim
that due to small size, "Farm output...remains low in comparison to
the country's enormous potential."[7] Furthermore, in the most recent
OECD (2006) country report on Turkey, it is stated that "stopping
land fragmentation and consolidating the highly fragmented land is
indispensable for raising agricultural productivity."[8]

However, no existing study examines the size-productivity nexus
in Turkish agriculture. The Turkish agricultural debates on farm size
revolve around identifying and choosing the optimal path for agrarian transformation as a means to modern economic development,
as larger farms are better for capital accumulation (Keyder 1984;
Bazoglu 1986; Boratav 1987; 2000; Akcay 1987; Aksit 1987; Aydin
1987; Toprak 1999).

Among the literature on Turkish agriculture, perhaps the only piece that underlines the importance of smallholder agriculture is by Kaldjian (2001). Kaldjian views the small farm as a strategic response to the path of economic development in Turkey. In this view, the small holder is a production unit in which the knowledge and skill base is experientially locally gathered, transferred from generation to generation, and designed to reduce risk and protect food and household security. Accordingly, small farms should be seen as rational responses to the economic realities of unemployment and food insecurity in the context of Turkey.

The following empirical investigation of IR for the case of Turkey is the first of its kind and employs a labor-based hypothesis. The setup used to test for the existence of IR in rural Turkey is a modification of classical equation (1). We used village fixed-effects regressions to control for unobservable village heterogeneity. We also employed type (2) regressions to analyze the relationship between labor and other nonlabor, nonland intermediate input use intensity and farm size.

3. Empirical Investigation

As we mentioned in chapter 3, despite the agroclimate homogeneity within regions in Turkey, it is not adequate to account for land heterogeneity only at the regional level; hence, we also control for village effects in the regional and national analysis. This approach accounts for any agroclimatic heterogeneity among regions as well as variability in other unobservable characteristics among villages in each region.

Using a 2002 World Bank Survey, our work is the first of its kind on Turkey that looks at the size-productivity nexus.

3.1. Descriptive Statistics of the Regression Variables and the Discussion of the Model

The data we are using is the Quantitative Household Survey for the year 2002 (QHS),[9] which includes 5,302 rural households from 7 regions, 73 provinces, 389 towns, and 517 villages in rural Turkey.

Eighty-nine percent of all the farms in Turkey are in the small or medium category (table 4.1). *Small* refers to an amount of land between 1 and 19.99 decares,[10] *medium* refers to 20 to 199.99 decares, *large* refers to 200 to 499.99 decares, and *very large* refers to an amount of land that is in excess of 500 decares. Turkish peasants work on farms that are, on average, 93 decares (table 4.1).

Table 4.1   Farm Size by Region, 2002

Regions	Small: 1–19.99		Medium: 20–199.99		Large: 200–499.99		Very Large: 500+		TURKEY	
	%	Avg. Size	%	Avg. Size	%	Avg. Size	%	Avg. Size	Total	Avg. Size
Mediterranean	24	10	68	63	7	267	2	837	633	79
Aegean	26	11	71	56	2	272	1	2,403	852	62
SE Anatolia	12	11	71	71	14	301	4	962	459	128
Marmara	18	10	73	73	7	275	1	808	758	118
Central An.	4	10	67	90	23	292	6	718	836	168
E. Anatolia	15	12	62	79	18	271	5	686	308	135
Black Sea	35	10	63	53	1	283	1	1,654	1,157	51
TURKEY	21	10	68	67	9	285	2	902	5,003	93

Source: Quantitative Household Survey, 2002.

Table 4.2   Land Fragmentation by Region, Rural Turkey, 2002

Regions		Small: 1–19.99	Medium: 20–199.99	Large: 200–499.99	Very Large: 500+	Avg.	N
Mediterranean		2.40	5.98	9.76	15.4	5.56	633
Aegean		3.00	7.81	19.64	7.80	6.77	852
SE Anatolia	Avg. Number of Land Plots	1.96	3.41	6.40	13.11	4.00	459
Marmara		3.07	9.72	19.15	17.77	9.32	758
Central An.		3.05	8.13	18.28	30.61	11.50	836
E. Anatolia		2.93	5.30	10.53	13.94	6.33	308
Black Sea		4.20	9.16	20.31	16.57	7.62	1,157
TURKEY		3.33	7.67	15.07	21.11	7.71	5,003

Source: Quantitative Household Survey, 2002.

Farms are fragmented in rural Turkey. The highest fragmentation is found on very large farms with an average of 21 different plots of land (table 4.2).

There is not a significant difference in ratio of irrigated land to total land between large and small farms. On average, small farmers irrigate 25 percent of their land holdings, 1 percent more than the large ones (table 4.3). However, there is significant regional heterogeneity in irrigation. Very large farms in the Mediterranean region

Table 4.3 Ratio of Irrigated Land to Total Farm Size by Region, 2002

		Farm Type					
		Small: 1–19.99 (%)	Medium: 20–199.99 (%)	Large: 200–499.99 (%)	Very Large: 500+ (%)	Avg. (%)	N
Regions	Percent of Irrigated Land						
Mediterranean		47	40	41	67	42	**633**
Aegean		38	34	41	1	35	**852**
SE Anatolia		41	27	31	27	29	**459**
Marmara		16	13	10	0	13	**758**
Central An.		38	20	17	19	20	**836**
E. Anatolia		50	33	21	29	33	**308**
Black Sea		8	12	22	1	10	**1,157**
TURKEY		**25**	**23**	**22**	**24**	**24**	**5,003**

Source: Quantitative Household Survey, 2002.

irrigate 67 percent of their farm, whereas small farms in the Black Sea region only irrigate 8 percent of their farm.

The sharecropping ratio is low in Turkey in general (4 percent). It is highest in South East Anatolia with 7 percent and lowest in the East Anatolia region with only 1 percent (table 4.4).

Farms in all regions are operated mostly with family labor and depict a declining pattern as land ownership gets larger. On average, 81 percent of all labor input for small farmers is from family members, as opposed to 68 percent in large farms (table 4.5).

Educational attainment of household heads in rural Turkey seems to show an interesting pattern based on farm size. Small farmers, interestingly, are not the group that is least educated. The percentage of household heads of small-scale farms who have a primary school degree is 72 percent, which is 2 percent more than the national average and 14 percent more than the average of the largest farmers. This difference is especially pronounced in Central Anatolia with 86% of the small farmers having primary school degrees, whereas this number is only 64 percent for the largest farmers (table 4.6).

The average age of the head of household is 50. Heads of small-farmer households are one year younger on average (table 4.7). In Turkey, a typical household has 5.7 members; however, the larger the farm, the more populated the household, with 7.7 for a very large farm. Most populated households are in Southeast Anatolia with 12.7, and the least in the small farms are in Marmara and the Aegean with 4 members (table 4.8).

Table 4.4 Percent of Sharecropped Land on the Farm by Region, 2002

		Farm Type				
		Small: 1–19.99 (%)	Medium: 20–199.99 (%)	Large: 200–499.99 (%)	Very Large: 500+ (%)	Avg. (%)	N
Regions						
Mediterranean		3	1	6	4	2	633
Aegean		6	4	2	0	4	852
SE Anatolia	Ratio of Sharecropped Land	4	8	7	5	7	459
Marmara		3	1	3	3	2	758
Central An.		0	3	10	16	5	836
E. Anatolia		0	2	0	1	1	308
Black Sea		4	3	0	0	4	1,157
TURKEY		4	3	7	8	4	5,003

Source: Quantitative Household Survey, 2002.

Table 4.5 Ratio of Family Labor in Total Labor by Region, 2002

		Farm Type				
		Small: 1–19.99 (%)	Medium: 20–199.99 (%)	Large: 200–499.99 (%)	Very Large: 500+ (%)	Avg. (%)	N
Regions						
Mediterranean		75	68	53	40	69	633
Aegean		80	77	68	89	77	852
SE Anatolia	Ratio of Family Labor	94	74	53	48	72	459
Marmara		83	83	76	74	83	758
Central An.		81	76	72	79	76	836
E. Anatolia		76	70	74	62	71	308
Blacksea		81	79	55	90	79	1,157
TURKEY		81	77	68	68	76	5,003

Source: Quantitative Household Survey, 2002.

Nationally, the dependency ratio is 1.45 mouths per pair of hands on average. Dependency ratio is highest among small farmers in South East Anatolia with 2.16 mouths for a pair of hands and lowest in Marmara with 1.16 for very large farms (table 4.9).

As can be seen from table 4.10, productivity per acre for small farms is substantially higher compared to large farms in all regions of Turkey. On average, small farms are nine times more productive per decare than the very large ones. This is very pronounced in the Black

Table 4.6 Educational Attainment of Household Heads by Region, 2002

| | Farm Size | | | | | | | | |
| | Small: 1–19.99 | | | Medium: 20–199.99 | | | Large: 200–499.99 | | |
Regions	Illiterate %	Primary %	High School %	Illiterate %	Primary %	High School %	Illiterate %	Primary %	High School %
Mediterranean	10	70	3	8	68	8	5	52	19
Aegean	5	80	1	6	77	4	0	47	29
SE Anatolia	17	74	2	20	61	3	13	55	8
Marmara	7	72	4	5	75	4	2	61	19
Central An.	5	86	3	8	74	5	6	72	7
E. Anatolia	17	59	0	10	65	5	11	73	2
Black Sea	8	69	7	9	64	5	13	63	0
TURKEY	**8**	**72**	**4**	**9**	**70**	**5**	**7**	**65**	**10**

| | Very Large: 500+ | | | Turkey | | |
Regions	Illiterate %	Primary %	High School %	Illiterate %	Primary %	High School %
Mediterranean	0	42	33	8	67	8
Aegean	0	80	0	5	77	4
SE Anatolia	6	53	12	5	77	4
Marmara	0	44	11	5	73	5
Central An.	0	64	9	7	73	6
E. Anatolia	6	50	25	11	65	5
Black Sea	0	71	0	9	66	5
TURKEY	**2**	**58**	**13**	**8**	**70**	**5**

Source: Quantitative Household Survey, 2002.

Table 4.7 Age Composition of Household Heads by Region, 2002

		Small: 1–19.99	Medium: 20–199.99	Large: 200–499.99	Very Large: 500+	Avg.	N
				Farm Type			
Regions							
Mediterranean		49	51	52	46	50	633
Aegean		46	49	47	47	48	852
SE Anatolia	Average Age of the Household Head	47	47	45	47	47	459
Marmara		51	52	50	57	52	758
Central An.		49	49	49	45	49	836
E. Anatolia		47	47	48	48	47	308
Black Sea		51	53	53	48	52	1,157
TURKEY		**49**	**50**	**49**	**47**	**50**	**5,003**

Source: Quantitative Household Survey, 2002.

Table 4.8 Household Size by Region, 2002

		Small: 1–19.99	Medium: 20–199.99	Large: 200–499.99	Very Large: 500+	Avg.	N
				Farm Type			
Regions							
Mediterranean		5.4	5.7	6.3	6.5	5.7	633
Aegean		4.0	5.0	4.7	2.8	4.7	852
SE Anatolia	Household Size	6.9	8.1	9.6	12.7	8.3	459
Marmara		4.0	4.6	5.5	6.6	4.6	758
Central An.		4.7	5.6	6.6	6.5	5.8	836
E. Anatolia		6.9	7.6	9.7	10.2	8.0	308
Blacksea		4.8	5.8	7.2	7.7	5.7	1,157
TURKEY		**4.8**	**5.8**	**7.2**	**7.7**	**5.7**	**5,003**

Source: Quantitative Household Survey, 2002.

Table 4.9 Dependency Ratio by Region, 2002

		Small: 1–19.99	Medium: 20–199.99	Large: 200–499.99	Very Large: 500+	Avg.	N
				Farm Type			
Regions							
Mediterranean		1.50	1.38	1.40	1.70	1.41	633
Aegean		1.36	1.36	1.37	1.24	1.36	852
SE Anatolia	Dependency Ratio	2.16	1.77	1.78	1.62	1.81	459
Marmara		1.31	1.31	1.31	1.18	1.31	758
Central An.		1.48	1.45	1.46	1.47	1.45	836
E. Anatolia		1.67	1.72	1.94	1.47	1.74	308
Black Sea		1.38	1.41	1.70	1.23	1.40	1,157
TURKEY		**1.44**	**1.44**	**1.54**	**1.47**	**1.45**	**5,003**

Source: Quantitative Household Survey, 2002.

Table 4.10   Productivity Per Decare by Region, 2002

		Small: 1–19.99 (%)	Medium: 20–199.99 (%)	Large: 200–499.99 (%)	Very Large: 500+ (%)	Avg. (%)	N
Regions							
Mediterranean		753	211	162	106	334	633
Aegean		405	220	102	34	265	852
SE Anatolia	Decare	1,231	146	59	55	259	459
Marmara		389	275	367	196	302	758
Central An.		547	119	61	45	121	836
E. Anatolia		225	59	19	45	121	308
Black Sea		499	156	103	2	275	1,157
TURKEY		**528**	**181**	**108**	**59**	**245**	**5,003**

Source: Quantitative Household Survey, 2002.

Table 4.11   Labor Input Per Decare by Region, 2002

		Small: 1–19.99	Medium: 20–199.99	Large: 200–499.99	Very Large: 500+	Avg.	N
Regions							
Mediterranean		23.0	3.2	1.1	0.9	7.7	633
Aegean		22.5	5.9	1.3	0.4	10.2	852
SE Anatolia	Labor Input Per Decr. in Mandays	8.6	2.2	0.6	0.5	2.7	459
Marmara		14.0	2.8	0.8	0.5	4.7	758
Central An.		12.3	1.6	0.5	0.3	1.8	836
E. Anatolia		8.4	2.0	0.4	0.3	2.6	308
Black Sea		17.0	3.8	0.6	0.1	8.4	1,157
TURKEY		**17.7**	**3.3**	**0.7**	**0.4**	**6.4**	**5,003**

Source: Quantitative Household Survey, 2002.

Sea region (279 times more) and in the South East Anatolia region (22 times).

The same inverse trend is also observed in labor and nonlabor input per decare (table 4.11). In Turkey, small farms are putting in 44 times more labor input per decare as compared to the largest ones, on average. In the Black Sea region, this ratio is strikingly high, with 170 times more man-days per decare. In addition, nationally, small farms spend six times more than the largest farms on nonlabor inputs. In the Black Sea region, this difference becomes striking, with smaller farms spending 88 times more than the largest farms (table 4.12).

Table 4.12   Nonlabor Input Per Decare by Region, 2002

| | | Farm Type | | | | |
		Small: 1–19.99 (%)	Medium: 20–199.99 (%)	Large: 200–499.99 (%)	Very Large: 500+ (%)	Avg. (%)	N
Regions							
Mediterranean		266	77	56	51	120	633
Aegean		185	67	56	6	98	852
SE Anatolia		64	38	21	32	38	459
Marmara	Nonlabor Nonland Expenditure	167	63	40	35	80	758
Central An.		364	52	25	20	57	836
E. Anatolia		80	34	14	10	36	308
Black Sea		88	35	27	1	53	1,157
TURKEY		153	54	28	23	72	5,003

Source: Quantitative Household Survey, 2002.

Table 4.13   Credit Per Decare by Region, 2002

| | | Farm Type | | | | |
		Small: 1–19.99	Medium: 20–199.99	Large: 200–499.99	Very Large: 500+	Avg.	N
Regions							
Mediterranean		40	6	3	5	14	633
Aegean		7	7	10	0.02	7	852
SE Anatolia		2	2	0	0.2	2	459
Marmara	Credit Per Decare	21	3	2	4	6	758
Central An.		0	1	2	1	1	836
E. Anatolia		0	1	0	1	1	308
Black Sea		16	4	0	0	8	1,157
TURKEY		16	4	2	1	6	5,003

Source: Quantitative Household Survey, 2002.

Small farmers also use more credit per decare than large ones (table 4.13). The national average for small farms is 16 New Turkish Lira (YTL) per decare, as opposed to YTL 6 for the very large ones. This is particularly pronounced in the Mediterranean, with YTL 40 for small farmers, as opposed to YTL 5 for very large farms.

One could say that the general demographic depicted by the dataset is a typical one for developing countries: middle-aged, male, uneducated household heads managing small family farms. From this initial analysis of the descriptive statistics of the regression variables, a clear pattern emerges—there is an inverse relationship between farm size and productivity, size and labor input, and size and nonlabor input.

3.2. Regression Model

Based on the observed patterns in the dataset, we undertake a village fixed effect OLS estimation of the form similar to the classical form (1). We test for pooled data (Turkey) and for each region: Mediterranean, Aegean, Marmara, Central Anatolia, East Anatolia, Southeast Anatolia, and Black Sea.[11] The model is as follows:

$$\text{Log}\,q = \alpha + \log(H) + \beta \log(X) + u, \tag{3}$$

where q is output per decare; α is the intercept; H is farm size; X is a matrix consisting of household head's age, household head's educational attainment, household size, provincial land ownership inequality, dependency ratio and its square, share of sharecropped land to total land holdings, share of family labor and its square, land fragmentation; and u is the error term.

Auxiliary to the main regression (3), to further analyze the role of labor input, we test to see if there exists an inverse relationship between labor input per decare and farm size utilizing the following log-log equation, which is a modification of type (2) equations:

$$\text{Log}\,l = \alpha + \log(H) + \beta \log(Y) + u, \tag{4}$$

where α is the intercept; l is total labor input per decare in man-days; H is farm size; matrix Y consists of household head's age, household head's educational attainment, household size, dependency ratio and its square, share of sharecropped land to cultivated land, regional average for agricultural wage rate, land fragmentation; and u is the error term.

To test whether other nonlabor inputs also exhibit an inverse-size relationship, we will test the following:

$$\text{Log}\,k = \alpha + \log(H) + \beta \log(W) + u, \tag{5}$$

where k is the monetary value of costs for nonlabor nonland input costs, such as fertilizer and pesticide use, irrigation, veterinary costs, and other infrastructure-related spending, such as electricity and gas for agricultural production;[12] α is the intercept; H is farm size; matrix W consists of household head's age, household head's educational attainment, household size, share of sharecropped land to cultivated land, credit per decare, land fragmentation; and u is the error term.

We expect k to have a negative relationship with farm size if markets are imperfect. If small farmers cannot buy land to utilize their labor and produce more, they might choose to spend more money on intermediary inputs to utilize their land and labor more, consequently resulting in IR.

Regressions (3), (4), and (5) are tested for the pooled sample (Turkey) and for each region.

It is necessary to elaborate each variable that is utilized in regressions (3), (4), and (5). The variable q is the total monetary value of farm production per decare. It includes value of total crops, animal sales, and secondary products produced on the farm, such as dairy products, or processed grains.[13] To overcome the problem of different valuation of the same products in different regions, we calculated a national average price for each crop, each secondary product item, and for animals by way of utilizing the dataset and employed these imputed prices to come up with the total value of farm output.[14] Farm size is the size of operational holdings: that is, the total area of land that is owned and leased-in (-out) by the household and not the net area under cultivation.

Household head's age and educational attainment are introduced to control for farmer heterogeneity. We expect the education level of the household head to be positively related to productivity per decare since better educated farmers may have improved access to knowledge and tools that may enhance productivity. We expect age to have a positive relationship since age is used as a proxy for experience and management skills. However, old age might pose disadvantages in agriculture because most of the work is physically demanding and also because older household heads might be too reluctant to try new, more efficient techniques than the younger ones.

The dependency ratio is the ratio of total number of household members to workers in the household.[15] To test Chayanovian claims of the peasant mode of production, we introduce the dependency ratio and its square to test if the ratio within a household makes a difference in the productivity per decare by adding extra stress, hence motivation to work more hours and harder, thereby resulting in higher yields. The square term of the ratio is introduced to test the possibility of a nonlinear, diminishing relationship between the dependency ratio and yield per decare, since too many mouths to too few hands might create a negative effect on output per decare if household labor is devoted mostly to reproduction of labor power and not to production of agricultural output. It is also important to note that women are very active participants in agricultural production in

Turkey, and caring for the elderly/sick/children is strictly the women's job. Hence, when the dependency ratio is high, availability of female labor might be limited, which would negatively impact labor input, hence productivity.

The variable, family labor ratio is the share of family labor input in total labor input. Labor supervision is an important factor in hiring decisions in agriculture; the more family members who work as supervisors, the more labor will be hired. Given agriculture is a labor-intensive production in countries such as Turkey; more labor input would increase productivity. Hence, we expect a positive relationship between family labor ratio and productivity per decare.

The ratio of sharecropped land to total cultivated land is introduced to control for land tenure type. Following the Marshallian disincentive argument, we expect a negative relationship between the ratio of sharecropped land and productivity per decare.

Credit per decare is the total amount of credit divided by the farm size and is used in regression (5) only. Credit access allows for better and more intermediary inputs (nonlabor and nonland), such as fertilizers, pesticides, and also more land access; therefore, we expect a positive relationship between credit per decare and intermediary input per decare. However, if credit is used for land access, then intermediary input per decare might fall since the farmer may not need to cultivate the land as intensively. In this case, the relationship may reverse.

Finally, fragmentation is claimed to reduce yield per decare not only because labor, fuel, and time is spent moving in between plots rather than on them, but also because larger plot size is more convenient for application of farm machinery (FAO 1999; OECD 2006). However, it is also argued that land fragmentation benefits farmers because it reduces the risks of drought, frost, floods, pests, and other uncertainties as a result of separated plots (Kaldjian 2001). Helburn[16] claims that for Central Anatolia, fragmentation benefits small farmers in terms of decreasing risk, since "having all one's land in a single soil type, in a single location and single exposure is considered risky." We introduce land fragmentation in our regression analysis to test which of these claims holds for Turkey.

4. REGRESSION RESULTS AND DISCUSSION

The results suggest a very strong inverse size-yield relationship (IR) in rural Turkey. The summary results of the regressions for Turkey and for each region are illustrated in table 4.14. The relationship prevails and is significant even after disaggregation of the data and controlling for village fixed effects. Doubling the farm size results in a 51 percent decrease in productivity per decare, nationally. The IR is most pronounced in the Black Sea region with -0.68 elasticity and least pronounced in the Marmara with −0.27.[17]

Contrary to the claims of the OECD (2006) and the FAO of the United Nations (1999) reports on Turkey, land fragmentation is positively and significantly correlated to productivity. Doubling the number of parcels results in approximately a 24 percent increase in output per decare at the 1 percent level of significance. Furthermore, when data is disaggregated based on geographical regions, significance still remains for the Aegean (5 percent), the Mediterranean (1 percent), Central Anatolia (5 percent), and the Black Sea (1 percent). In all other regions the coefficient is not significant; however, it stays positive indicating a positive correlation between land fragmentation and productivity per decare. Our findings support Helburn's claims (Kaldjian 2001) in his observation that fragmentation positively affects productivity in Central Anatolia.

In addition to the findings discussed above, other interesting findings emerge from the analysis. The Chayanovian argument of a life cycle hypothesis, which is captured by the dependency ratio in the regressions, is not significant nationally, but shows dramatic regional variation. In the Mediterranean and Central Anatolia, the relationship is negative and significant; in the Black Sea and East Anatolia, it is positive and significant; and in all others, it is positive but not significant. Nationally, there is a diminishing relation between the dependency ratio and IR; which suggests that after a certain point, the presence of too few hands to work for too many mouths limits the hours for farm production, negatively impacting productivity.[18]

Other demographic variables are significant as well. Household size and the household head's educational attainment are positively related to productivity, whereas the household head's age is negatively related nationally and regionally.

The ratio of family labor is significant at the 10 percent level for farm productivity. A 1 percent increase in the ratio results in a 0.6 percent increase in productivity for Turkey. When we disaggregate the data regionally, the coefficient stays positive, except for the Black Sea. However, it is not significant in any of the regions. To our surprise, there is also a nonlinear relationship between the family labor ratio and productivity per decare, both nationally and regionally. Up to a threshold point (>.95), family labor has a positive impact

Table 4.14 Summary Results for Regression (3), 2002

Region	Constant	ln Farmsize	ln HH size	ln HHHH Education	ln HHH Age	ln Dependency Ratio	ln Share Family Labor	ln Ratio Shrcrp	ln Fragmentation	Adj. R²	N
Turkey	19.52***	−0.51***	0.34***	0.13**	−0.24***	1.41	0.60*	−0.41*	0.24***	0.46	5,003
Mediterranean	28.09***	−0.43***	0.46***	0.18	−0.38*	−22.15*	0.47	−0.44	0.29***	0.38	633
Aegean	17.95**	−0.49***	0.29***	0.09	−0.25*	4.45	1.11	0.22	0.17**	0.43	852
SE Anatolia	16.24**	−0.47***	0.26*	−0.09	−0.42*	10.65	1.21	−0.19	0.21	0.38	459
Marmara	14.99***	−0.27***	0.11	0.08	−0.27	11.2	0.99	0.16	0.15	0.36	758
Central Anatolia	27.49***	−0.48***	0.43***	0.30	−0.42**	−18.52*	0.50	−1.87*	0.23**	0.33	836
East Anatolia	10.27**	−0.60***	0.40**	0.41**	−0.30	18.31*	1.38	−0.74	0.31	0.49	308
Black Sea	16.13**	−0.68***	0.36***	0.11	−0.11	12.63*	−0.23**	−0.23	0.26**	0.45	1,157

Note: *significant at the 10% level; ** significant at the 5% level; *** significant at the 1% level. Robust standard errors. Controlled for village fixed effects.

on productivity. This relationship inverts as the family labor ratio gets closer to one. The nonlinearity of the relationship may point to the fact that when farmers cannot employ hired labor during extremely busy times such as harvest, they might be losing a large portion of their output since harvesting crops is an extremely time-sensitive process, hence the negative relationship.

The estimate of the relationship between the ratio of sharecropped land and per decare productivity confirms our expectations. The coefficient for sharecropping ratio is negative and significant at the 10 percent level nationally, with regional variation. It is only significant in Central Anatolia at the 10 percent level, and not significant in other regions. However, the relationship is negative in five out of seven regions. Using type (4) regressions, we explore possible causes of the sharecropping-productivity relationship.

Examining the determinants of labor input per decare using regression (4) suggests that labor input per decare does not present a significant and consistent relationship based on the tenure type (table 4.15). All else equal, the ratio of sharecropping is not significant anywhere, with the exception of Marmara. Our results make a case against the Marshallian disincentive explanation of inefficiency in sharecropping.

On the contrary, when one studies the regression results for (5) in table 4.16, the ratio of sharecropping is significantly negative for determining variations in nonlabor, nonland input expenditures per decare in Southeast Anatolia, where land inequality is among the highest and feudal relations are prevalent (Yakin 1981). These findings are in support of arguments made by Sen (1981), Cornia (1985), and Rao (2005) that the landlord's choice of input and crop type, not the tenant's choice of labor input, is the explanation for lower productivity on sharecropped land.

Another important finding pertains to land fragmentation. All else equal, for Turkey, a 1 percent increase in land fragmentation results in a 0.19 percent increase in labor input per decare. This relationship is significant at the 1 percent level. The relation stays positive across all regions and stays significant in all but Marmara. In all other regions except Southeast Anatolia, the relationship is significant at the 1 percent level and at the 5 percent level in Southeast Anatolia.

It is clear that the culprit of IR is the intensive labor use per decare as farm size gets smaller, as indicated by regression results for equation (4) (table 4.15). On average, a 1 percent rise in farm size results in a 0.75 percent decline in labor input per decare. The inverse relation and its magnitude seem to be similar across all regions, ranging

Table 4.15 Summary Results for Regression (4)

Region	Constant	ln Farmsize	ln HH Size	ln HHHH Education	ln HHH Age	Independency Ratio	ln Wage Rate	ln Ratio Shrcrp	ln Fragment	Adj. R²	N
Turkey	17.97***	−0.75***	0.24***	0.16***	−0.06	−7.83***	−0.61***	0.04	0.19***	0.69	5,003
Mediterranean	9.94***	−0.66***	0.25***	0.16	−0.19	6.41**	−0.06	−0.03	0.22***	0.50	633
Aegean	15.26***	−0.80***	0.32***	0.17	−0.15	−3.49	−0.53***	0.04	0.19***	0.61	852
SE Anatolia	5.05	−0.71***	0.24***	0.16	−0.02	−2.13	−0.11	0.09	0.21*	0.55	459
Marmara	−3.06	−0.65***	0.25***	0.35***	0.18	3.53	0.33	0.73*	0.01	0.66	758
Central Anatolia	14.03***	−0.77***	0.24***	0.09	−0.18	−20.03***	−0.17	−0.13	0.23***	0.55	836
East Anatolia	−1.10	−0.74***	0.13	0.06	0.01	−4.14	0.32**	−1.17	0.33***	0.76	308
Black Sea	11.25***	−0.81***	0.23***	0.15**	0.07	5.48**	−0.16	0.04	0.17***	0.64	1,157

Note: *Significant at the 10% level; ** Significant at the 5% level; *** Significant at the 1% level. Robust standard errors; Controlled for village fixed effects.

Table 4.16 Summary Results for Regression (5)

Region	Constant	ln Farmsize	ln HH Size	ln HHHH Education	ln HHH Age	Credit Per Acre	ln Ratio Shrcrp	ln Fragmentation	Adj. R²	N
Turkey	4.84***	−0.47***	0.27***	0.18***	−0.12**	0.01***	−0.07	0.16***	0.46	5,003
Mediterranean	4.93**	−0.49***	0.21**	0.1	−0.32***	−0.003	0.10	0.28***	0.42	633
Aegean	4.40***	−0.49***	0.40***	0.25**	−0.002	0.01***	0.12	0.18***	0.44	852
SE Anatolia	3.85***	−0.29***	0.14	0.21**	0.06	0.02*	−0.74**	0.06	0.35	459
Marmara	5.11***	−0.352***	0.31***	0.18	−0.24	0.01	0.46	−0.003	0.32	758
Central Anatolia	4.81***	−0.43***	0.25***	0.1	−0.22**	0.01	0.12	0.12	0.41	836
East Anatolia	2.81***	−0.55***	0.19	0.36**	0.44**	−0.01	−1.19**	0.17	0.41	308
Black Sea	5.37***	−0.56***	0.25***	0.14*	−0.15	0.01**	−0.01	0.18***	0.44	1,157

Note: *significant at the 10% level; ** significant at the 5% level; *** significant at the 1% level. Robust standard errors; Controlled for village fixed effects.

between 0.81 (Black Sea) and 0.65 (Marmara) at the 1 percent level of significance.

One further finding of regression (4) is that nationally, the wage rate in agriculture has a negative impact on labor input per decare; that is, as the wage rate increases by 1 percent, labor input per decare decreases by 0.61 percent. This negative relation could be the result of farms hiring fewer hands because price is higher.

There is also a consistent and widely observed negative and significant relationship between farm size and intermediary input, as illustrated by the results of regression (5) (table 4.16). For Turkey, a 1 percent increase in farm size results in a 0.47 percent decrease in nonlabor input usage per decare. The relationship is significant at the 1 percent level for all regions, between the range of −0.56 (Black Sea) and −0.29 (Southeast Anatolia). This finding is in agreement with Berry and Cline (1979) and Cornia (1985), where both studies find a significant inverse relationship between per acre nonlabor input and farm size for different developing countries.

5. CONCLUSION AND POLICY IMPLICATIONS

Several interesting conclusions came out of this chapter. First is the affirmation of a very strong inverse relationship in the case of Turkey. Clearly, our findings do not confirm the claims by FAO (1999), Cakmak (2004), and OECD (2006) on the need to consolidate land to reach higher productivity in agriculture.

Second, our results suggest that labor-based hypotheses conform well to the Turkish data. Labor input per decare seems to be driving the IR. Third, the Chayanovian argument of peasant mode of production and farmer heterogeneity are only small parts of the IR puzzle for Turkey. Both educational attainment and dependency ratio are significant nationally but not for every region. Fourth, even though land heterogeneity explains part of the IR, it is still very robust and significant despite controlled land heterogeneity. Fifth, land fragmentation seems to be impacting land productivity positively for Turkey in general. At the very least, our regional analysis does not support OECD (2006) and FAO (1999) claims of a negative relationship between fragmentation and productivity.

The findings with this exercise suggest that most recently market-friendly reforms, namely, Agricultural Reform Implementation Program (ARIP) is an ill-advised policy for Turkish agriculture.

Given the inverse productivity-size relationship in agriculture, what is needed for increased productivity in agriculture and overall growth does not seem to be so-called market-friendly reforms but land redistribution supported by a comprehensive reform package, including technical and financial assistance for farmers. Given current macroeconomic policy on agriculture, in our point of view, Turkey will experience rising inequality and poverty in the years to come. Indeed, as we have illustrated in chapter one that this is already be the case. Agrarian transformation initiated by the implementation of ARIP may be occurring but at the expense of a great majority of the people. Transformation ought not and need not be accompanied by the crippling of agriculture. As argued, there is no economic justification to pursue development policies that inflict economic crisis on the vast numbers of people who depend on this crucial sector. Inflicting hardship on rural people is what market-friendly reforms seem to be doing despite evidence of market failures in the form of an inverse relationship between farm size and yield per acre.

REFERENCES

Agarwal, B. 1994. *A Field of One's Own: Gender and Land Rights in South Asia*. Cambridge: Cambridge University Press.

Akcay A. 1987. "Turkiye tariminda buyuk toprakli isletmelerin olusum surecleri uzerine notlar." In *11. Tez Kitap Dizisi: Turkiye'de Tarim Sorunu 7*: 47–58. Istanbul: Belge Yayinlari.

Aksit, Bahattin. 1987. "Kirsal Dönüsüm ve Köy Arastirmalari: 1960–1980." In *11. Tez Kitap Dizisi: Turkiye'de Tarim Sorunu 11–29*. Istanbul: Belge Yayinlari.

Alderman, H., J. Hoddinott, L. Haddad, and C. Udry. 1995. "Gender Differentials in Farm Productivity: Implications for Household Efficiency and Agricultural Policy." Discussion Paper Series, No. 6, Food Consumption Nutrition Division (FCND), International Food Policy Research Institute, Washington DC.

Alvarez, Antonio and Carlos Arias. 2004. "Technical Efficiency and Farm Size: A Conditional Analysis." *Agricultural Economics* 30(3): 241–50.

Aresvik, O. 1975. *The Agricultural Development of Turkey*. New York, Washington, London: Praeger.

Assuncao, J. J. and L. H. B. Braido. 2004. "Testing Among Competing Explanations for the Inverse Productivity Puzzle." Accessed on March 9, 2005, available at: http://www.econ.pucrio.br/PDF/seminario/2004/inverse.pdf

Aydin, Z. 1987. "Turkish Agrarian Debate: New Arguments or Old Acores." *New Perspectives on Turkey* 1(1): 81–109.

————. 1986. "Kapitalizm, tarimsorunuve azgelismis ulkeler: (I). *11*" In *Tez Kitap Dizisi* 4:126–56. Istanbul: Belge Yayinlari

Aysu, A. 2002. *1980–2002 Turkiye Tariminda Yapilanma(ma):Tarladan Sofraya Tarim*. Istanbul: Su.

Banerjee, A. V. 1999. "Land Reforms Prospects and Strategies." Paper presented at the 1999 Annual World Bank Conference on Development Economics, Washington, DC. Accessed on April 12, 2005, available at: http://www.eldis.org/static/DOC7128.htm.

Bardhan, P. K. 1973. "Size Productivity, and Returns to Scale: An Analysis of Farm-Level Data in Indian Agriculture." *The Journal of Political Economy* 81(6): 1370–86.

————. 2003. *Poverty, Agrarian Structure and Political Economy in India: Selected Essays*. New Delhi: Oxford University Press.

Barret, C. B. 1996. "On Price Risk and the Inverse Farm Size-Productivity Relationship." *Journal of Development Economics* 51(369): 193–215.

Bazoglu, Nefise. 1986. "Iscilesmeye Karsi Koylulugun Devami Tartismasi ve Dusundurdukleri." In *11. Tez Kitap Dizisi*, 30–4. Istanbul: Belge Yayinlari.

Benjamin, Dwayne. 1995. "Can Unobserved Land Quality Explain the Inverse Productivity Relationship?" *Journal of Development Economics* 46(1): 51–84.

Benjamin, D. and L. Brandt. 2002. "Property Rights, Labour Markets, and Efficiency in a Transition Economy: The Case of Rural China." *The Canadian Journal of Economics* 35(4): 689–716.

Berry, A. and W. Cline. 1979. *Agrarian Structure and Productivity in Developing Countries*. Baltimore, MD: Johns Hopkins University.

Bhalla, S. S. 1979. "Farm Size Productivity and Technical Change in Indian Agriculture." In *Agrarian Structure and Productivity in Developing Countries*, edited by A. Berry and W. Cline, 141–193. Baltimore, MD: Johns Hopkins University.

Bhalla, S. S. and P. Roy. 1988. "Mis-Specification in Farm Productivity Analysis: The Role of Land Quality." *Oxford Economic Papers, New Series* 40(1): 55–73.

Bharadwaj, K. 1974. *Production Conditions in Indian Agriculture: A Study Based on Farm Management Surveys*. Cambridge, UK: Cambridge University Press.

Binswanger, H. and J. McIntire. 1987. "Behavioral and Material Determinants of Production Relations in Land-Abundant Tropical Agriculture." *Economic Development and Cultural Change* 36(1): 73–99.

Binswanger, H. P., K. Deininger, and G. Feder. 1995. "Power, Distortions, Revolt and Reform in Agricultural Land Relations." In *Handbook of Development Economics, Vol. III*, edited by J. Behrman and T. N. Srinavasan, 2661–763. Amsterdam: Elsevier Science.

Binswanger, H. P. and M. Elgin. 1988. "What are the Prospects for Land Reform?" In *Agriculture and Governments in an Interdependent World: Proceedings of the Twentieth International Conference of Agricultural*

Economists, edited by A. Maunder and A. Valdés, 739–54. Dartmouth, UK: Aldershot.

Boratav, Korkut. 1987. "Eski bir Tartismanin Yansimalari Uzerine." In *11. Tez Kitap Dizisi*, 185–92. Istanbul: Belge Yayinlari.

————. 2000. "Birikim Bicimleri ve Tarim." In *Turkiye'de Tarimsal Yapilar*, edited by S. Pamuk and Z. Toprak, 237–56. Istanbul:Yurt Yayinlari Dergisi.

Boserup, E. 1965. *The Conditions of Agricultural Growth: The Economics of Agrarian Change under Population Pressure*. London: George Allen & Unwin.

Brambilla, I. and G. P. Guido. 2005. "Farm Productivity and Market Structure: Evidence from Cotton Reforms in Zambia." Discussion Paper Series, No. 919, Economic Growth Center, Yale University.

Cakmak, E. 2004. "Structural Change and Market Opening in Agriculture: Turkey Towards EU Accession." In *ERC Working Papers in Economics*, No. 04–10, Department of Economics, Middle East Technical University.

Carter, M. 1984. "Identification of the Inverse Relationship Between Farm Size and Productivity: An Empirical Analysis of Peasant Agricultural Production." In *Oxford Economic Papers, New Series* 36(1): 131–45.

Chayanov, A. 1966. *The Theory of Peasant Economy*. Homewood, IL: R. D. Irwin.

Conning, J. 2000. "Do Better Functioning Factor Markets Reduce Inequality: A Simplified Exposition." Panel on Asset Ownership, Redistribution, and Rural Growth at the Annual World Bank Conference on Development Economics, Washington DC, April 18. Accessed on March 2, 2007, available at: http://www.worldbank.org/research/abcde/washington_12/agenda_12.html

Cornia, G. A. 1985. "Farm Size, Land Yields and the Agricultural Production Function: An Analysis for Fifteen Developing Countries." *World Development* 13(4): 513–34.

Deere, C. D. and L. Magdalena. 2001. *Empowering Women: Land and Property Rights in Latin America*. Pittsburg, PA: University of Pittsburgh.

De Janvry, A., V. Renos, S. Elisabeth, and C. Carlo. 2004. "Testing for Separability in Household Models with Heterogeneous Behavior: A Mixture Model Approach." In *CUDARE Working Papers*, Department of Agriculture and Resource Economics, University of California, Berkeley.

Deolikar, A. B. 1981. "The Inverse Relationship Between Productivity and Farm Size: A Test Using Regional Data from India." *American Journal of Agricultural Economics* 63(2): 275–79.

Eastwood, R., M. Lipton, and A. Newell. 2004. "Farm Size." Paper prepared for *Volume III of the Handbook of Agricultural Economics*. Accessed on June 2, 2005, available at: http://www.ids.ac.uk/ids/aboutids/Seminarseries2005/Eastwood.pdf

Eswaran, Mukesh and Ashok Kotwal. 1986. "Access to Capital and Agrarian Production Organization." *Economic Journal* 96(382): 482–98.

Food and Agriculture Organization of the UN. 1999. "Country Profile: Turkey." *New Agriculturalist Online*. Accessed on June 1, 2006, available at: http://www.new-agri.co.uk/00-3/countryp.html

Feder, Gershon. 1980. "Farm Size, Risk Aversion and the Adoption of New Technology Under Uncertainty." *Oxford Economic Papers, New Series* 32(2): 263–83.

———. 1985. "The Relation Between Farm Size and Farm Productivity: The Role of Family Labor, Supervision, and Credit Constraints." *Journal of Development Economics* 18(2–3): 297–313.

Gozenc, S. 2006. "Turkiye'nin Toprak Ozellikleri." Accessed on March 3, 2007, available at http://www.aof.edu.tr/kitap/IOLTP/2291/unite04.pdf

———. 2006. "Turkiye'nin Iklim Ozellikleri." Accessed on March 3, 2007, available at: <http://www.aof.edu.tr/kitap/IOLTP/2291/unite03.pdf>

Griffin, K., A. R. Khan, and A. Ickowitz. 2002. "Poverty and Distribution of Land." *Journal of Agrarian Change* 2(3): 279–330.

Heltberg, R. 1998. "Rural Market Imperfections and the Farm Size-Productivity Relationship: Evidence from Pakistan." *World Development* 26(10): 1807–26.

Herring, R. 1983. *Land to the Till—The Political Economy of Agrarian Economy in South Asia*. New Haven and London: Yale University.

Kaldjian, P. 2001. "The Smallholder in Turkish Agriculture: Obstacle or Opportunity?" In *Rural Development in Eurasia and the Middle East: Land Reform, Demographic Change, and Environmental Constraints*, edited by K. Engelmann and V. Pavlakovic, 239–78. Seattle and Washington: University of Washington.

Kevane, M. 1996. "Agrarian Structure and Agricultural Practice: Typology and Application to Western Sudan." *American Journal of Agricultural Economics* 78(1): 236–45.

Keyder, C. 1984. "Paths of Rural Transformation in Turkey." *Journal of Peasant Studies* 11(1): 34–49.

Khusro, A. M. 1974. *Economics of Land Reform and Farm Size in India*. Delhi: McMillan Press.

Kutcher, G. P. and P. L. Scandizzo. 1981. *The Agricultural Economy of Northeast Brazil*. Baltimore, MD: World Bank and Johns Hopkins University.

Lamb, Russell L. 2003. "Inverse Productivity: Land Quality, Labor Markets, and Measurement Error." *Journal of Development Economics* 71(1): 71–95.

Lewis, A. 1954. "Economic Development with Unlimited Supplies of Labour." *Manchester School of Economic and Social Studies* 22(2): 139–91

Masterson, T. 2005. *Productivity, Gender and Land Rental Markets in Paraguayan Rural Development*. Doctoral Dissertation, Department of Economics, University of Massachusetts, Amherst, Massachusetts.

Mazumdar, D. 1965. "Size and Farm Productivity: A Problem of Indian Peasant Agriculture." *Economica, New Series* 32(126): 161–73.

OECD. 2006. Economic Surveys, Turkey.

QHS. 2002. Quantitative Household Survey. Ministry of Agriculture, ARIP office, Ankara Turkey.

Rao, J. M. 1986. "Agriculture in Recent Development Theory." *Journal of Development Economics* 22(1): 41–86.

———. 2005. "The Forms of Monopoly Land Rent and Agrarian Organization." *Journal of Agrarian Change* 4(1) and (2): 161–90.

Rao, V. and T. Chtotigeat. 1981. "The Inverse Relationship between Size and Land Holdings and Agricultural Productivity." *American Journal of Agricultural Economics* 63(3): 571–74.

Rosenzweig, Michael and Hans Binswanger. 1993. "Wealth, Weather Risk, and the Composition and Profitability of Agricultural Investments." *Economic Journal* 103(416): 56–78.

Rudra, A. and B. Bandapadhyaya. 1973. "Marginalist Explanation for More Intense Labour Input in Smaller Farms." *Economic and Political Weekly* 8(22): 989–1004.

Schultz, T. W. 1964. *Transforming Traditional Agriculture*. New Haven: Yale University.

Sen, Abhijit. 1981. "Market Failure and Control of Labor Power: Towards an Explanation of 'Structure' and Change in Indian Agriculture." *Cambridge Journal of Economics* 5(3–4): 201–28 and 327–50.

Sen, A. K. 1962. "An Aspect of Indian Agriculture." *Economic Weekly* 14(4–6): 243–246.

———. 1966. "Peasants Dualism with or without Surplus Labour." *Journal of Political Economy* 74(5): 425–50.

———. 1999. *Employment, Technology, and Development*. Oxford: ILO and Clarendon Press.

Sender, J. and J. Deborah. 2004. "Searching for a Weapon of Mass Production in Rural Africa: Unconvincing Arguments for Land Reform." *Journal of Agrarian Change* 4(1) and (2): 142–64.

Sirman, N. 1966. "From Economic Integration to Cultural Strategies of Power: The Study of Rural Changes in Turkey." *New Perspectives on Turkey* 14: 115–25.

Srinivasan, T. N. 1972. "Farm Size and Productivity: Implications of Choice Under Uncertainty." *The Indian Journal of Statistics* 34(4): 409–20.

Stock, J. and M. Watson. 2003. *Introduction to Econometrics*. New York: Pearson Education.

Toprak, Z. 1999. "Turkiye Tarimive Yapisal Gelismeler 1900–1950." In *75 Yilda Koylerden Sehirlere*, edited by Oya Baydar, 19–37. Istanbul: TC. Is Bankasi Yayinlari, Tarih Vakfi Yayinlari.

Viner, Jacob. 1957. "Some Reflections on the Concept of Disguised Unemployment." *Indian Journal of Economics* 38: 17–23.

Yakin, Erturk, 1981. *Rural Change in Southeastern Anatolia: An Analysis of Rural Poverty and Power Structure as a Reflection of Center-Periphery Relations in Turkey*. Unpublished Dissertation, Cornell University.

5

MARKET FAILURE AND
LAND CONCENTRATION
IN TURKEY

1. INTRODUCTION

According to the conventional theory in economics, it is presumed that perfectly competitive markets allow the full utilization of land, labor, and capital, and their efficient allocation across alternative uses. This assertion provides a theoretical as well as a normative benchmark for economic outcomes in terms of aggregate income, poverty, and inequality (Rao 2005). However, markets of developing countries do not conform to the conditions of perfect markets; neither do markets of developed countries.

Markets have always been an important mechanism to mediate agricultural policies. As we have discussed in chapter 1, starting with the 1980s—markets began to claim a more central role in distributing economic opportunities to people; for the first time, the role of markets have shifted from being mediators of policy to decision makers of production and consumption in agriculture.

Markets indeed allocate resources between people and nations; they are deemed to be effective to the extent that they offer economic opportunities to people. However, the extent to which they offer such opportunities depends on how markets function and on the distribution and structure of the assets and income people have (Sarris 2001).[1]

In the face of imperfect markets, efficiency of resource use depends crucially on the distribution of assets, particularly land assets (Sen 1981; Binswanger and Rosenzweig 1986; Griffin et al. 2002; Rao 2005).

The major inquiry of this chapter is to look at the link between the most important asset in agriculture: land ownership inequality and the functioning of rural factor markets in Turkey. We suggest an analytical method to measure market malfunction. In so doing, this research fills an important empirical gap in the development of literature that looks at market failure mostly via theoretical models. In this chapter, we argue that rural factor markets have a tendency to perpetuate initial land and land-related inequalities rather than ameliorate them. The main question we will answer is the following: Is land ownership inequality positively associated with factor market malfunctioning?

In doing so, the structure of the rest of this chapter is as follows: In the next section, we review the literature on the rural factor markets-inequality nexus and claim that heterodox approaches provide a more powerful understanding of the functioning of factor markets in the context of developing countries where markets are less developed and land concentration is high; In the third section, we detail the methodology; in the fourth section, we test our hypotheses by utilizing a World Bank survey on rural Turkey for 2002; finally, in the last section, we take account of our empirical inquiry and then conclude.

2. LITERATURE REVIEW

In the literature, studies of inequality and rural markets can be divided into three different strands with respect to where they locate inequality in relation to factor markets. The first strand is the pure neoclassical view in which inequality is an outcome of the efficient functioning of competitive factor markets. The second strand, transactions cost/asset dependency theory, locates inequality outside of markets as a factor that prevents market participation (i.e., inequality in the ownership of certain assets prevents full participation of agents), thereby impeding perfect competition and resulting in inefficient resource allocation in the economy. The third strand, the heterodox view, locates inequality within the exchange process. In the heterodox view, inequality is both an outcome and a force that affects the process that produces the outcome.

2.1. Pure Neoclassical Theory

In the pure neoclassical view, income inequality maps to endowment inequality perfectly. Through perfectly competitive markets, all factors of production are fully utilized and receive their marginal contribution; consequently, resources are allocated efficiently across alternative uses (Schultz 1964; Conning 2000). In short, mainstream economics disregards the distribution of assets or resources and exclusively focuses on efficiency through free markets. Inequality is a result of perfect competition in which the most efficient producer wins and the outcome is reflected in efficient resource allocation.

Schultz's (1964) study evaluating developing country agriculture as "poor but efficient" is perhaps the most well-known study of "traditional agriculture" from a pure neoclassical standpoint where "efficiency," not inequality, is the focus. Schultz (1964) argues that in farming communities bound by the behavior of traditional agriculture, all factors of production are allocated efficiently because all resources are fully utilized; hence, poverty in traditional agrarian societies is not due to underutilization of resources but due to lack of productivity-increasing technology. According to Schultz (1964), these "efficient but poor" farmers respond to prices, which bring about allocative efficiency. Since prices transfer the information about marginal productivities of land and labor, intervention with the market mechanism creates not only impediments to integration of larger markets with local ones, but also generates problems in disseminating information about factors and products that help in reducing imperfections in capital markets, such as pricing of irrigation and other facilities at marginal costs.

Schultz's (1964) ultra neoclassic work sheds no light on the relation between inequality and rural factor markets, neither does it aim to do so; however, another work within the same paradigm does. Based on a two factor (land and labor), two household (land-rich and land-poor) trade model, Conning (2000) argues that factor market participation reduces inequality through market exchange since increases in marginal productivity of land (labor) would be very significant for land-rich (land-poor) farmers.

2.1.1. Asset Dependency and Transaction Cost Theory

A second strand of thinking on inequality within the framework of mainstream theory on agriculture emerges from including the transaction costs into the analysis of rural markets and inequality. Transaction costs could be defined as various costs, such as registration fees, titling costs, and information costs, which make market participation costly for the poor, thereby making the poor settle for the second-best option, leading to market failure in efficiently allocating resources. Some of the studies within this paradigm are more holistic in their approach to the imperfect markets-inequality nexus since they look at more dimensions, such as differentiation in agrarian organization as outcomes resulting from imperfections in rural factor markets (Bardhan 1984, 1998; Eswaran and Kotwal 1986; Carter and Wiebe 1990; Barham et al. 2000) rather than one dimension, such as outcomes pertinent to one asset only (Dercon 1998; Carter and Zegarra 2000; Carter and Zimmermann 2000, 2003; Renkov, Hallstrom, and Karanja 2004).

Within the first group, in their influential study, Eswaran and Kotwal (1986) model the impact of credit access and supervision cost on the organization of class structure and agricultural production. Subject to credit and supervision constraints, farmers optimize between different choices of working on or off the farm, which then determine their class position and thereby the agrarian organization. Their study is important, because it shows the importance of land distribution, and thus agrarian organization as partly an outcome of imperfect rural factor markets.

The "asset or endowment dependency theorem," as it is called by Barham et al. (2000), looks at the problem of inequality over time and over different sets of endowments and activities. The theorem posits inequality as a result of production and investment decisions made by people based on the nature of endowments they hold. Their study on the Peruvian Amazon considers two different types of endowments: reproducible and fixed. For example, fishing nets and land are related to two different activities: fishing and agriculture. The reproducibility of fishing nets as opposed to the fixed nature of land creates endowment dependency. Despite showing how the structure of endowments (i.e., assets before entering the market exchange) affects asset accumulation (i.e., assets after the market exchange), their study does not shed light on *how* rural markets correct, retain, or create inequalities.

Other studies on transaction costs focus on the link between the distribution of one main asset and rural factor markets (Dercon 1998; Carter and Zimmermann 2003; Renkow, Hallstrom, and Karanja 2004). A well-known study within this category is by Dercon (1998) on the patterns of activity choice and asset accumulation between rich and poor farmers in Western Tanzania. The central point of Dercon's work is that most profitable investments are constrained by entry, which is eased by credit, and credit access is eased by land ownership. His conclusions suggest that when investment is a necessity to participate in high-yield-returning economic activity, market imperfections widen the gap between rich and poor farmers.

A common point in the transactions costs/asset dependency view that constitutes a major difference from the pure neoclassical view is that the efficiency of the outcome is rejected under market imperfections. Despite its contribution to modify the neoclassical theory to include market imperfections as reflected in transaction costs, in our view, the asset dependency approach is mainstream. It is mainstream not only in the sense that it uses mainstream methodological individualism and fails to recognize power structures within markets, but also in the message it gives. Either as countries develop over time, or by the efforts of market-friendly policy intervention (which is generally through a multinational institution, such as the World Bank), the problem of rural economies would be solved by smoothing the functioning of markets. In short, the policy's suggestion to increase efficiency is to correct for market failures that are exogenous to the system and not produced by markets as a result of the existing power imbalances.

2.2. Heterodox Approach

Heterodox literature departs from mainstream studies in two major ways. First, inequality is not only an outcome of a malfunctioning market as conceived in mainstream theory, but inequality is a major determining factor that creates malfunctioning. Second, markets are part and product of a larger entity, in which not everything can be explained by the fundamentals of economics.

The seminal paper that started a great deal of discussion not only within the mainstream paradigm but also among heterodox thinkers is the contribution of Griffin, Khan, and Ickowitz (2002) on monopoly land power and how it affects rural land and labor markets, thus inequality and poverty.[2] Griffin et al. (2002) include power as a factor that creates market imperfections. Rural factor markets are fragmented, "law of one price" (i.e., small and large farmers facing the same price for goods and services) does not apply due to the latter's ability to exercise monopoly power, thereby resulting in increased inequality and poverty.

Monopoly land power also affects rural labor markets. Maybe more than in any other market, there are systems of labor control in rural markets because relatively isolated local, rural markets are more prone to abuse by local powers than a centralized market. Labor control systems affect those who can participate to what extent and the relative bargaining power of certain groups that are engaged in labor market transactions. Griffin et al. (2002) claim that land concentration particularly is a form of institutional (as opposed to environmental and cultural) labor control in the context of fragmented local markets, because monopoly in land market gives the landlord monopsony power in labor markets in which they operate (i.e., when there is only one landlord to work for, he sets the rules). They further argue that it is the economic outcome of monopsony power within labor markets that are responsible for production inefficiencies, surplus labor, and rural inequality and poverty through low wages, low levels of employment, and low levels of output.

The major difference between mainstream theories and Griffin et al.'s (2002) approach to the rural markets-inequality nexus is that in Griffin et al.'s study, markets are recognized as entities where power plays a role. In mainstream conceptualization, markets are perceived as entities where the major role belongs to individuals who are independent of demographic, ethnic, or cultural features who act rationally to maximize utility given exogenous constraints (i.e., endowments). If inefficiencies occur, it is because asset-poor agents cannot compete due to transaction costs—that are, again, exogenous imperfections in markets. Griffin et al.'s (2002) approach suggests that it is not the imperfections in the market that result in persisting inequalities and inefficiency; it is inequality that results in imperfections in the markets that generates inequality and inefficiency. In short, two major differences between Griffin et al. (2002) and mainstream studies looking at the nexus of inequality and rural factor markets are the following: first, causality and, second, a broader understanding of the functioning of rural markets as being impacted by inequalities.

However (as pointed out by many economists), methodologically, Griffin et al.'s (2002) study has a limited scope for power in their analysis; power is only confined within the structure of the markets, not outside of what constructs that structure. Therefore lacks a multidimensional inquiry into history, culture, and the relations of production that are reflective of classes in agriculture (Byres 2004; Rao 2005).

Rao (2005) takes Griffin et al.'s (2002) analysis on monopoly land markets a step further and puts it in a broader framework. Rao's contribution to the literature is to delineate a framework within which rural factor markets function and agrarian organization is shaped based on three major determinants: economic (degree of land inequality), political (effectiveness of supervision given the social structure of both parties engaged in labor contracts), and technical (labor productivity given the technology). Constrained by these three structural variables, large landowners maximize their surplus—which Rao (2005) defines as economic rent—and decide among different tenure types, such as sharecropping, fixed-rent tenancy, wage labor, and labor rent.[3] In his work, Rao (2005) emphasizes the relations of production rather than the relations of exchange, and he directs the reader into thinking more about noneconomic fundamentals in shaping agrarian societies.

In short, the contribution from Rao (2005) is the dialectical analysis of the nexus of inequality and market imperfection. In the neoclassical paradigm, causality is from market imperfections to inequality; in Griffin et al.'s thinking (2002), it is from inequality to market imperfections. Rao's (2005) theoretical analysis combines the two conclusions rather than excluding either of them: pronounced land inequality is a cause of (monopolistic) imperfections, as for Griffin et al. (2002), but it is not the sole cause of income inequality. Market imperfections, for any given level of land inequality, work through the relations of production and exchange as the other key determinant of income inequality.

In this chapter, we locate inequality both within and outside of factor markets. We look at the causes of rural inequality both as an outcome of malfunctioning rural markets and as a factor that induces malfunctioning in factor markets. As such, the central concept in our study is the connectedness[4] between land ownership inequality and factor market malfunctioning.

3. THE METHODOLOGY

To define malfunctioning, one needs to define "well-functioning," which will serve as the norm of proper functioning. The norm we use in this book is *perfect markets* as defined by conventional theory. There are two main assumptions for perfect markets. The first assumption is about the macro context: all factors are fully utilized (e.g., there exists no unemployment). The second is about the micro context: all markets function within a perfectly competitive framework (e.g., there are no transaction costs, no information costs, and no fragmented markets). In other words, all agents have equal opportunity in the exchange process in which all factors get exactly their marginal contribution as a reward. The wage rate is equal to the marginal productivity of labor, and rent is equal to the marginal productivity of land. If there is income inequality in the society where such markets function, it must be due to endowment inequality. In other words, perfect markets perfectly map endowment inequality to income inequality.

After setting up the norm, we can move on to the discussion of the analytical framework this research employs, which is a combination of

Rao (2005), Benjamin and Brandt (1997), and Sen (1981). In their 1997 paper on rural China, Benjamin and Brandt develop a simple analytical model that serves two main functions. The first function is to assess if the factor markets are functioning as suggested by the neoclassical model (i.e., whether or not rural markets are perfect). The second function is to evaluate the functioning of the factor markets as either increasing or decreasing inequality. Both of these points require more detailed elaboration that will be provided in the following pages, as we simultaneously build the analytical framework.

The basic idea of the model by Benjamin and Brandt (1997) is to construct a neoclassical account of the functioning of rural markets and of incomes derived from such markets, and then compare the theoretically predicted outcomes with the actual outcomes. Following this, they estimate an inequality index for both incomes (predicted and actual) and then utilize the gap among the incomes and the indices. They do this by evaluating the functioning of the factor markets as inequality increasing or decreasing, while being able to point out the ways in which markets fail.

Benjamin and Brandt's (1997) evaluation of the functioning of factor markets is based on using trade variables as proxies to measure the markets' ability to function. The two variables are (1) the ratio of leased (in or out) land to total land holdings and (2) the ratio of adults participating in the labor markets in agriculture and in nonagriculture. Hence, their norm, or evaluation of the markets' functioning, is based on the markets' depth. We think use of such variables representing market depth is circular in logic since Benjamin and Brandt (1997) try to explain the well-functioning of actual factor markets with variables endogenous to the well-functioning of markets.

The model we utilize here differs from Benjamin and Brandt's model in various ways. First and foremost in this study, evaluating the impact of factor markets is an inquiry into the connectedness, aiming to look at the relation between the inequality of land ownership distribution and the factor market failure. This is measured by comparing the norm to the actual by utilizing income inequality indices. Perfect markets should map endowment inequality to income inequality perfectly; to the extent that they do not, markets malfunction. We further argue that the higher the land inequality, the poorer rural markets function, and also that the relationship between inequality and market malfunctioning is dialectical.

The mathematical modeling of the framework we employ follows the same setup of Benjamin and Brandt's (1997) neoclassical agrarian

economy; however, the utilization of the model differs in the aforementioned ways.

Basic assumptions of the normative model (markets functioning
under the neoclassical ideal) are as follows:

- Homogeneity of agricultural output across households where
  output can be sold in the market for price, p, or consumed at
  home:

$$Q = F(T, L), \tag{1}$$

where Q is output, T is land, and L is labor used in production.

- Households can hire labor or hire themselves out into the labor
  market at the wage rate, w, and also land can be rented in or
  rented out at the same rental rate, r. Markets are perfect, thus p,
  r, and w are given and there is perfect substitution between the
  family and hired factors, which suggests household income will
  not change, for example, due to the owner's preference of cultivating or leasing out one's own land.
- Households decide the optimal level of land and labor to be used
  in the production from a mixture of hired-in and family inputs,
  that is, on-farm production is a result of hired-in and family
  inputs.

$$L^* = L^F + L^H \text{ and } T^* = T^F + T^H \text{ and} \tag{2}$$

$$Q^* = F(T^*, L^*), \tag{3}$$

where the superscript F stands for family, and H stands for hired
factors.

- Household income then can be written as the sum of returns on
  land, labor, and farm profits. And since working on or off the farm
  does not make a difference, a simplified version of income is:

$$\tilde{Y} = wLn + rTo + \Pi(w, r, p), \tag{4}$$

where Π is the farm profits, Ln is the labor time endowment, and
To is the amount of owned land. Π could be written more elabo-
rately as:

$$\Pi(w, r, p) = pF(T^*, L^*) - wL^* - rT^*, \tag{5}$$

- Farm profits are assumed to be zero, for simplicity, which redefines the net farm income as:

$$pF(T^*, L^*) - wL^H - rT^H = wL^F + rT^F, \tag{6}$$

Equation (5) suggests that net farm income is the returns-to-family inputs used in farm production; if we add hired-out factors into this equation, we come up with the net household income, which is an elaborated form of equation (3):

$$\tilde{Y} = wL^F + rT^F + wL^M + rT^M = wLn + rTo, \tag{7}$$

As mentioned by Benjamin and Brandt (1997), equation (7) suggests an accounting identity that would hold only under a strictly neoclassical model (i.e., under perfect factor markets where income equals the market value of the endowments of land and labor). In the real world, one of the reasons this identity might not hold is due to imperfect markets. For example, the household's actual labor earnings might be less than the market value of their labor endowment if the labor markets are not clearing due to high unemployment. Then a more precise valuation of the household endowments would be at shadow prices rather than market prices:[5]

$$Y = w^*L^F + r^*T^F + wL^M + rT^M = w'Ln + r'To, \tag{8}$$

where w^* and r^* are the shadow wage and rental rate; w and r are market wage and rental rates; w' and r' are weighted averages of the shadow market wage and rental rates; and Y is the actual income. This suggests that neoclassical income ($\tilde{Y}$) will diverge from the actual income (Y) when there is inequality between shadow and market wage and rental rates. However, w^* and r^* (the shadow wage rate and the shadow rental rate, respectively) are not observed variables. In this equation, we are predicting an approximation of neoclassical income per household by using the average market land rental and average market wage rates and multiplying that with the land and labor endowments from the data set. On the basis of these approximations of the neoclassical income, a neoclassical inequality index, or the neoclassical Gini coefficient ($G_{\tilde{Y}}$) can be computed. We can calculate the actual income inequality index, or G_Y, from the actual income obtained from the data set. We then take the distance between the two Gini coefficients (predicted and actual) and normalize this distance with the predicted Gini coefficient to arrive at an index, which we call *the market-malfunctioning measure* (MMM).

$$MMM = (G_Y - G_{\hat{Y}})/G_{\hat{Y}}, \tag{9}$$

Our general hypothesis is that, in Turkey, as in any labor surplus economy, labor is not fully utilized and what lies behind this is the malfunctioning of markets, which is connected to land ownership inequality. Thus, when there is an improvement in the functioning of factor markets, labor utilization improves; the presumption is that labor utilization improves relatively more. Therefore, whenever markets function better, effective demand for labor will be higher. This demand will cause the earnings of labor to be greater. Any improvement in land earnings will be comparatively smaller than the improvement in labor earnings. In all, this hypothesis indicates that any improvement in market functioning reduces inequality of income.

It is obvious that the poor are those with relatively little land endowment and are also those who supply a plethora of labor. Conversely, the rich are those who have a lot of land and supply relatively little labor. Finally, by definition, markets function best at the neoclassical ideal from which it follows that income inequality will be lowest under neoclassical market conditions.

On the basis of the preceding arguments, it can be expected that when markets function perfectly in the neoclassical sense, then MMM=0; otherwise MMM will be positive for a labor-abundant economy.[6] There may be some exceptions to this.

In an ideal world of neoclassical economics, it is reasonable to expect inequality of income to be necessarily less where there are perfect markets (i.e., no asymmetric information, no transactions costs, and no interdependence of preferences). There are some cases that may or may not support this hypothesis. First, there may be noneconomic arguments regarding familial, or quasi-familial relationships, in which poor families may get priority in labor, land, or credit market transactions in the actual world but not in a neoclassical world. This situation then causes inequality to rise in a neoclassical world as opposed to the actual world.

In addition to the noneconomic arguments, an economic argument could be made based on land underutilization in large farms. In large farms, there will be more land underutilization as compared to the small farms. Thus, when household income is calculated with the average land rental rates, there could be cases where neoclassical income for the land-rich households could be much greater than its actual level. When this is the case, the rich would become richer and the poor would be better off, but the income gap maybe larger than before. Hence, the distribution of income could worsen, depending on the land underutilization of land-rich farms compared to labor underutilization of labor-rich but land-poor farms. In such a case, MMM could be negative. Keeping these points in mind, we now move on to test if markets are perfect in rural Turkey.

First, we examine whether or not factor markets are neoclassical in rural Turkey. In other words, whether MMM=0 or Y–Ỹ=0. The test is a statistical paired t-test on the means of Y and Ỹ. It is important to note that the major contribution of this chapter is not to show markets are imperfect in Turkey, as this is no secret to anyone in any developing country. In particular, rural markets in developing countries are far from functioning perfectly, as they are prone to imperfect information, transaction costs, inadequate infrastructures, and high unemployment. The novelty in this inquiry is to show that land ownership inequality distorts market functioning in the direction as it is predicted by the theory.

We show this distortion by testing the connectedness between land inequality and market malfunctioning utilizing the following equation:

$$MMM = \beta 0 + \beta 1^* \, G_{TO} + \beta 2^* \text{ population density} + \text{error}, \qquad (10)$$

where $\beta 0$ is the constant term, G_{TO} is the Gini coefficient for owned land.

This is the hypothesis of "connectedness" put forth by Sen (1981) and Rao (2005).[7] Our argument is that even though factor markets serve to reduce inequality, the reduction in equality will be small when markets widely malfunction. Conversely, well-functioning markets will produce large reductions in inequality. Our main argument is not that factor markets may not diminish inequality; rather our argument is that while factor markets do in fact diminish inequality, the extent of reduction in inequality depends on how well the markets function. However, because market malfunctioning is itself connected to endowment inequality, the inequality reducing the role of markets is structurally limited. Hence, we expect a positive relationship between land ownership inequality and MMM.

We expect the population density to have a negative impact on MMM. Boserup (1965) argues that population density creates a pressure to introduce intensive cultivation techniques to meet food requirements. This suggests that a higher population density brings about higher land yields and even higher average incomes. In addition, it is plausible that in densely populated areas, work and land leases may be accessed with lower transaction costs from within proximate neighborhoods, which could be an impediment to monopoly power in local land markets.

In addition to MMM, which is a measure based on outcomes in terms of household incomes, we assess the malfunctioning of markets via process measures. For assessing land markets, we look at the relation between land holding inequality and land ownership inequality and test the connectedness between the two by the following regression:

$$G_T = \beta 0 + \beta 1\ G_{TO} + \beta 2^* \text{ population density} + \text{error term,} \qquad (11)$$

where G_T stands for Gini coefficient for land holding, and G_{TO} stands for Gini Coefficient for land ownership.

3.1. Calculations and Assumptions of Actual and Neoclassical Income

3.1.1. Calculations of Actual Income

Actual net farm household income is the summation of two major components. The first component is the summation of gross income from crop production, secondary production, such as dairy and animal sales, net of farm expenditures such as fertilizers, pesticides, irrigation, veterinary, and utility bills for the barns, and homestead. The second component is net rental income from land (both fixed rent and sharecropping), and net labor income (wages earned minus wages paid).

3.1.2. Calculations and Assumptions of Neoclassical Income

Given factor endowments, income inequality may not be necessarily the result of malfunctioning factor markets. It may be the result of preferences to participate in the markets or due to factor price differences in different markets. To address different preferences regarding off-farm labor market participation and differing wage rates for seasonal and permanent employment within and outside of agriculture, we have estimated five different per capita neoclassical incomes, hence five different MMMs. In all the estimations, labor markets are assumed to be perfectly neoclassical in the sense that there exist no fragmented markets, no transactions costs, and no unemployment.

First, we have assumed that all adult members of the household prefer to work full time and are indifferent to working on or off the farm.[8] Labor endowment is then multiplied by a market wage rate, which is the average of agricultural and nonagricultural wage rates for full-time, permanent employment.[9]

The second calculation addresses gender preferences about market work within the household. These preferences could be due to noneconomic factors regarding gender roles that may be limiting off-farm labor force participation of females. To account for such preferences, we have deflated the total female labor endowment by 0.25. Wage rate is the same as in the first calculation (model one).

The third calculation of neoclassical income addresses the issue of love for one's own farm. It is argued that lack of off-farm labor market participation (labor supply response) in rural agrarian economies is due to one's love for one's own farm (Visaria 1970). Hence, the third calculation differs from the ones above in the sense that total family labor days on the farm are assumed to be the households' work preference. The wage rate that is used to calculate the value of labor endowment is a daily agricultural wage rate.[10]

The fourth and fifth calculations differ from the third in terms of the wage variable only. Rather than using agricultural seasonal income, we have used nonagricultural seasonal income as the daily wage rate. For the fifth calculation, we took the market value of permanent value of full-time employment (both agricultural and nonagricultural) and divided this annual figure into 330 work days to arrive at a daily wage rate.

Now that we have detailed assumptions regarding the estimations and have set up the model, it is time to move forward with the actual empirical investigation.

4. DATA AND SAMPLE CHARACTERISTICS

The data we use in this research is QHS 2002. The QHS survey allows us to look at the degree of land and income inequality at the household level on a per capita basis. We have utilized 5,280 of the observations to calculate the Gini coefficients and, when expanded by the household members, there are 30,242 observations.

Table 5.1 provides sample means of the key components of the variables we used in the analysis for the whole sample. Earnings from crop production comprise 78 percent of total household income. Income from agricultural sidelines, such as animal sales, husbandry, secondary production, sales of dairy and flour products, constitutes 12 percent of

Table 5.1 Selected Household Characteristics

	Mean	Min	Max
Crop Production[a]	6,260.0	0	751,000
Agricultural Sidelines[b]	994.0	0	90,300
Income from Land Rent (Agr)	25.3	0	15,000
Land Rent Paid (agr)	219.3	0	30,000
Given Crop Share	183.0	0	133,000
Taken Crop Share	1.8	0	3,600
Labor Income from Market[c]	765.0	0	30,000
Wages Paid	382.8	0	45,000
Other Expenses	3,422.3	0	154,000
Net Income	3,839	−0.02	753,000
Household Size	5.7	1	37
Land Owned (in Decares)	68.5	0	3,800
Land Operated (in Decares)	91.6	0	3,884
Sample Size	5,280		

Note: All income and expenses are in YTL. [a]Net of sharecropping. [b]Secondary production and animal sales. [c]Includes both agricultural and non-agr. labor income.
Source: Quantitative Household Survey, 2002.

the total household income, followed by labor income from hired-out labor (10 percent). An average household pays 383 YTL per year for labor hired on the farm and spends more than half of its gross crop income on expenses, such as fertilizer, pesticide, irrigation-related expenses, veterinary costs, and electricity and gas bills.

The descriptive statistics for five different MMMs at three different levels of analysis (province, town, and village) can be seen in table 5.9 in appendix A. First of all, there is not even a single case where MMM index has the value zero in any, including all models and all three levels of analysis.

The means of provincial MMMs are higher for the first two models, 2.76 and 2.61, but lower for the others, 0.67 for the third and 0.74 for the fourth and fifth (table 5.9). It is reasonable to see a smaller MMM for the third, fourth, and fifth models, as the labor endowment estimation for these are only the total number of days worked on one's own farm. When labor endowment is taken only as the total number of days worked on the farm, it is normal to see that the neoclassical income distribution gets closer to the actual one. Neoclassical income will be much closer to the actual one since the labor income gap between the actual and the neoclassical household income would be simply due to wage differences and not differences in labor endowments. Hence, market-malfunctioning index gets smaller. The same pattern is also visible for town and village level MMMs.

5. REGRESSION ANALYSIS

5.1. Province Level Analysis

Province level results suggest a positive relationship between land ownership inequality and market malfunctioning (table 5.2). In all the models, the coefficient of land ownership inequality is positive and statistically significant in the first three models. There is a 1 percent change in provincial land ownership inequality resulting in approximately 1 percent increase in the market-malfunctioning measurement for models I and II, and a 2 percent increase for model III at the 5 percent significance level, for models IV and V, the positive relationship still holds but with no significance.

In model I, population density is significant and negative, as expected, at the 10 percent level. An increase of 1 percent in population density results in a 0.10 percent decrease in market-malfunctioning measurement.

We extend the analysis by dropping the most developed and populated province in Turkey: Istanbul. A good reason to drop Istanbul is the fact that it accounts for 50 percent of all economic activity and is home to 23 percent of the Turkish population. A village that is under the jurisdiction of Istanbul is very different than villages elsewhere since this giant city's effective urban boundaries include its villages. Therefore, looking at the relationship without Istanbul provides a better picture of the inequality-factor market nexus in rural Turkey. The results of this reduced sample are illustrated in table 5.3.

Table 5.2 Province Level Results for Market Malfunctioning Measure

	I	II	III	IV	V
	(ln)MMM1	(ln)MMM2	(ln)MMM3	(ln)MMM4	(ln)MMM5
(ln) City	1.02	0.97	2.09	1.13	1.13
Land Gini	(0.51)*	(0.52)*	(0.94)**	−0.93	−1.06
(ln) Population	−0.10	−0.09	0.02	−0.19	−0.25
Density	(0.06)*	−0.06	−0.11	−0.15	−0.18
Constant	1.02	0.96	−1.28	0.25	0.54
	(0.40)**	(0.38)**	(0.75)*	−0.95	−1.13
Observations	73	73	70	71	71
Adjusted R-squared	0.15	0.13	0.09	0.13	0.15

Note: *significant at 10%; **significant at 5%; ***significant at 1%. All regressions are controlled for regional variation. Robust standard errors in parentheses.
Source: Quantitative Household Survey, 2002.

Results change dramatically without Istanbul (table 5.3). Not only does the significance of land ownership increase compared to the full sample, but land ownership distribution becomes significant in all the models. Population density, however, loses its significance in all the models.

5.2. Town and Village Level Analysis

We also ran the same regressions at town and village levels; however, for some of the towns and villages, the index of MMM takes a negative value, suggesting that actual income distribution is better compared to the neoclassical income distribution, particularly for the models in which we assumed the quantity of labor supplied to the market and the farm were equal. As we have discussed earlier, values of MMM can be negative under certain circumstances including: when land is not utilized fully by large-scale landlords, when the gap between rich and poor households would be smaller compared to the neoclassical, and where familial preferences are given to the very poor. Hence, it is reasonable to see some of the index values turn negative. Out of 363 towns, 8 turn negative in models I and II, and the number of negative MMMs are 50, 35, and 32 for models III, IV, and V respectively. Overall, a maximum 98 percent and a minimum 86 percent of all towns predict a positive MMM. It is reasonable to see more negative values for MMMs for models III through V, as labor

Table 5.3 Province Level Results for Market Malfunctioning Measure without Istanbul

	I	II	III	IV	V
	(ln)MMM1	(ln)MMM2	(ln)MMM3	(ln)MMM4	(ln)MMM5
(ln) City Land Gini	1.08 (0.52)**	1.04 (0.53)*	2.09 (0.97)**	1.59 (0.82)*	1.70 (0.90)*
(ln) Population Density	−0.08 −0.07	−0.06 −0.06	0.02 −0.11	−0.02 −0.09	−0.04 −0.09
Constant	−1.79 (0.43)**	0.79 (0.40)*	−1.28 (0.75)*	−0.74 −0.59	−0.70 −0.59
Observations	72	72	70	70	70
Adjusted R-squared	0.16	0.14	0.09	0.12	0.13

Note: *significant at 10%; **significant at 5%; ***significant at 1%. All regressions are controlled for regional variation. Robust standard errors in parentheses.
Source: Quantitative Household Survey, 2002.

endowment is assumed to be identical to the actual days worked on the farm. In an economy where land is concentrated but labor is not, returns to labor should have an equalizing effect on the distribution of income. In our estimation of MMMs in models III through V, we have reduced the impact of labor endowment and, hence, reduced the equalizing impact of labor endowment; hence, there are more negative MMMs. One drawback of the regression analysis of the MMM index is that when MMM turns negative, the interpretation of the coefficients becomes challenging; so, we narrowed the analysis to the observations with positive MMMs. Basically, where the MMMs are positive, the possibility of their meaningful interpretation and explanation exists within the framework adopted in this chapter. Otherwise, for villages with negative MMMs, one must conclude that the relevant universe is distinct.

For villages, in models I through V similar to town-level calculations, a small number of MMMs turn negative; only 5 out of 500 villages. For models III through V, however, the number of negative MMMs is 75, 50, and 42, respectively. Overall, a maximum 99% and a minimum 85% of all villages depict a positive MMM.

5.2.1. Town-Level Results

For town-level analysis, we have excluded the population density variable since it cannot be disaggregated to the town level, and we have added the distance-to-cities variable. It is hypothesized that the closer a household is to a larger market in cities, the less impact land ownership inequality will have on market malfunctioning since larger markets provide opportunities of alternative employment.[11]

As illustrated in town-level regressions in all the models, land ownership inequality depicts a positive relationship with the MMM; in models I, II, and VI, this relationship is statistically significant (table 5.4). In model I, 1 percent change in land ownership Gini is correlated with 0.57 percent change in MMM at the 5 percent significance level. In model V, town land ownership distribution is significant at the 10 percent level (p value = 0.08). A change of 1 percent in land ownership distribution is correlated with 0.73 percent increase in the MMM.

The regression results for the reduced sample (exclusive of Istanbul) are not significantly different for town-level analysis. Only magnitude effects change slightly (table 5.5).

5.2.2. Village Level Results

In village level regressions along with population density variable, we excluded the distance-to-cities variable since disaggregation of this

Table 5.4 Town Level Results for Market Malfunctioning Measure

	I	II	III	IV	V
	(ln)MMM1	(ln)MMM2	(ln)MMM3	(ln)MMM4	(ln)MMM5
(ln) Town	0.57	0.51	0.43	0.64	0.73
Land Gini	(0.28)**	(0.28)*	−0.46	−0.40	(0.39)*
(ln) Distance	−0.01	−0.01	0.007	−0.01	0.02
	−0.02	−0.02	−0.04	−0.03	−0.03
Constant	0.70	0.66	−0.74	−0.58	−0.88
	(0.17)***	(0.17)***	(0.30)**	(0.24)**	(0.25)***
Observations	355	355	313	325	331
Adjusted R-squared	0.11	0.10	0.00	0.05	0.03

Note: *significant at 10%; **significant at 5%; ***significant at 1%. All regressions are controlled for regional variation. Robust standard errors in parentheses.
Source: Quantitative Household Survey, 2002.

Table 5.5 Town Level Results for Market Malfunctioning Measure without Istanbul

	I	II	III	IV	V
	(ln)MMM1	(ln)MMM2	(ln)MMM3	(ln)MMM4	(ln)MMM5
(ln) Town	0.61	0.56	0.44	0.66	0.74
Land Gini	(0.28)**	(0.28)**	−0.46	−0.40	(0.39)*
(ln) Distance	0.004	0.01	0.01	−0.01	0.02
	−0.02	−0.02	−0.04	−0.03	−0.03
Constant	0.67	0.63	−0.75	−0.60	−0.89
	(0.17)***	(0.17)***	(0.30)**	(0.24)**	(0.25)***
Observations	353	353	312	324	330
Adjusted R-squared	0.12	0.10	0.00	0.05	0.03

Note: *significant at 10%; **significant at 5%; ***significant at 1%. All regressions are controlled for regional variation. Robust standard errors in parentheses.
Source: Quantitative Household Survey, 2002.

variable at the village level is not possible, given the data. Also, there exists no linear relationship between the distance from villages and towns, and adding distance-to-cities would not add much explanatory power.[12]

As illustrated in table 5.6, there is a positive and significant correlation between land ownership inequality and the market-malfunctioning index in all the models. For models I and II, a 1 percent increase in land ownership inequality in a village is positively correlated with a 0.6 percent increase in MMM at the 5 percent

Table 5.6 Village Level Results for Market Malfunctioning Measure

	I	II	III	IV	V
	(ln)MMM1	(ln)MMM2	(ln)MMM3	(ln)MMM4	(ln)MMM5
(ln) Village	0.59	0.58	1.13	1.07	1.36
Land Gini	(0.27)**	(0.27)**	(0.43)***	(0.41)***	(0.39)***
Constant	0.69	0.61	−0.97	−0.86	−1.21
	(0.13)***	(0.13)***	(0.24)***	(0.21)***	(0.23)***
Observations	495	495	423	450	457
Adjusted R-squared	0.11	0.1	0.03	0.03	0.03

Note: *significant at 10%; **significant at 5%; ***significant at 1%. All regressions are controlled for regional variation. Robust standard errors in parentheses.
Source: Quantitative Household Survey, 2002.

significance level. For models III, IV, and V, this impact is larger, and it is more significant for models IV and V at the 1 percent level (p value 0.008 and 0.001). A 1 percent increase in village land ownership inequality is correlated with more than a 1 percent increase in the market-malfunctioning index: 1.13, 1.07, and 1.36 for models III, IV, and V, respectively.

For the reduced sample, the results are similar to the regular sample, except with slightly larger coefficients for the land ownership distribution variables (table 5.7).

After establishing the positive correlation between land ownership inequality and market-malfunctioning measurement, it makes sense to look at the connectedness between land ownership inequality and land holding inequality, as land markets seem to be the culprit in market malfunctioning.

For assessing if land ownership inequality is instrumental in land access, we tested the connectedness between the two via utilizing QHS 2002 on province, town, and village levels, by the following regression:

$$G_T = \text{constant} + \beta 1\, G_{TO} + \beta 2^* \text{ population density} + \text{error term}.$$

The results suggest a very strong connectedness between land holding distribution and land ownership distribution in rural Turkey (table 5.8).

For all levels of analysis, a 1-unit change in land ownership Gini results in approximately 0.5-unit change in land holding Gini. The relationship is significant at the 1 percent level in all levels. Contrary

Table 5.7 Village Level Results for Market Malfunctioning Measure without Istanbul

	I	III	VI	VII	VIII
	(ln)MMM1	(ln)MMM2	(ln)MMM3	(ln)MMM4	(ln)MMM5
(ln) Village	0.62	0.62	1.137	1.09	1.36
Land Gini	(0.28)**	(0.28)**	(0.43)***	(0.41)***	(0.39)***
Constant	0.671	0.60	−0.971	−0.87	−1.22
	(0.132)***	(0.13)***	(0.24)***	(0.21)***	(0.23)***
Observations	493	493	422	449	456
Adjusted R-squared	0.12	0.11	0.02	0.03	0.03

Note: *significant at 10%; **significant at 5%; ***significant at 1%. All regressions are controlled for regional variation. Robust standard errors in parentheses.
Source: Quantitative Household Survey, 2002.

Table 5.8 Connectedness in Land Market

	City Land Holding Gini	Town Land Holding Gini	Village Land Holding Gini
	I	II	III
Land Ownership Gini	0.48	0.51	0.46
	(0.11)**	(0.05)**	(0.05)**
lnpopdens	0.02	0.01	0.004
	−0.01	−0.01	−0.01
Constant	0.20	0.19	0.20
	(0.08)*	(0.04)**	(0.08)*
Observations	73	363	500
Adj R-squared	0.47	0.48	0.41

Note: *significant at 5%; **significant at 1%. All regressions are controlled for regional variation. Robust statistics in parentheses.
Source: Quantitative Household Survey, 2002.

to our expectations, population density is neither significantly nor negatively related to the distribution of land holdings in any of the samples. It seems like land ownership distribution is the driving factor behind land holding distribution.

6. CONCLUSION

One of this chapter's major contributions to the existing inequality-factor markets literature is to suggest an analytical method to look at the connectedness between market malfunctioning and asset distribution. We further fill in an important empirical gap in the literature that studies asset inequality and markets. In places where the scope of markets is mostly local, such as in rural factor markets in developing countries, looking at the inequality-market functioning nexus becomes even more crucial. Markets with a local scope not only are more prone to abuses of local powers but, more often than not, they are the only livelihood alternative poor people have. In developing countries where a large majority of the population relies on agriculture, the role of factor markets in distributing economic alternatives becomes very crucial not only for the people engaged in agriculture but also for the country's resource allocation.

In this chapter, we showed that rural factor markets are structurally limited in their functioning, which is positively correlated with unequal distribution of owned land in agriculture. The empirical investigation into the relationship between land ownership inequality and rural factor market functioning illustrates that there is strong evidence in support the "connectedness" between land ownership inequality and market malfunctioning in agriculture that results in failure to distribute economic opportunities.

Further, our findings suggest that when markets are already non-neoclassical, it would be unrealistic to expect efficient outcomes. No country markets, particularly rural ones in developing countries, follow the dictates of neoclassical economics textbooks. Given these findings, we argue that in the presence of structural problems, such as land concentration, rural factor markets left to their own devices will be very ineffective in achieving allocative efficiency and will further add to the existing problems of rural unemployment and income and asset inequality.

REFERENCES

Bardhan, P. K. 1984. *Land, Labor, and Rural Poverty: Essays in Development Economics.* New York: Columbia University Press.

Barham, B. L., Y. Takasaki, and O. T. Coomes. 2000. "Are Endowments Fate? An Econometric Analysis of Multiple Asset Accumulation in a Biodiverse Environment." Research Paper for the Award for Outstanding Research on Development Second Annual Global Development Network Conference Tokyo, Japan, December 11–13. Accessed on September 9, 2006, available at: http://www.gdnet.org/pdf/890_Yoshito.pdf.

Benjamin, D. 1995. "Can Unobserved Land Quality Explain the Inverse Productivity Relationship?" *Journal of Development Economics* 46(1): 51–84.

Benjamin D., and L. Brandt. 1997. "Land, Factor Markets, and Inequality in Rural China: Historical Evidence." *Explorations in Economic History* 34 (4): 460–94.

Binswanger, Hans P. and Mark R. Rosenzweig. 1986. "Behavioural and Material Determinants of Production Relations in Agriculture." *The Journal of Development Studies* 22(3): 503–539.

Boserup, E. 1965. *The Conditions of Agricultural Growth: The Economics of Agrarian Change Under Population Pressure.* London: George Allen and Unwin.

Byres, T. 2004. "Neo-Classical Neo-Populism 25 Years On: *Déjà Vu* and *Déjà Passé.* Towards a Critique." *Journal of Agrarian Change* 4(1–2): 17–44.

Cakmak, E. 2004. "Structural Change and Market Opening in Agriculture: Turkey Towards EU Accession." *ERC Working Papers in Economics*, No. 04–10. Ankara, Turkey: Middle East Technical University, Department of Economics.

Carter, M., and E. Zegarra. 2000. "Land Markets and the Persistence of Rural Poverty in Latin America: Conceptual Issues, Evidence and Policies in the Post-Liberalization Era." In *Rural Poverty in Latin America*, edited by A. Valdes and R. Lopez, 65–86. London: MacMillan.

Carter, M., and F. J. Zimmermann. 2000. "The Dynamic Cost and Persistence of Asset Inequality in an Agrarian Economy." *Journal of Development Economics* 63(2): 265–302.

Carter, M., and F. J. Zimmermann. 2003. "Asset Smoothing, Consumption Smoothing and the Reproduction of Inequality under Risk and Subsistence Constraints." *Journal of Development Economics* 71(2): 233–60.

Carter, M. R., and K. D. Wiebe. 1990. "Access to Capital and Its Impact on Agrarian Structure and Productivity in Kenya." *American Journal of Agricultural Economics* 72(5): 1146–50.

Conning, J. 2000. "Do Better Functioning Factor Markets Reduce Inequality: A Simplified Exposition." Panel on Asset Ownership, Redistribution, and Rural Growth at the Annual World Bank Conference on Development Economics, Washington DC, April 18. Accessed on March 2, 2007, available at: http://www.worldbank.org/research/abcde/washington_12/agenda_12.html

Dercon, S. 1998. "Wealth Risk and Activity Choice: Cattle in Western Tanzania." *Journal of Development Economics* 55(1):1–42.

Eswaran, M., and A. Kotwal. 1986. "Access to Capital and Agrarian Production Organization." *The Economic Journal* 96(382): 482–98.

Griffin, K., A. R. Khan, and A. Ickowitz. 2002. "Poverty and Distribution of Land." *Journal of Agrarian Change* 2(3): 279–330.

QHS. 2002. *Quantitative Household Survey.* Ankara: Ministry of Agriculture, ARIP office.

Rao, J. M. 2005. "The Forms of Monopoly Land Rent and Agrarian Organization." *Journal of Agrarian Change* 4(1–2): 161–90.

Renkow, M., D. Hallstrom, and D. Karanja. 2004. "Rural Infrastructure, Transactions Costs and Market Participation in Kenya." *Journal of Development Economics* 73(1): 349–67.

Sabates-Wheeler, R. 2005. "Asset Inequality and Agricultural Growth: How are Patterns of Asset Inequality Established and Reproduced?" WDR

Background Paper on Asset Inequality and Agricultural Productivity, Washington DC: World Bank

Sarris, A. H. 2001. "The Role of Agriculture in Economic Development and Poverty Reduction: An Empirical and Conceptual Foundation." Paper Prepared for the Rural Development Department of the World Bank Rural Action Plan 2001–2006. Washington DC.

Schultz, T. W. 1964. *Transforming Traditional Agriculture.* New Haven, CT: Yale University.

Sen, Abhijit. 1981. "Market Failure and Control of Labor Power: Towards an Explanation of 'Structure' and Change in Indian Agriculture." *Cambridge Journal of Economics* 5(3–4): 201–28 and 327–50.

Visaria, P. 1970. "The Farmers' Preference for Work on Family Farm." In Report of the Committee of Experts on Unemployment Estimates. New Delhi: Planning Commission, Government of India.

World Bank. 2004. *Turkey: A Review of the Impact of the Reform of Agricultural Sector Subsidization.* Washington, DC: World Bank.

6

CONCLUSION

1. MAIN FINDINGS

In this book, we have conducted an exhaustive empirical analysis to document how rural factor markets function and to investigate how landownership inequality impedes this functioning using Turkey as a case study. As in many parts of the developing world, Turkey's transition to a market economy is marked by a neoliberal policy package with a particular focus on the agricultural sector. With the introduction of the Agricultural Reform Implementation Program (ARIP) in 2001, markets have been given a central role within the sector, which employs 30 percent of the labor force. The so-called aim for ARIP was to eliminate inefficiencies in agriculture by "getting the prices right" while increasing the fiscal soundness of the government budget through eliminating subsidies, a typical neoliberal recipe. The reforms would help increase the low productivity of the agricultural sector through crop switching and markets redistributing land to those who are more productive farmers. Land fragmentation and small farming were perceived to be the two most important causes for low land productivity (Cakmak 2004; DSI 2009; FAO 1999). Thus, one of the natural outcomes of ARIP would be the consolidation and concentration of agricultural land through markets. Despite an abundance of data, lack of empirical studies on the productivity-size nexus is surprising in a country such as Turkey that has a significant agricultural sector. But what is more surprising is the confidence in the policy advice from international and national institutions without scientific evidence.

It is true that in a pure neoclassical world where markets work perfectly, factor proportions are distributed efficiently in agriculture. In other words, markets would bring both technical and allocative efficiency. In agriculture, given constant returns to scale, if there is optimal allocation of resources, there should not be any evidence of an inverse size-yield relationship (IR). Markets ought to distribute resources to the more efficient producers by allocating more land to the farms where land is more productive and more labor to the farms where labor is more productive. In such societies where markets function perfectly, market-centered policies produce efficient outcomes.

However, markets are not capable of producing efficient outcomes in Turkey. One of the important contributions of this book is to show that there is indeed allocative inefficiency in the Turkish economy by demonstrating inefficient utilization of factors of production, such as land and labor, as evidenced by the IR in agriculture. This is the first and only empirical study on Turkish agriculture on IR. Utilizing the latest rural survey for 2002, our results suggest that the small unproductive farmer is an urban myth for every single region in Turkey. Small farmers are far more productive in utilizing their land compared to the large ones, and they still stay small. It is because Turkish land markets do not allocate land to those with higher land productivity (i.e., the small farms) and labor markets do not allocate labor to those with higher labor productivity (i.e., the large farms).

The observation of an IR raises the question of which factors are at play in driving the relationship in Turkey. Our results suggest two very important findings that contribute to the literature. First, land fragmentation has a positive impact on productivity in Turkey. Land fragmentation increases spatial diversity and reduces the risks of drought, frost, floods, pests, and other uncertainties, thereby helping to increase land yields. Impact of land fragmentation on productivity is an understudied issue, and the few existing empirical studies suggest a significantly negative impact of land fragmentation on productivity (Nguyen et al. 1996; Cheng and Wan 2001; Rahma and Rahmana 2009). Second, we found that the most important factor in driving the IR is labor. Labor is a relatively cheaper input for smaller farmers; hence they use it intensively. In chapter 4, we have shown that a small farmer operating a farm with fewer than 20 decares of land uses, on average, 44 times more man-days per decare than the largest ones (i.e., those larger than 1,000 decares) in Turkey. Why small farms use so much labor input on their own farm as opposed to selling their labor in the labor market has a straightforward answer for most developing countries: it is because those who cannot adjust their land margin to employ their labor adjust their labor margin and put in extra days to make a living. If labor markets were perfect, rather than adjusting their labor margin on their own farm, small farmers would be able to work off farm. Hence, in developing countries, off-farm employment opportunities are crucial in rural areas to increase labor productivity. Turkey has some deep-rooted inequality problems, which may pose challenges to rural development and job creation. As we have discussed in chapter 1, the Ottoman Empire's landownership structure evolved through a set of policies that privileged local elites with the ownership rights to land. Particularly in some regions, such as Southeast and East Anatolia, historical legacy in landownership inequality when combined with social inequalities and geographic and agroclimatic hardships created a much taller fence to jump over for the poor and the small farmer to benefit from economic opportunities. Most importantly, our findings in chapter 5 suggest that rural factor markets perpetuate existing inequalities rather than redressing them because of existing inequalities in landownership.

Another finding of this research is the rising poverty in rural Turkey. Our findings suggest that poverty in rural areas is particularly concentrated in the agricultural sector. There has been a slight reduction in some classes linked to the poverty of policies for the agricultural sector. Policies such as ARIP, without the support of scientific inquiry and with no economic justification, are ill advised for the sector given the sector's structural problems of high land ownership inequality.

2. CHALLENGES AND OPPORTUNITIES IN A GLOBAL WORLD: ALTERNATIVES FOR DEVELOPING COUNTRIES IN THE SHADOW OF CHINA AND INDIA

When such structural imbalances cause inefficiency problems and if markets function on existing structures, it is unreasonable to expect markets to provide the solution to the low productivity problem in agriculture. Economic inequalities create social classes whose members exert power in rural markets, distorting allocative efficiency of markets. Particularly in rural markets where markets are localized, the outcomes of distorted markets are even more detrimental to the people and to the economy because people lack alternatives. From a political economy perspective, maybe one of the most challenging issues for a country with a large agricultural base and high landownership inequality is to change the status quo, which favors haves over have-nots. Since existing socioeconomic structure serves those who have economic privileges and power, those with power would use it to keep the status quo regardless of the economic reform implemented.

As also confirmed by economic history, this is why effective interventions by a third party are often the answer to change the status
quo. Except in violent revolutions, that third party is often the state
machinery.

However, the effectiveness of states in bringing improved living
conditions to masses through increased socioeconomic opportunities depends on the degree of infestation of the state machinery by
the privileged. The economic transition of Russia from a planned
economy to a market-oriented one provides an excellent example for
how underlying structural imbalances within the old system produce
worse outcomes for masses when not addressed in the new one.

Since its inception, the Turkish Republic has been trying to transition away from an agrarian society to an industrialized one through
various reforms without addressing its structural problems. Countries
who have addressed their initial landownership inequalities have done
much better in achieving higher levels of modernization and incomes
when compared to Turkey, such as South Korea. Still a middle-income
developing country in 2011, Turkey was 3.2 times more affluent
than South Korea in 1960 in monetary terms with a GDP per capita
of $497 as opposed to South Korea's $155 per capita GDP. Today,
South Korea is twice as rich as Turkey with $20,757 per capita GDP as
opposed to Turkey's $10,0094 in 2010 (World Bank 2011b)[1]. Today,
it is hard to imagine that South Korea was an agrarian-based poor
country with limited natural resources, low savings rate, and a small
domestic market trying to emerge out of a civil war some 50 years
ago. Countries who have transformed their agrarian structures into
an egalitarian system of individual peasant farming before unleashing
the so-called efficiency of free markets are also the ones who have
been successful on the modern economic growth path.

In our day, to industrialize in the presence of giants like India and
China in an open world economy is a much taller order than before.
Turkey, along with other developing countries, faces major challenges
and opportunities specific to the twenty-first century. To address
the challenges and opportunities, one has to realize how the world
is different now when compared to the first half of the twentieth
century.

For starters, the world is a much more integrated place now
through trade, financial flows, travel, communications, and information technology. Furthermore, today's global macroeconomic
framework is characterized by labor-saving technological change in
production, deregulated factor and goods markets, increased exposure to financial and economic crisis in the face of shrinking social

protection from the state, limited fiscal space for national govern-ments due to reduced tariff revenues, and increased concentration of economic power within markets by multinational corporations. Even though insightful and brilliant, the economic development models of the twentieth century, therefore, do not provide clear answers to today's challenges. In Kuznet's (1955) and Lewis's (1954) conceptualizations, economic development is a transformation of resources of a country away from a low productivity activity, such as agriculture, to a high productivity one, such as industry. Since productivity in industry is higher than agriculture in the initial stages of development, economic activity gravitates toward cities and away from rural areas with development. Also known as the traditional Kaldorian model of endogenous growth, a shrinking rural labor force has to increase its productivity, and thereby its income, because it has to support an increasing urban working class. In such a world, economic growth is endogenous because structural change in pro-duction and employment induces productivity growth in agriculture through backward linkages. Even if in the initial stages of develop-ment, poverty, unemployment, or rising income inequality emerge, it is through these rural-urban channels that, despite significant transformation of resources away from agriculture, disproportionate social and economic cost to the rural populations is avoided (Palanivel and Unal 2011).

However, for the reasons we cited above, particularly since the 1980s, the overall framework within which developing countries operate is quite different to the degree that traditional channels of Kaldorian endogenous growth theory break in most of today's developing countries. First, in open economies the backward link-age between domestic demand for food stuffs and agricultural pro-duction may disappear due to cheap food imports (Ghosh 2008; Heintz 2009). This may eliminate the incentive to improve produc-tivity in the agricultural sector due to low price signals and, in some extreme cases, such as in Haiti, destroy the agricultural sector, cre-ating an unmanageable rural-urban migration. Second, as countries develop, the changing structure of production toward industry and manufacturing may not be accompanied by an equal rise in manufac-turing employment due to capital deepening in production. Such has been the episodes of "jobless growth" in almost all the developing countries recently (Heintz 2009; Palanivel and Unal 2011). Third, due to the availability of cheap manufactured imports from China, the experience of structural transformation in many developing coun-tries has been skipping manufacturing and industrialization from agriculture to services directly, such as the case in India. Therefore, for many developing countries, structural change may mean passing by industrialization and concentration of employment in the services sector or in agriculture (Ghosh 2008; Heintz 2009; UNRISD 2010). Unless addressed by social protection policies, developing countries in such a macro framework will be faced with increasing poverty and inequality (Palanivel and Unal 2011).

If structural change is shifting productive resources away from agriculture, which is labor intensive in developing countries, to manufacturing or industry, which is more capital intensive, then one would expect to see a negative relationship between the decreased share of agriculture in production and increased inequality given that nonfarm formal job creation would be at a lower rate than the rate at which the agricultural sector sheds labor. This has been the case in many developing countries, including Turkey. When such is the case, the poor are crowded into urban informal sectors, particularly into services. According to Heintz (2009), informal service sector employment rises and prevails much faster than manufacturing or industrial jobs during structural transformation due to four main reasons. First, since income elasticity for services is higher, demand for services would be higher as incomes rise, and because most marketed services are nontradable, increases in domestic income would result in increase in domestic demand for services. Second, service sector productivity does not rise as fast as in the manufacturing and industrial sector; hence service sector jobs tend to increase with output. Third, due to cheap manufactured imports and/or higher productivity in the manufacturing sector, employment creation would lag behind output growth, and hence unemployed urban workers would crowd into informal urban jobs. Finally, the rate of urbanization almost always exceeds the rate of labor absorption by industrial jobs, although exceptions to this are prevalent, particularly in such countries as Bolivia and Thailand (Heintz 2009).

Inevitably, the structure of employment will change with development or, more generally, sectoral patterns and techniques of production. However, as discussed by Heintz (2009), quantity and quality of employment affect economic growth in turn as well. Low productivity activities and limited employment opportunities would retard domestic markets, resulting in even fewer employment opportunities. Furthermore, countries where the majority of employment is in the informal sector, even under the scenario of service sector–led growth, such as in India, income inequalities will increase because tradable service sector jobs would get paid more because tradable goods and services tend to enjoy higher returns (Heintz 2009). The poor tend to crowd into nontradable service sector jobs due to inequalities in access to education and other related factors such as networks. Added to these are the rise of China and India as the new economic powers, which make all of the above challenges more difficult to overcome for small- and medium-sized developing economies. According to Kray (2007) one of the most distinguishing features of the modern era globalization is the rise of China and India from their self-imposed isolation. In our view, the rise of China and India is particularly distinctive of this century because never before in economic history has such sizable low-cost labor had such dynamism. In the recent past particularly, the countries that were developing fast were much smaller in size, such as Japan or the Asian tigers namely, Hong Kong, Taiwan, Singapore, and South Korea. Today, besides India and China, Brazil and Russia, two other very populous economies, are also growing fast economically, even though Brazil has slowed down significantly in the recent year.

However, Asia, particularly East Asia, has been growing faster than any other developing region in the world, and the growth has been accelerating. From the 1970s to the 2000s, for East Asia, annual average per capita decade-wise growth has risen from 5.03 in the 1970s to 5.97 in the 1980s, to 6.82 in the 1990s, and to 8 percent in the 2000s (World Bank 2011b). Whereas growth rate in the developing countries of MENA has been volatile and negative at times and has changed from 3.53 to −0.62, 2.03, and 2.47, respectively, during the same period (World Bank 2011b). The fast and increasing pace of the Asian growth has had many economists thinking that the twenty-first century will be the "Asian Century," in which led by China and India, Asians would dominate the socioeconomic and cultural life just like the United States did in the twentieth century (Kray 2007, ADB 2011).

According to Asian Development Bank (ADB) (2011) projections, by 2050 there will be no poor nation left in Asia whose income per capita levels are below $1,000. In 2050, Chinese per capita income will be as high as the income levels of today's EU, around $38,000 in purchasing power parity (PPP). In this new world, urban areas would be home to 70 percent of the total population, and we will be 2 billion people more. If Asia, led by China, keeps growing as fast as it has been, the region will command half of the world's GDP by 2050. Assuming the United States, the EU, Brazil, and Russia would also claim significant shares from the global pie, an interesting question would be, "What is left for the rest of the developing countries?"

The purpose of the rest of this chapter is an attempt to answer this challenging question, particularly given pressing exigencies of climate change and its implications on the world's peoples, lands, and water resources. We have chosen four countries to explore possible alternatives for development in the shadow (or on the shoulders) of these two Asian giants. Since most of the issues covered in this book so far have been about the Middle East economies, we have selected Tunisia, Egypt, and Turkey from MENA and Pakistan from South Asia. Different sizes and endowments of these economies would provide us a richer discussion to offer for developing countries because Tunisia is a relatively small country with a population of fewer than 10 million, whereas Pakistan is a large country with a population of over 170 million, and Egypt and Turkey are each about 70 million. All four have significant shares of labor force employed in agriculture. In our attempt to explore their possibilities in economic development, we have structured the rest of the chapter as follows. In section 2.1, we will briefly look at the similarities and differences of the Indian and the Chinese growth trajectories and follow this discussion with the rising opportunities of today's world in agriculture and the changing role and nature of agriculture. We will then conclude the chapter with possible paths of development for the countries we have proposed to study.

Because of the unmatched scale of their production capacity due to their vast populations—and thereby their market size—the two Asian giants have been shaping, and will continue to shape, the socioeconomic landscape of the developing and the developed world in the twenty-first century. To understand through which channels this change may influence other developing countries and the world at large, one needs to take a closer look at their economies. At this point, let us mention that the following analysis is nowhere near an exhaustive account of the Chinese and the Indian economic growth models. For the interested reader, there is an immense and an everincreasing literature. Here, we would like to distinguish the two economies based on a few fundamental issues besides traditional discussions of sectoral shifts, such as the impact of economic growth on poverty, and specific policies of the agrarian sector.

2.1. China and India

The two engines of the Asian economic growth differ in their economic histories, their sociopolitical structures, and their growth trajectories. China has been growing based on manufactured exports and India on tradable service sector. Chinese social structure is much more egalitarian with its roots in the communist era practices when compared to the cast system of India.

Based on cheap manufactured exports, China has been growing with an average annual per capita rate of 8.8 percent since 1977, the year that marks the beginning of its ongoing high growth (World Bank 2011b). Even though many economists and laymen attribute China's economic success to the reforms that liberalized its economy, the Chinese industrial and technological infrastructure was built during the Maoist era, before China started to rise as a major global player (Li 2008). Even in the 1960s, long before the reforms, China had been a predominantly industrial economy: industry was 45 percent of the country's GDP, as opposed to 33 percent for services, and 22 percent for agriculture (World Bank 2011b). In 2010 the service sector accounted for 45.5 percent of total GDP, while industry stayed the same at 45 percent, and agriculture's contribution shrank to 9.5 percent (World Bank 2011b). Since 1977, agriculture has been growing at an average annual rate of 4.4 percent, whereas the other two sectors have been growing at 12 percent annually (World Bank 2011b).[2]

When China's economic performance is evaluated by the criterion of poverty reduction (i.e., how much of the economic growth has been translated into better lives for its vast numbers of poor)—it is considered a miracle. China managed to reduce the number of people living in extreme poverty ($1.25 or less per day) by 500 million from 1981 to 2005, or from 84 to 16 percent of the population (www.povcal.net). When measured by the official poverty line, the ratio of poor people living in poverty has declined from 53 percent in 1981 to only 2.8 percent in 2004, a tremendous success by all measures (Ravallion and Chen 2007). As rightly stated by the China Human Development Report in 2008, "The speed, scope and magnitude of the improvements in the lives of 1.3 billion people rank among the most stunning achievements in the history of human development" (HDR China 2007–08, iii).

However, this stunning achievement of poverty reduction was not due to manufacturing growth. It was the result of a policy focus on the country side during market reforms. During 1979–1984, land was distributed equally to rural households, however without ownership rights. Since credit markets were not well developed, the Chinese government prevented land concentration that could arise as a result of credit market imperfections. In other words, since credit markets are imperfect and require collateral, especially in the initial years of the reform, land was not changing hands toward those who might not be the most efficient producers. This constraint on land ownership rights provided a major pillar of pro-poor growth, as market reforms had a wider base to reach to the poor segments of society.

The second policy implemented during those years was to encourage farmers to diversify their crops away from a quota-based, grain-only system to a more market-oriented one by liberalizing agricultural prices. This shift was to take place in steps, using a "dual-track pricing system" (Ravallion and Chen 2007). After fulfilling their grain quotas, farmers could produce other products that they would sell in the market. This opportunity created incentives to increase productivity without generating price instability in the grain markets. In the initial years of the reforms, both total agricultural production and productivity increased dramatically due to the use of high-yielding hybrid rice varieties. Between 1978 and 1994, incomes rose by 15 percent a year in rural China (Savanti and Sadoulet 2008). By ensuring a sustainable and affordable supply of grain through the dual-track pricing system, combined with production quotas for grain, the government ensured low labor costs for the industry, as wages for the urban working class depended on the price of food.

The second period of high growth and high poverty reduction was also a result of agricultural policies. From 1995 to 2000, China raised commodity price supports along with increasing fertilizer supplies to farmers (Cornia 2006). From 1994 to 2000, the number of absolute poor decreased from 80 million to fewer than 30 million as a result of the Poverty Reduction Plan (Chandrashekar and Ghosh 2006). Additionally, the Chinese government provided the macroeconomic environment to support economic growth by the prevalence of public banks, which fostered capital accumulation at the municipal and local level. The overall macroeconomic environment was supported by a controlled capital account and managed exchange rate to decrease exposure to global financial volatility and ensure accumulation of foreign exchange reserves (Chandrashekar and Ghosh 2006).

If China had embarked upon its reforms without addressing its vast rural poverty problem, it would have crippled its great potential for sustainable economic growth, as Brazil did. The slowdown in Brazil's economic growth is attributed to existing socioeconomic inequalities and poverty. According to an article in *The New York Times* (September 5, 2010),[3] the low level of so-called social capital in the Brazilian economy has put a lid on its growth. In sum, Chinese economic growth and its accompanying success due to the increased well-being of vast numbers of people are not simply the result of shock therapy policies to transition away from a command economy, as it has been often narrated by the popular media and by mainstream economics. On the contrary, the government played a significant role in reducing poverty and mobilizing rural sources through agricultural policies that eased market failures. One of the true accomplishments of the Chinese agricultural policies was therefore, the combination of state-led and market-oriented economic policies. This combination motivated farmers to increase productivity and thereby their living standards, and ensured stability of wages for industry simultaneously the industrial sector.

India, on the other hand, only recently joined the "turnpike of Asian growth"[4] in the 1990s, although it had started to accelerate in the 1980s (Basu and Maertens 2007). Unlike Chinese economic growth, India's growth has not been accompanied by impressive results in poverty reduction. According to the 2011 estimates of the World Bank, there were 411 million people—or 56 percent of India's total population—living in extreme poverty in 1983. By 2005 that number had only declined to 42 percent. In absolute terms, however, poverty has actually increased because of population growth. Today, India is home to 420 million poor people, as opposed to 411 million in 1983, the majority of whom live in rural areas.

Compared to China, India has been pursuing a significantly different growth path despite having a massive agrarian base. Fifty percent of India's lands are arable. The majority of its population is employed in agriculture—approximately 56 percent in 2005 (World Bank 2011b). However, the acceleration in the economic growth in India has mainly come from a rapid growth in the service sector. In 1960 India was a predominantly agrarian economy with 43 percent of its GDP coming from agriculture, followed by 38 percent from the services sector and 20 percent from industry (World Bank 2011b). Today, 55 percent of value added to India's GDP is from the service sector, followed by industry at 28 percent and agriculture at 16 percent (World Bank 2011b). This structural shift in the composition of the economy is largely due to policy reforms that have discouraged and ignored the agricultural sector. Since the agricultural sector has been neglected in India, it is registering low growth rates, as low as 0.2 percent in 2009, whereas the service sector grew at about 8.5 percent annually for the same period (World Bank 2011b). However, this structural shift in output has not been reflected in the level of employment, as the majority of the labor force continues to work in the agricultural sector, thereby reducing labor productivity. The latest available data from 2005 show that the share of agriculture in total employment was approximately 56 percent, compared to services at 26 percent. The remaining share of 19 percent was in industry (World Bank 2011b). As Basu and Maertens (2007) argued, a one-to-one match between output and employment shares of sectors is not expected, but the gap between the output and employment shares of the service sector is alarming. Such a large gap confirms the phenomenon of jobless growth in India. Furthermore, India's employment-to-population ratio, the ratio of employed adults to the total number of working-age adults, has been much lower—55 percent—when compared to China's 73 percent, which is one of the highest in the developing world (World Bank 2011b). This further raises a red flag about the unemployment problem in the Indian economy.

According to Chhibber and Palanivel (2009), the high savings and investment rates, combined with respectable rates of technological progress, have been a main driver for India's capital-intensive, nonagricultural-led growth. However, it is important to note that, at least initially, what made high savings and investment rates possible was the penetration of nationalized banks in remote rural areas during Indira Gandhi's leadership (Basu and Maertens 2007). Traditionally, low savings and investment rates, which were around 15 percent in the 1960s, rose during the 1970s and finally crossed the 20 percent mark during 1978 to 1979 (Basu and Maertens 2007). Additionally, India's long colonial past had been instrumental in providing the comparative advantage of the English language for attracting overseas information and communications technology (ICT) companies, when compared to other low-labor-cost countries. Unlike the China's, India's economic growth model is a nontraditional one in the sense that it has skipped the manufacturing stage and has relied on the ICT sector for economic growth.

This pattern of economic growth has not served the poor in India well (Chhibber and Palanivel 2009). On the contrary, the tradable service sector–led model of economic growth tends to create high inequalities and has a limited ability to reduce poverty. India's tradable service sector–led growth increased demand for high skilled laborers, who are less likely to be poor, further leading to increased inequalities through widening wage gaps between unskilled and skilled workers. Since the majority of the poor live and work in rural areas or concentrated in cities, growth in the service sector rarely trickled down to the poor. Thus, despite high economic growth, India has been failing to reduce its very high poverty rates.

However, even though they are following different growth paths, the two Asian giants, China and India, have one thing in common;

rising income inequality, not poverty, particularly between urban and rural areas. The widening gap between the rich and the poor has already been posing challenges in both countries. In India, for example, overall income inequality rose from 0.32 in 1983 to 0.37, as measured by the Gini coefficient (WIID 2010). China has registered a dramatic increase in inequality, from a highly equal income distribution of 0.23 in 1981 to one in which the Gini coefficient had risen to 0.42 in 2005 (World Bank 2011b).[5]

Regardless of its consequences in terms of increasing inequalities, the economic opportunities brought by the fast growth of these two giants have been a hope for many of the poor countries in the region. Nonetheless, to follow the footsteps of one or the other may be to fall into the "fallacy of composition", especially for manufacturing led growth aspirations. For a smaller-size developing country, it is difficult, if not impossible, to attain the economies of scale that China or India have. Hence, what has been successful for the Chinese or the Indian economy may be a failure for another developing country. In our view, then, countries that treat their options for economic growth only through the lens of traditional growth models and fail to see other emerging opportunities are highly likely to be part of the fallacy of either the Chinese or the Indian composition. Such countries may become trapped in a stage of nontransformation of its economy and increasing poverty, as China and India already have a tremendous comparative advantage in the manufacturing and service sectors, respectively. Or, in a best-case scenario, those countries may be stuck in a middle-income trap under the shadow of these giant economies.

One may ask, then, what are the alternatives, if there are any, for developing countries with agrarian economies? One of the answers, in our view, is agriculture, but not your grandmothers' agriculture.

2.2. Twenty-First-Century Agriculture and Agricultural Markets

Today, agriculture is significantly different from what it was in the 1960s and 1970s. Since the 1980s, and particularly in the past two decades, agricultural produce markets have changed profoundly on the demand side, the supply side, and on the governance side (IFAD 2011).

On the demand side, changes have come through quantity effects, through quality effects, and through purely speculative channels. Increasing population coupled with increasing incomes has been changing the structure of demand for agricultural products.

According to the United Nations, the 7-billionth baby will be born somewhere on the planet in October 2011, and if this baby happens to be born in a relatively high-income country, that child will exert more pressure on the world's agricultural resources. As a result of rising incomes in many developing countries, demand for higher-value agricultural products such as fruit, vegetables, and animal products have increased significantly. According to FAO (2009a), compared to the early 1960s, the world's per capita egg consumption has increased fivefold, milk per capita consumption has doubled, and meat consumption has tripled. In particular, increase in red meat consumption exert greater pressure on grain production, as one kilogram of red meat requires seven kilograms of grain for animal feed (UNCTAD 2011). Assuming that the world will be a much wealthier place by 2050, we can expect increasing demand for high-value-added agricultural products. Rising income levels will be combined with the addition of two billion people, of whom more than 70 percent will live in urban areas (FAO 2009b). According to FAO (2009b), net of biofuels, the world will have to produce 70 percent more food products than it is producing today to meet the demands of this richer and more urban population. In quantity terms, "annual cereal production will need to rise to about 3 billion tons from 2.1 billion today, and annual meat production will need to rise by over 200 million tons to reach 470 million tons" (FAO 2009b, 2). Furthermore, to realize this 70 percent food production hike by 2050, developing countries need to increase their already low and declining yields by 80 percent, and their arable land by 20 percent (FAO 2009b). Given the limited amount of arable land in China (only 12 percent) and low land productivity of agriculture in India due to "Green Revolution fatigue" these two economies have been finding a partial solution to feed their populations through outsourcing arable land—in other words, land grabbing (Rowden 2011).

However, land grabbing is not always for food. Between 2006 and 2009 in developing countries, ownership of a land area equivalent to the total arable land of France has been negotiated to be transferred from peasants or the state into the hands of Western investors. Some of these investors include Wall Street banks, private hedge funds, and other entities that see land as a hedge against inflation or other risky investments, as well as for speculative purposes with the expectation of higher future land prices (De Schutter 2009). Among developing nations, China and India are spearheading land grabbing. For example, India holds the largest amount of leased land in Ethiopia. In 2008, 300,000 hectares of land were leased to Karuturi, a private

Indian company that is the world's largest producer of cut roses.[6] China started its land grabbing in Cuba and Mexico much earlier than India, in the late 1990s (von Braun and Meinzen-Dick 2009). On top of rising food demand and land grabbing for commercial and financial purposes, another significant factor that has been putting pressure on arable land is the issue of so-called energy security: namely, the production of biofuels. Use of biofuels has been regulated by governments as mandatory targets to be mixed with fossil fuels in areas such as the United States, the European Union, Brazil, and India. There is no economic or efficiency justification for the use of biofuels, particularly from corn, as the energy required to produce corn-based biofuels is higher than the energy released by their consumption. However, the use of biofuels is subsidized through corn farmers, who wield significant political clout in some of the biofuel-producing countries, including the United States. Since biofuel use is legal in these countries, there is unlikely to be a dramatic change in the practice for the near future, since changing legal procedures is generally time consuming. Biofuels have a significant impact on price increases for corn, which are sometimes as high as 75 percent (Mitchell 2008). As incomes rise and cars become part of the consumption basket in China, India, and the rest of the developing world, there is no doubt that demand for biofuels, and thus the price of arable land and whatever is produced on that land, is likely to increase significantly. In an economic system governed by free markets, there is a good chance that poor consumers and small farmers could be marginalized when entitlements to land are distributed on the basis of purchasing power.

In agricultural markets, however, there may be a counterbalancing trend against this marginalization. In both the developed and the developing world, demand for agricultural products has been differentiated significantly. In the developed world, due to rising awareness for socially responsible consumption and health concerns, organic farming has become the fastest-growing industry. In fact, today many large corporations go out of their way to convey to their customers that they are not exploiting natural or human resources in the developing world. The change in Starbucks's labor practices after the company came under fire for its exploitative treatment of its laborers is a case in point. Consumer behavior has become a much more credible threat in the Northern economies as a result of the development of virtual markets and communication systems such as the Internet and the cell phone, through which people have access to alternative markets and suppliers without incurring large transaction costs. Consumers can also raise awareness against a certain corporation using social media. In other words, low-cost technology access has been counteracting the negative outcomes of low-cost production practices.

On the supply side, agricultural production has gone through significant changes as well. Perhaps the most important change is that traditional food markets have been replaced by supermarket chains in many parts of the world (IFAD 2011). This shift in food distribution from traditional local markets to a centralized system has allowed consumers in some countries to transcend growing seasons due to the availability of fruit and vegetables from around the world throughout the year (IFAD 2011). Even though some of these supply chains have been offering small farmers new opportunities with high profit potential, market access for small farmers is still minimal due to the regulations regarding standardization and packaging of products or processes by Northern retailers (IFAD 2011).

To sum up, agriculture and agricultural product markets are evolving in such sophisticated ways that they can pose significant challenges for small farmers. They can also, however, offer significant opportunities, particularly now that the advantages of small farming in sustainable agriculture are widely recognized. In addition, most of the developing countries' small farms are more productive than large-scale farming, and the global environment of agriculture also offers greater opportunities for small farmers through ease of access to larger markets.

2.3. Can Tunisia, Pakistan, Turkey, and Egypt Benefit from This New World Order in Agriculture?

As we briefly discussed in the case of MENA in chapter 1, climate change and the shrinking land base for agriculture due to urbanization are considered the most pressing issues for food security and, therefore, for the future of the region. Supply of agriculture has to accommodate these changes. So the first interesting question we could raise would be the following: could developing countries such as Turkey, Egypt, Tunisia, and Pakistan take advantage of their agrarian resource base to benefit from the new world order in agriculture?

For starters, if we look at these countries' agricultural and economic indicators, as shown in table 6.1, all four countries have significant shares of their populations living in rural areas with high shares of employment in agriculture. Overall, however, the value added to the economy by agriculture is low, except in Pakistan and Egypt. In Pakistan and Egypt, agriculture contributes approximately 21 and

Table 6.1 Chosen Indicators for Agricultural Production

	Rainfall Index (mm/Year) (2002)	Area Harvested (in Arable Land) (2009) (%)	Share of Rural Pop (2010)	Share of Econ Active Pop in Agr. (2010)	Share of Agr. in GDP (2009)	Share of Arable Land/ Total Land (2008) (%)	Irrigation Share in Arable Land & Permanent Crops (2008)	Agr. Pop/Total Pop (2010) (%)	Share of Agr. in Total Emp.	Land Gini	Income Gini
China	1119	80	54.8	61	8.9	12	52	61	44	n/a	42 (2005)
Egypt	107	110	57.2	25	13.7	3	100	28	31	69 (2000)	34 (2004)
India	1432	64	69.9	54	16.5	53	37	48	60	60 (1996)	37 (2005)
Pakistan	438	66	63.0	39	20.8	26	94	43	44	60 (2000)	31 (2005)
Tunisia	355	31	32.7	21	9.8	18	9	21	26	69 (1995)	41 (2000)
Turkey	614	55	30.4	32	8.3	28	21	20	26	58 (2001)	41 (2006)

Source: FAOSTAT (2011), except Share of Agriculture in Total Employment is from World Development Indicators (2011). Income Gini coefficient for China is also from World Development Indicators.

14 percent, respectively, whereas in Turkey and Tunisia it contributes 10 and 8 percent, respectively. Low GDP shares combined with high employment shares suggest low productivity and hidden unemployment in the sector.

The country with the highest level of land underutilization is Tunisia, with only 30 percent of harvested land in total arable land, and the highest ratio is in Egypt, with 110 percent, signaling multi harvesting (i.e., harvesting the same area twice in a calendar year).

In Egypt and Pakistan, it is surprising to see such a large gap between the ratio of rural population and the population of people who are economically active in agriculture (table 6.1). In Egypt, since only 3 percent of all the land is arable, such an outcome may not be too surprising, but for Pakistan, it is—at least at first sight. However, a closer look at land ownership distribution reveals possible explanations for low economic agricultural activity among rural population in Pakistan. Despite the FAO coefficient of 0.60 Gini for land holdings, land ownership inequality is high in rural Pakistan. According to a 2007 World Bank Report, Pakistan's land ownership Gini is one of the highest in the world at 0.86, accompanied by a landlessness ratio of 63 percent. The agricultural sector employs a high share of the labor force (44 percent); however, it is because of this high inequality that the benefits of agricultural growth are not shared by the poor (Zaman et al. 2010; World Bank 2007). This skewed land ownership is also reflected in the income composition of rural households: only 40 percent of rural household incomes are from agriculture in Pakistan (World Bank 2011a). Since the majority of Pakistani people still live in rural areas, and a significant proportion of them are employed in agriculture, land inequality in rural areas has important consequences for the lives of the majority in the country. Pakistan has many young, unskilled, and unemployed people. Even though high concentration poses challenges for its utilization, Pakistan also has significant land area. Its current political climate is not attractive to foreign direct investors due to ongoing conflict, so Pakistan has to rely on domestic resources to get on the "turnpike of Asian growth." Given the rising importance of agriculture and Pakistan's strategic location as a close market to India and China, Pakistan could very well mobilize its agrarian base and crowded labor force as fuel for economic takeoff.

The countries under inquiry here face yet another challenge: not one is food self-sufficient. That is, their relevant food production ratios are smaller than their consumption shares. The least food self-sufficient country is Tunisia at 50 percent, followed by Egypt at

57 percent, while the most food self-sufficient country is China at 81 percent. As we have discussed, food security is a more important issue in human well-being than food self-sufficiency. However, given the volatility in food prices and the prospects for their high levels in the future, countries like Turkey and Pakistan in particular would benefit from reconsidering their crop choices and moving toward high-value food crops, especially staples. Since the 2006–2008 crisis, food crops have been highly profitable, but unfortunately not many farmers in the developing countries have been able to take advantage of this opportunity. According to the IFAD (2011) report, the majority of the increase in food production after the food crisis came from the developed world (13 percent), while developing countries increased food production by only 2 percent.

Table 6.2 shows that since 2000 only China has increased its per capita agricultural production significantly, by 27 percent. It seems as if none of the other countries has responded to the price signals from the food crisis, as their production index has remained stagnant since 2000 despite significant increases in food inflation (as illustrated by food CPI in table 6.2). There is already an existing literature on the reasons that farmers in developing countries may not respond to prices by increasing their output (Taylor and Adelman 2003). In a nutshell, because farmers are both producers and consumers of their goods, their response to price changes varies according to their ability to produce marketable surplus. Farmers' failure in developing countries to respond to price hikes signals that they may not be as connected to the markets in the developing world, either because it is too costly for them to do so, or because they have no surplus due to their small size, or a combination of the two.

Egypt is one of the countries hurt significantly by the most recent food crisis, even seeing some food riots. Some of the most fertile lands in the world lie in Egypt's Nile Delta, and cotton production is a significant source of foreign exchange reserves in the country. Since the food crisis, however, Egypt has been decreasing the amount of its land devoted to cotton cultivation. Yet even if Egypt converts all of its 3 percent arable land to food crops, it is unrealistic to expect that such a narrow land strip along the River Nile could feed over 70 million people. Therefore, in the new agricultural order of the world, Egypt's role may become more sophisticated in its textile industry, as its high-yield cotton crops would have a greater advantage in the world markets as more and more lands were devoted to food crops elsewhere.

Tunisia is a relatively small country when compared to the rest in our small sample. One of the strengths in Tunisian agriculture, however,

Table 6.2 Selected Indicators for Agricultural Trade, Consumption, and Production Patterns

	Per Capita Agr. Prod. Index[a] (2009)	Agr./ Total Imports (2008)	Agr./ Total Exports (2008)	Share in World Food Prod. (2007)	Share in World Food Cons. (2007)	CPI Total (2009)	CPI Food (2009)	Share in Agr. Trade in GDP Imports (2008)	Share In Agr. Trade In GDP Exports (2008)	Food Imports/ Total Agr. Imports (2008)	Food Exports/ Total Agr. Exports (2008)
China	127	4.6	1.7	17.6	21.5	n/a	n/a	2.50	1.22	70.95	70.54
Egypt	117	17.9	7.0	0.8	1.4	208	188	6.53	1.17	89.53	82.23
India	106	2.8	8.9	10.1	15.0	152	173	1.03	1.60	76.32	60.78
Pakistan	107	12.5	12.9	1.4	2.2	206	230	3.51	1.71	64.83	87.14
Tunisia	106	10.4	8.1	0.1	0.2	134	138	7.76	4.46	82.39	89.28
Turkey	103	5.1	8.0	1.1	1.4	461	168	1.92	1.59	65.46	84.40

Note: a: base year 2000.
Source: FAOSTAT (2011).

is that Tunisia has a significant number of agricultural researchers in public institutions (IFPRI 2006). The government supported agricultural growth by significantly increasing public spending on agriculture and thereby increasing productivity from the 1970s through the mid-1980s, with an average annual growth rate of 7.2 percent (Bibi and Chatti 2005). Public spending was particularly oriented toward irrigation and drainage and reuse of treated water in agriculture. In an era when agricultural production has to be coupled with efficient use of water and high technology, Tunisia may carve itself a niche in agricultural markets. However, this would be far too insignificant to climb the development ladder unless Tunisia finds a way to combine its highly skilled experts in agriculture with manufactured high-end agricultural machinery, particularly on water treatment.

As we have been discussing in the majority of this book, Turkey is an important agricultural producer, and if more equal access could be provided to farmers, it could become even a more prominent producer. More than any other country we have discussed so far, Turkey's geostrategic location combined with its relatively abundant land and water resources and ease of access to major world markets would situate Turkey in the driver's seat for reaping the benefits of a new agricultural order in not only the MENA region, but also in Europe. The rising tide of agricultural prices is an opportunity for Turkey and other developing countries to jump to the next level of development. Furthermore with the changing dietary habits of, particularly the Europeans toward more vegetables and fruits, Turkey also has an advantage to catch many niches in the fruits and vegetables markets for producing and marketing high-end agricultural products, and transporting them at lower cost to both developed Europe and developing MENA and Asia.

2.4. A Final Question

In every transformation, two aspects require particular scrutiny: first, the political and economic mechanisms of transformation; and second, the historical context of the transformation process because of internal (domestic) and external (international) processes (Oya 2009). According to Oya (2009), agrarian transformation is particularly important for any given country for two reasons. First, the efficiencies/inefficiencies or completeness/incompleteness in the fundamentals of this transformation can be seen to have a continuing effect on capitalist development. Second, diversity in economic development cannot be understood without understanding how the agriculture sector is supporting the overall economy and how it is changing. As has been discussed by many in the literature, the question of sustainability in agriculture cannot be raised in isolation from the broader development processes, particularly without an analysis of industry-agriculture relations (Oya 2009).

The challenges and opportunities of the twenty-first century have created such dynamism between industry and agriculture that each is becoming indispensable to the other. Agriculture's reliance on new technologies has been increasing tremendously, since technological changes in water desalination, drought-resistant food crops, and special chemicals to replenish lost minerals from the soil are absolutely necessary for the future of the world. As noted in IFAD (2011), investments in agricultural R&D continue to be one of the most productive investments, with rates of return between 30 and 75 percent. Perhaps even more necessary would be a mechanism to allow equal access to food by all. The fact is, never in the history of the world has food scarcity been due to a lack of production. The problem has always been distribution.

We think it is time for the world to see that modern, urbanized development and the dogmatic belief that one could only achieve development through industrialization may pose more challenges than opportunities. Rural places must be considered hubs of development and sociocultural and economic life where young people can achieve their aspirations.

We also think it is time to ask another important question to ourselves: How can we structure world agricultural production and markets so there will be global food security? Answering this question may require rendering possible of a new model of agricultural production that necessitates a supranational institution to oversee the production of the world's agriculture that could intervene during food emergencies. This may sound like a utopian concept, but it has been implemented since 1944 for money and credit through the IMF, so why not for agriculture?

REFERENCES

Asian Development Bank. 2011. "Asia 2050: Realizing the Asian Century." Accessed on September 25, 2011, available at: http://www.adb.org /documents/reports/asia-2050/default.asp

Basu, Kaushik, and Annemie Maertens. 2007. "The Pattern and Causes of Economic Growth in India." *BREAD Working Paper* 149.

Bhaduri, Amit. 1973. "A Study in Agricultural Backwardness Under Semi-Feudalism." *Economic Journal* 83(329): 120–37.

Bibi, S. and Rim Chatti. 2005. "Public Policy and Poverty Reduction in the Arab Region: Public Spending, Pro-Poor Growth, and Poverty Reduction in Tunisia: A Multilevel Analysis." IFPRI/API Collaborative Research Project.

Cakmak, Erol. 2004. "Structural Change and Market Opening in Agriculture: Turkey Towards EU Accession." *ERC Working Papers in Economics*, No. 04–10. Ankara: Middle East Technical University.

Chandrasekhar, C. P., and Jayati Ghosh. 2006. "Macroeconomic Policy, Inequality and Poverty Reduction in Fast-Growing India and China." In *Pro-Poor Macroeconomics Potential and Limitations*, edited by G. A. Cornia, 248–81. New York: Palgrave McMillan.

Cheng, Enjian, and Wan G. H. 2001. "Effects of Land Fragmentation and Returns to Scale in the Chinese Farming Sector." *Applied Economics* 33(2): 183–94.

Chibber, A., and Thangavel Palanivel. 2009. "India Manages Global Crisis but Needs Serious Reforms for Sustained Inclusive Growth." Accessed on July 2, 2010, available at: http://data.undp.org.in/FinancialCrisis/India-,Manages-Global-Crisis-But-Needs-Serious-Reforms-for-Sustained-Inclusive-Growth.pdf.

Cornia, G. A. 2006. "Potential and Limitations of Pro-Poor Macroeconomics: An Overview." In *Pro-Poor Macroeconomics Potential and Limitations*, edited by G. A. Cornia, 3–25. New York: Palgrave McMillan.

De Schutter, Oliver. 2009. "Responsibly Destroying the World's Peasantry." Accessed on September 5, 2011, available at: http://www.project-syndicate.org/commentary/deschutter1/English

DSI. 2009. "Temel Politikalarve Oncelikler, Toprakve Su Kaynaklari." Accessed on September 7, 2011, available at: http://www2.dsi.gov.tr/topraksu.htm.

Enjiang, Cheng, Christopher Findlay, and Tin Nguyen. 1996. "Land Fragmentation and Farm Productivity in China in the 1990s." *China Economic Review* 7(2): 169–80.

Food and Agriculture Organization of the UN. 1999. "Country Profile: Turkey." *New Agriculturalist Online*. Accessed on June 1, 2006, available at: http://www.new-agri.co.uk/00-3/countryp.html.

———. 2009a. "The State of Food and Agriculture: Livestock in the Balance." Accessed on September 22, 2011, available at: http://www.fao.org/docrep/012/i0680e/i0680e.pdf

———. 2009b. "How to Feed the World in 2050." Accessed on September 17, 2011, available at: http://www.fao.org/fileadmin/templates/wsfs/docs/expert_paper/How_to_Feed_the_World_in_2050.pdf

———. 2011. "AQUASTAT: The Global Information System on Water and Agriculture." Developed by the Land and Water Development Division of the Food and Agricultural Organization. Accessed on September 2, 2011, available at: http://www.fao.org/AG/AGL/aglw/aquastat/main/index.stm.

Ghosh, Jayati. 2008. "Growth, Macroeconomic Policies, and Structural Change." In UNRISD's "Flagship Report on Poverty." Available at: http://www.unrisd.org/80256B3C005BB128/%28httpProjectsForResearch Home-en%29/791B1580A0FFF8E5C12574670042C091?OpenDocument &category=Thematic+Papers.

Heintz, James. 2009. "Employment, Economic Development, and Poverty Reduction: Critical Issues and Policy Challenges." In UNRISD's "Flagship Report on Poverty." Accessed on December 7, 2010, available at: http://www.unrisd.org/80256B3C005BB128/%28httpProjectsFor ResearchHome-en%29/791B1580A0FFF8E5C12574670042C091? OpenDocument&category=Thematic+Papers.

Human Development Report China. 2008. "Human Development Report China 2007/08: Access for All: Basic Public Services for 1.3 Billion People". United Nations Development Programme, China and China Institute for Reform and Development.

International Food Policy Research Institution. 2006. "Agricultural Science and Technology Indicators: Country Brief No: 29: Tunisia." Accessed on September 3, 2011, available at: http://www.asti.cgiar.org/pdf /TUNISIA_CB29.pdf

International Fund for Agricultural Development. 2011. "New Realities, New Challenges: New Opportunities for Tomorrow's Generation." Rural Poverty Report 2011, Rome, Italy. Accessed September 10, 2011, available at: http://www.ifad.org/rpr2011/.

Kray, Dollar. 2007. "Asian Century or Multi-Polar Century." *Policy Research Working Paper Series* 4174. Accessed on September 1, 2011, available at: http://wwwwds.worldbank.org/servlet/WDSContentServer/WDSP/IB /2007/03/20/000016406_20070320112343/Rendered/PDF /wps4174.pdf.

Kuznets, Simon. 1955. "Economic Growth and Income Inequality." *The American Economic Review* 45 (1): 1–28

Lewis, Arthur. 1954. "Economic Development with Unlimited Supplies of Labor." *Manchester School of Economic and Social Studies* 22(2): 139–91.

Li, Minqi. 2008. *The Rise of China and the Demise of the Capitalist World Economy.* New York: Monthly Review Press.

Martinez-Alier, J. 1983. "Sharecropping Some Illustrations." In *Sharecropping and Sharecroppers,* edited by Terence J. Byres, 95–105. London: Frank Cass and Company.

Mitchell, Donald. 2008. "A Note on the Rising Food Prices." Policy Research Working Paper 4682. Accessed on September 12, 2011, available at: http://www-wds.worldbank.org/external/default/WDSContentServer /IW3P/IB/2008/07/28/000020439_20080728103002/Rendered /PDF/WP4682.pdf

Oya, Carlos. 2009. "The World Development Report 2008: Inconsistencies, Silences, and the Myth of 'Win-Win' Scenarios." *The Journal of Peasant Studies.* 36(3): 593–601.

Palanivel, Thangavel, and Fatma Gul Unal. 2011. "Inclusive Growth and Policies: The Asian Experience." Unpublished mimeo. New York: UNDP.

Patnaik, Utsa. 1983. "Classical Theory of Rent and Its Application to India: Some Preliminary Propositions with Some Thoughts on Sharecropping." In *Sharecropping and Sharecroppers*, edited by Terence J. Byres, 71–87. London: Frank Cass and Company.

Pearce, R. 1983. "Sharecropping Towards a Marxist View." In *Sharecropping and Sharecroppers*, edited by Terence J. Byres, 42–70. London: Frank Cass and Company.

Rahma, Minazur, and Sanzidur Rahmana. 2009. "Impact of Land Fragmentation and Resource Ownership on Productivity and Efficiency: The Case of Rice Producers in Bangladesh." *Land Use Policy* 26(1): 95–103.

Ravallion, Martin and Shaohua Chen. 2007. "Measuring Pro-Poor Growth." World Bank Development Research Group Working Paper. Accessed on December 14, 2010, available at: http://econ.worldbank.org/external /default/main?pagePK=64165259&theSitePK=475520&piPK=641654 21&menuPK=64166093&entityID=000094946_01092004013092.

Rowden, Rick. 2011. "India's Role in the New Global Farmland Grab an Examination of the Role of the Indian Government and Indian Companies Engaged in Overseas Agricultural Land Acquisitions in Developing Countries." Accessed on September 1, 2011, available at: http://www .grain.org/bulletin_board/entries/4342-india-s-role-in-the-new-global -farmland-grab

Savanti, Paula and Elisabeth Sadoulet. 2008. "Agriculture's Special Powers in Reducing Poverty." Accessed on September 25, 2011, available at: http:// elibrary.worldbank.org/docserver/download/1020797x-10-3-16-19.p df?expires=1317589222&id=id&accname=guest&checksum=9D08C9 D6838E420C2AC64F10A25AEADD

Taylor, Edward J. and Irma Adelman. 2003. "Agricultural Household Models: Genesis, Evolution, and Extensions." *Review of Economics of the Household* 1: 33–58.

United Nations Conference on Trade and Development. 2011. "Price Formation in Financialised Commodity Markets: The Role of Information." A Study prepared by the Secretariat of the United Nations Conference on Trade and Development. Accessed on September 5, 2011, available at: http://www.unctad.org/en/docs/gds20111_en.pdf

UNRISD. 2010. "Combating Poverty and Inequality: Structural Change, Social Policy, and Politics." Geneva: United Nations Research Institute for Social Development. Accessed on February 7, 2011, available at: http://www.unrisd.org/publications/cpi.

Von Braun Joachim and Ruth Meinzen-Dick. 2009. "'Land Grabbing' by Foreign Investors in Developing Countries: Risks and Opportunities." Accessed on September 18, 2011, available at: http://www.ifpri.org /sites/default/files/publications/bp013all.pdf

World Bank. 2007. "Pakistan: Promoting Rural Growth and Poverty Reduction." Sustainable and Development Unit, South Asia Region Report No. 39303-PK. Accessed on September 20, 2011, available at: http://siteresources.worldbank.org/PAKISTANEXTN/Resources/293051 -1177200597243/ruralgrowthandpovertyreduction.pdf

World Bank. 2011a. "Pakistan: Data Projects and Research." Accessed on September 20, 2011, available at: http://web.worldbank.org/WBSITE /EXTERNAL/COUNTRIES/SOUTHASIAEXT/PAKISTANE XTN/0,menuPK:293057~pagePK:141159~piPK:141110~theSiteP K:293052,00.html.

World Bank. 2011b. World Development Indicators Database. Accessed September 8, 2011, available at: http://databank.worldbank.org/ddp /home.do?Step=12&id=4&CNO=2

World Income Inequality Database (WIID). 2010. Accessed on October 17, 2010, available at: http://www.wider.unu.edu/research/Database/en_GB /database/

Zaman, Khalid, Muhammad Mushtaq Khan, Mehboob Ahmad, and Waseem Ikram. 2010. "An Empirical Analysis of Growth, Inequality and Poverty Triangle in Pakistan: Co-Integration Approach (1964–2006)." *International Research Journal of Finance and Economics* 46: 32–46. Accessed on January 4, 2011, available at: http://www.eurojournals.com /IRJFE_46_03.pdf

APPENDIX A

Table 3.3 Descriptive Statistics of the Regression Sample

	Variable	Mean	Std. Dev.	Min	Max
	Sample Size (N)	4,995			
DEMOGRAPHICS	Household Size	5.8	3.1	2	37
	Head's Education	2.9	0.9	1	7
	Head's Age	49.9	13.3	18	96
	Average Age Female[a]	39.7	12.8	13	94
	Average Age Male[a]	40.1	13	14	96
	Female Ratio[b]	0.5	0.14	0.09	1
	Dependency Ratio	1.45	0.52	0.8	7
	Self Sufficiency Rate	0.26	0.29	0	1
WEALTH	Total Land Owned	69.8	161.4	0	3800
	Per Capita Consumption[d]	1150	584	30.5	7350
	Total Cattle (HH)	2.4	4.5	0	80
	Total # of Tractors	0.4	0.5	0	3
MARKET	Population Density	145.8	293.2	10.4	1754
	Village Land Distribution (Gini)	0.46	0.17	0	1
	Share of Marketed Crops	0.65	0.36	0	1
	Per Capita Credit	64.6	222	0	4250
	Infrastructure Index[e]	67.7	5.6	36	83
	Agr. Income/Total Income	0.28	0.3	0	1

Source: Quantitative Household Survey, 2002.

Table 3.4 Descriptive Statistics of the Agrarian Sample

	Variable	Mean	Std. Dev.	Min	Max
	Sample Size (N)	3,801			
DEMOGRAPHICS	Household Size	5.8	3.1	2	37
	Head's Education	3.0	0.9	1	7
	Head's Age	48.8	13.2	18	96
	Average Age Female[a]	39.0	12.6	13	94
	Average Age Male[a]	39.3	12.5	14	96
	Female Ratio[b]	0.50	0.14	0.13	0.92
	Dependency Ratio	1.46	0.53	0.8	7
WEALTH	Self Sufficiency Rate	0.26	0.3	0	1
	Total Land Owned	74.1	160.1	0	3,800
	Per Capita Land Owned	14.9	48.1	0	1,900
	Per Capita Consumption[d]	1,150	580	31	7,350
	Total Number of Cattle	2.6	4.9	0	80
MARKET	Total # of Tractors	0.5	0.51	0	3
	Population Density	151.2	306.8	10.4	1,754
	Village Land Distribution (Gini)	0.46	0.16	0	0.96
	Share of Marketed Crops	0.7	0.33	0	1
	Per Capita Credit	73.3	237	0	4,250
	Infrastructure Index[c]	68.3	5.4	36	83
	Agr. Income/Total Income	0.13	0.15	0	0.5

Notes: [a]Calculated for Adults Older Than 15. [b]Ratio of Females in Total Earners. [c]Protein and Carbohydrates Only. [d]In Annual Million TLs. [e]Max 100.

Source: Quantitative Household Survey, 2002.

Table 5.9 Descriptive Statistics for MMMs

Variable	N	Mean	Std. Dev.	Min	Max
TOWN LEVEL					
MMM I	73	2.76	1.26	0.74	8.51
MMM II	73	2.61	1.07	0.71	6.86
MMM III	73	0.67	0.51	−0.25	2.47
MMM IV	73	0.74	0.52	−0.26	2.53
MMM V	73	0.74	0.53	−0.25	2.52
TOWN LEVEL					
MMM I	363	2.77	2.12	−0.1	31.05
MMM II	363	2.58	1.62	−0.13	17.19
MMM III	363	0.66	0.8	−0.48	6.79
MMM IV	363	0.76	0.86	−0.5	7.42
MMM V	363	0.74	0.76	−0.49	5.81
VILLAGE LEVEL					
MMM I	500	2.71	2.03	−0.4	31.05
MMM II	500	2.52	1.60	−0.39	17.19
MMM III	500	0.66	0.82	−0.61	6.79
MMM IV	500	0.78	0.83	−0.5	6.30
MMM V	500	0.74	0.78	−0.49	5.81

Source: Quantitative Household Survey, 2002.

Appendix B

Chapters 2, 3, 4, and 5

QHS 2002: According to the World Bank Turkey Report (2004): Quantitative Household Survey employs cluster sampling, prepared according to eight project crops: wheat, tobacco, hazelnut, sugarbeet, maize, cotton, olives, and tea. Four hundred and ninety-nine villages were selected by random sampling from the lists of State Institute of Statistics (SIS) that are divided according to regions where crops are grown. The sample has 71 provinces: 11 in the Marmara region, 13 in Central Anatolia, 6 in the Aegean, 12 in the Mediterranean, 6 in Southeast Anatolia, 10 in East Anatolia, and 13 in the Black Sea region. Random selection of the farm holders was based on a "village list" generated after an interview with the *muhtar* (village headman). After completion of the village *muhtar* questionnaire, eleven households were selected for interviewing. Agricultural-business households were randomly selected from the village household list with a systematic sampling method while implementing the survey (World Bank Turkey Report 2004).

Chapters 4 and 5

Calculation of Family Labor Input in Crop Production

Within the labor input category, total number of man-days that family members put into production is reported under two sections; first one is family-labor-only, and the other is a mixture of family labor and wage labor with no specification of the exact share of either. Hence, we have assumed half of the mixed category is family labor and multiplied the amount reported in this section by half and added this with the family-labour-only category to arrive the total number of man-days used in crop production. This may be a conservative assumption given that small rural households usually hire only when the family members are not adequate; so it is reasonable to expect that this ratio in reality would be more than the half.

Calculation of Family Labor Input for Agricultural Sidelines

Reported labor input in QHS is only for crop production but work on a farm is rarely confined to crop production only. Agricultural sidelines such as cattle grazing, household food processing and providing services to reproduce labor power in the household are all significant parts of on-farm labor input. Therefore, we have taken all these additional activities into consideration since labor input if not used in such activities can be sold in the market. For households that own cattle, we have added man-days to total labour input based on the following assumptions: for households who own more than 0 but less than 10 cattle, we have added 2 additional man-days per week; for households who own more than 10 but less than 20 cattle we added 3 man-days per week; for households who own more than 20 but less than 30, we have added 4 man-days per week; for households who own more than 30 but less than 50 cattle, we have added 5 man-days per week; for households who own more than 50 but less than 81, we have added 6 man-days per week. Maximum number of cattle owned by any household in the dataset is 80. We have added the numbers based on our interviews with farmers in Central Anatolia.

We further added man-days to account for household production based on the household size: for households with more than one and less than 5 members we have added 3 man-days per week; for households who have more than 6 and less than 9 members we have added 4 man-days per week; for households with more than 9 and less than 14 members we have added 5 man-days per week; for households who have more than 14 and less than 19 members we have added 6 man-days per week; for households who have more than 19 and less than 24 members we have added 7 man-days per week; for households who have more than 24 and less than 29 members we have added 14 days per week; for households who have more than 29 and less than 38 members we have added 21 man-days per week. The maximum household in the dataset is 37.

NOTES

PREFACE

1. Connectedness is a term first coined by Abijit Sen in his pioneering work of 1981 on market failure in India.
2. Also from my conversations with Prof. Mohan Rao, who was my dissertation advisor.

1 INTRODUCTION: WHY AGRICULTURE?

1. "Lady, Lady."
2. "Land reform is a many splendored thing" is a quotation from Griffin (2002).
3. From, E., *To Have or To Be*.
4. Data for 2008.
5. When we refer to MENA in this book, it includes the following countries: Algeria, Bahrain, Egypt, Iran, Iraq, Israel, Jordan, Lebanon, Libya, Morocco, Occupied Palestinian Territory, Oman, Qatar, Saudi Arabia, Sudan, South Sudan, Syria, Tunisia, Turkey, UAE, and Yemen.
6. Despite South Sudan having gained its independence in July 2011, its statistics are still combined with Sudan's.
7. Self-sufficiency refers to the domestic supply of food products in meeting domestic demand.
8. Food security: demand does not need to be met through domestic supply, and hence, it differs from food self-sufficiency.
9. Calculated by the author from the most recent statistics available. Internal renewable water resources is defined as the long-term average annual flow of rivers and recharge of aquifers generated from endogenous precipitation. Double counting of surface water and groundwater resources is avoided by deducting the overlap from the sum of the surface water and groundwater resources.
10. Data refers to most recent available data, which is 2009.
11. Term quoted from chief economist, Oxfam England, CAPORDE 2005 discussions.
12. In IFAD's 2011 Rural Poverty Report, MENA countries include all countries in our poverty sample except Iran.
13. Another credit was extended to agriculture in 2001 though this credit was given the neutral-sounding name "economic reform credit."

14. Source: http://www.oib.gov.tr/portfoy/portfoy_genel.htm (Turkish Republic Privatization Administration General Directorate website), accessed September 1, 2011.
15. Earlier or later dates are not available.
16. 1 *donum* = 1,600 square meters.
17. According to Aricanli (1976), the reasons for stagnation and the "failure" to transition to capitalism were related to the institutional significance of the state in economic organization and the state's need to control labor and not the land. Even in the most fertile Anatolian plains, the land–labor ratio was quite high (Aricanli 1976). In contrast to other arguments in the literature, Aricanli argues that the struggle between the state, the elite, and the peasants were *not about land ownership* but rather about *labor ownership* because plenty of high-quality "free" agricultural land was available. The fact that neither land nor labor had been controlled privately in the Ottoman system enhanced the institutional significance of the state in economic organization.
18. Today the existing legal system regarding land rights in Turkey goes back to these laws issued in 1858.
19. Discussion in Koymen (1999).
20. Please refer to Ziya Meral (2010) for a detailed discussion on how AKP's Islamic identity has been perceived by different Turkish constituencies.
21. The Turkish government refuses to recognize the Republic of Cyprus until the political and economic blockade on the Turkish Republic of Northern Cyprus is removed, which has led to problems with the Customs Union and hence, the EU progression. According to the Customs Union, Turkey is obligated to open its transportation hubs to the Republic of Cyprus. However, Turkey refuses to open its seaways and airways until the economic blockade is lifted from Northern Cyprus, which would help ease Northern Cyprus dependence on Turkey and its international isolation (Meral 2010; Morelli 2011).

2 A PORTRAIT OF TURKISH AGRICULTURE: INEQUALITY AND ITS DISCONTENTS

1. Unless otherwise noted, all information regarding Turkey's agroclimatic features is from official documents accessed through the Web from the State Water Work's 2009 report (DSI 2009) and the State Meteorology Directorate's DMO (2011) brief about the climate of Turkey.
2. www.cografyabirtutkudur (accessed on September 14, 2011)
3. 1 decare = 1 donum = 0.24 acre
4. Based on TUIK (2011) 24 percent and based on FAOSTAT (2010), 30 percent of the total population live in rural areas in Turkey.
5. Per capita values are per capita per household, not per capita per region (i.e., we have estimated these values by dividing total household income by total members in the family and then taking a regional average).

6. For more information on the early mechanization in agriculture in Turkey, see "Tarimsal Teknolojide Ilk Gelismeler: Ilk Makinelesme." Ilhan Tekeli, Selim Ilkin, in 75 Yilda Koylerden Sehirlere, 1999.

3   SHARECROPPING OR FIXED-RENT TENANCY?

1. This was argued given three conditions; the labor input is not negotiable, the landlord has no control over the amount of land to be leased out, and the rental rate (share in this case) is customarily fixed.
2. See Bardhan and Srinivasan (1971), Bell and Zusman (1976), Eswaran and Kotwal (1985a), and Otsuka et al. (1992) on this issue.
3. The factors we have chosen to include in this variable are education services (high school and equivalent), drinking water, irrigation, agricultural marketing support, canals and roads, agricultural education extension services, and veterinary services. Each household is asked to evaluate the services compared to five years ago in the village. Based on the household's evaluation, each category is given a number (by the household) from 1 to 5, one referring to positive improvements in the service, 5 referring to its absence, and 4 referring to no opinion. Since this kind of response does not give any quantitative measurement, we chose to form an index. Admittedly, this index is better at indicating changes over time within a single village than it is at indicating differences among villages. However, rather than omitting this variable totally, we assumed that service improvements could proxy for an overall evaluation of the infrastructure in a village, Hence I decided to include it rather than face the problem of omitted variable bias. Since the higher the number the worse the overall infrastructure, we aggregated these reported numbers and deducted them from 100. After this transformation, the index reflects a better level of infrastructure with a higher number.
4. We further ran the regressions for Central Anatolia only since his reference was for that region. But our results show no statistical significance in support of his argument (results not shown here).
5. For purposes of sample consistency, we dropped the observations of households who are not engaged in crop production on their farm and hence, have a missing value for their crop marketization ratio.

4   TESTING FOR INVERSE SIZE-YIELD RELATIONSHIP IN TURKISH AGRICULTURE

1. One of the first questions to be answered regarding IR assessment is whether increasing, decreasing, or constant returns to scale prevail in agriculture. However, I am not including this discussion in the main

body of the chapter because it has been established elsewhere that constant returns to scale characterize a developing country's agriculture. For further discussion on the topic, see Berry and Cline (1979) and Cornia (1985).

2. Cornia (1985) observes the opposite in Brazil. He argues that most of the large-land holders have the better quality land. This argument seems reasonable when one considers the opportunities of a wealthy farmer compared to a poorer one.

3. Even though canals are man-made, they are considered exogenous because their location is determined by government mandate, not by farmers themselves.

4. The argument assumes that the farmer is an arrow type risk averse person, i.e., as his/her wealth gets smaller he/she will become more risk averse, hence he/she will devote most of his/her time on his/her land to maximize farm income.

5. Labor is more expensive for large farms due to supervision and/or worker search cost (Eswaran and Kotwal 1986), and credit is cheaper and more accessible for large farmers due to the need for collateral, which small farmers lack.

6. However, the zero marginal productivity assumption—along with the existence of surplus labor in agriculture—was later discredited by Viner (1957) by referring to the impossibility of such an assumption given the nature of agricultural work: An additional worker always adds something positive, which would not be there in the absence of the worker, such as better weeding, better soil preparation, etc. The solution to the bottleneck of positive marginal productivity of labor (MPL) is offered by Sen (1962; 1966) who proposed that labor effort, not labor, of an individual worker should be included in calculations of MPL. None of the studies in this paper refer to zero MPL.

7. FAO Turkey (1999), online: country profile, Turkey: http://www.new-agri.co.uk/00-3/countryp.html. Accessed on July 4, 2005.

8. OECD Economic Surveys Turkey (2006), p.186.

9. The sampling method employed was cluster sampling, prepared according to eight project crops: wheat, tobacco, hazelnut, sugar beet, maize, cotton, olives, and tea. Four hundred and ninety-nine villages were selected by random sampling from the lists of State Institute of Statistics (SIS) that are divided according to regions where crops are grown. The sample has 71 provinces: 11 in the Marmara region, 13 in Central Anatolia, 6 in the Aegean, 12 in the Mediterranean, 6 in Southeast Anatolia, 10 in East Anatolia, and 13 in the Black Sea region. Random selection of the farm holders was based on a "village list" generated after an interview with the *muhtar* (village headman). After completion of the village muhtar questionnaire, 11 households were selected for interviewing. Agricultural-business households were randomly selected from the village household list with a systematic sampling method while implementing the survey (World Bank Turkey Report 2004).

10. One decare= 0.2474 acres.

11. We further tested this relationship after disaggregating the data into nine agricultural regions, and will discuss the findings in the following sections.

12. In calculating the value of k, we were not able to apply the same price rule as we did in estimating farm output due to data-related issues. We believe this does not create a problem, since electricity, oil, fertilizers, and pesticide prices do not fluctuate as much. Fertilizers and pesticides are provided by six major producers who command 70 percent of the market, and electricity is a state monopoly in Turkey. Oil prices also do not fluctuate among geographical regions and it could be said that law of one price holds for oil in Turkey.

13. Output can be measured in two units: physical weight (volume) or in monetary units; that is, in terms of "value." Measuring output in terms of weight or volume could only be plausible for highly specialized monocrop or monoproduct farms. Most farms produce multicrops and dairy products, therefore this is not a convenient method to be used for the developing-country agrarian context, definitely not for the Turkish context.

14. We also ran the regressions with given prices; discussion on this will be in the following sections.

15. We calculated the number of workers in the household, assuming members younger than 15 but older than 11 as "half workers." The same method was applied to people who are older than 65 and younger than 75. People who are on the two extremes of these ranges are considered full dependents.

16. Discussion in Kaldjian (2001).

17. Even though this chapter focuses on the broader question of resource utilization, we further tested the IR relationship based on different definitions of farm size, such as area cultivated rather than area held, and also via using different definitions of farm output, such as crop production only, crop and animal production only, and tested for seven regions, and nine agricultural regions under two main assumptions; one with varying prices for each household and the other with national average prices. In the model that we calculated the crop value only via using national prices, in the Marmara region, even though the sign stayed the same, farm size lost its significance; in the third subregion, the IR also lost its significance and the sign also is reversed when the denominator of the dependent variable was area cultivated and the numerator was the value of crop production or crop and animal production only. In all others, IR relationship prevails and was significant at the 1 percent level. When we used farm gate prices as reported by each household, the IR relationship prevailed at 1 percent significance in all regions and in Turkey, except one; in the third subagricultural region farm size's significance reduced to 10 percent, and in the Marmara region, when the denominator was cultivated area and the numerator excluded secondary production, IR

relationship stayed significant, but at 5 percent. We also tested IR via using physical output versus area cultivated for specific crops in all seven regions and saw that the IR relationship prevails and it is significant for all the crop types, except corn. For corn, the sign was reversed, but it was not statistically significant. The crops we ran regressions for are: wheat, alfalfa, barley, tea, tobacco, sugar beet, corn, hazelnut, sun flower, raw cotton, and lint cotton. All the results on these aforementioned regressions can be provided upon request.

18. Results of the square of dependency ratio are not reported in the tables.

5 Market Failure and Land Concentration in Turkey

1. Reference in Sabates-Wheeler (2005).

2. See *Journal of Agrarian Change*, (2004). Vol. 4, Issue 1 and 2 for the debate.

3. The direct exchange of land for labor time includes key characteristics of both fixed rent (control over the allocation of farmer's labor time and the output) and wage labor (supervision is required to control the rent).

4. The term "connectedness" is first coined by Sen (1981) in pioneering work on agrarian market failure.

5. Following Benjamin and Brandt (1997), this is still assuming identical returns for each factor for all the households, ignoring land and labor heterogeneity among households.

6. However, one should be careful to evaluate equality of MMM to zero as market perfection without further analysis, as in rare cases, imperfections in land markets could cancel out imperfections in labor markets. One way to overcome this shortcoming is to conduct a closer analysis of MMMs when they turn out to be zero to make sure that the source of zero value of MMM is not due to two imperfections canceling each other out.

7. From conversations on the topic with Prof. Mohan Rao.

8. For a more realistic estimation of labor input, we have added man-days to total number of man-days reported in the dataset as the reporting only addressed crop production. Please see appendix B for details.

9. Wage rates are averaged for each unit of analysis (i.e., village, town, and province). In the first model, unlike the calculations offered by Benjamin and Brandt (1997), we did not assume the length of the work week, such as 40 hours per week. Rather, we used the annual average wage income as reported in the dataset. This freed us from assuming total hours worked for annual or seasonal wage employment. Hence, total neoclassical wage income of the household is calculated by multiplying the annual wage rate by the number of working-age adults. We have also conducted same calculations with seasonal agricultural wage rates and obtained very similar results. Results could be furnished upon request.

10. Since wage income is reported annually, we have estimated a daily wage rate via dividing this number by 90 days, assuming the season to be three months. In addition, the amount of leased-out labor income is included to account for household members who are already earning wages from off-farm employment. Hence, we did not have to include them in the category of estimated income.

11. The distance-to-cities variable measures the distance (in kilometers) to the city center of which the town is under the jurisdiction. Ideally, it is true that not political but geographical proximities to the city centers would be a better indicator of how close the town is to the nearest city center; however, due to data unavailability, we have used the jurisdiction level distances from towns to the cities of which they are a municipality.

12. Regressions including distance and population density are also conducted, and the significance results for land ownership inequality do not change. Moreover, including these variables does not add much to the goodness of fit.

6 CONCLUSION

1. GDP per capita is in current USD.

2. Author's own calculations from World Bank (2011) database.

3. Educational Gaps Limit Brazil's Reach. Available at: http://www.nytimes.com/2010/09/05/world/americas/05brazil.html?scp=2&sq=brazil&st=nyt

4. Term coined by Mr. Ajay Chhibber, UNDP Under Secretary General, and director, Regional Bureau for Asia and the Pacific, during Pakistan Economic Growth Conference in Islamabad, July 13–15, 2011.

5. For a detailed discussion of reasons for rising inequality in India and China as well as Asia-Pacific countries, please refer to Palanivel and Unal (2011) UNDP Working Paper.

6. Source: Karuturi website. Accessed on September 14, 2011, available at: http://www.karuturi.com/index.php?option=com_content&task=view&id=12&Itemid=31.

INDEX

Note. Page numbers in **bold** denote illustration.

water problems—*Continued*
  solutions to, 7–9
  virtual water, 7–8
  wastewater, recycling, 8
  water ratio, MENA, 6
WB, *see* World Bank
wealth variables of
  households, fixed-rent
  tenancy, 76
welfare subsidies, 30
Western European Union, 31
worker search cost, 103,
  188n5

World Bank
  agricultural policies, 15
  guidance of, 14
  influence on development
    policies, 4
  interventions by, 28
  Quantitative Household Survey
    (QHS), 47, 106, 142, 184
  2007 Report, 170
World Bank Survey, 106, 130

zero marginal cost of labor, 103,
  188n6